마이갓 5 Step 모의고사 공부법

● **Vocabulary** 필수 단어 암기 & Test
① 단원별 필수 단어 암기 ② 영어 → 한글 Test ③ 한글 → 영어 Test

 ● **Text** 지문과 해설
① 전체 지문 해석 ② 페이지별 필기 공간 확보 ③ N회독을 통한 지문 습득

 ● **Practice 1** 빈칸 시험 (w/ 문법 힌트)
① 해석 없는 반복 빈칸 시험 ② 문법 힌트를 통한 어법 숙지
③ 주요 문법과 암기 내용 최종 확인

 ● **Practice 2** 빈칸 시험 (w/ 해석)
① 주요 내용/어법/어휘 빈칸 ② 한글을 통한 내용 숙지
③ 반복 시험을 통한 빈칸 암기

5 ● **Quiz** 객관식 예상문제를 콕콕!
① 수능형 객관식 변형문제 ② 100% 자체 제작 변형문제 ③ 빈출 내신 문제 유형 연습

영어 내신의 끝
마이갓 모의고사 고1, 2

1 등급을 위한 5단계 노하우
2 모의고사 연도 및 시행월 별 완전정복
3 내신변형 완전정복

영어 내신의 끝
마이갓 교과서 고1, 2

1 등급을 위한 10단계 노하우
2 교과서 레슨별 완전정복
3 영어 영역 마스터를 위한 지름길

마이갓 교재
보듬책방 온라인 스토어 (https://smartstore.naver.com/bdbooks)

마이갓 10 Step 영어 내신 공부법

Vocabulary

필수 단어 암기 & Test
① 단원별 필수 단어 암기
② 영어 → 한글 Test
③ 한글 → 영어 Test

Grammar

단원별 중요 문법과 연습 문제
① 기초 문법 설명
② 교과서 적용 예시 소개
③ 기초/ Advanced Test

Text

지문과 해설
① 전체 지문 해석
② 페이지별 필기 공간 확보
③ N회독을 통한 지문 습득

Practice 3

빈칸 시험 (w/ 해석)
① 주요 내용/어법/어휘 빈칸
② 한글을 통한 내용 숙지
③ 반복 시험을 통한 빈칸 암기

Practice 2

빈칸 시험 (w/ 해석)
① 주요 내용/어법/어휘 빈칸
② 한글을 통한 내용 숙지
③ 반복 시험을 통한 빈칸 암기

Practice 1

어휘 & 어법 선택 시험
① 시험에 나오는 어법 어휘 공략
② 중요 어법/어휘 선택형 시험
③ 반복 시험을 통한 포인트 숙지

Quiz

객관식 예상문제를 콕콕!
① 수능형 객관식 변형문제
② 100% 자체 제작 변형문제
③ 빈출 내신 문제 유형 연습

Final Test

주관식 서술형 예상문제
① 어순/영작/어법 등
   주관식 서술형 문제 대비!
② 100% 자체 제작 변형문제

전체 영작 연습

직접 영작 해보기
① 주어진 단어를 활용한
   전체 서술형 영작 훈련
② 쓰기를 통한 내용 암기

학교 기출 문제

지문과 해설
① 단원별 실제 학교 기출
   문제 모음
② 객관식부터 서술형까지
   완벽 커버!

마이갓

2024 고2

6월

WORK BOOK

2024년 고2 6월 모의고사 내신대비용 WorkBook & 변형문제

CONTENTS

2024 고2 6월 WORK BOOK

보듬영어

| ❶ voca | ❷ text | ❸ [/] | ❹ ____ | ❺ quiz 1 | ❻ quiz 2 | ❼ quiz 3 | ❽ quiz 4 | ❾ quiz 5 |

18	resident	주민		overestimate	과대평가하다; 과대평가
	take advantage of	~을 활용[이용]하다		accurately	정확히, 정밀하게
	parking lot	주차장		discern	식별[분별]하다, 인식[파악]하다
	plant	(묘목 등을) 심다; 식물, 공장		unlock	열다, ~을 밝히다, 누설하다
	weed	잡초; 풀을 뽑다, 제거하다		potential	가능성이 있는, 잠재적인; 가능성, 잠재력
	decoration	장식(품), 훈장	21	trappings	장식
	regard	간주[주목]하다, 관련있다; 관심, 존경, 관계		be forced to V	~하도록 강요받다
19	relay	전달[중계]하다, 교대시키다; 중계, 교대		in return	대신에, 답례로
	spot	발견하다, 찾아내다; 장소, 반점		suit	정장, 소송; 적합하다, (알)맞다
	perform	수행하다, 행동하다, 공연[연주]하다		depend on	~에 의존하다, ~에 달려 있다
	make a mistake	실수하다		attend	참석하다, 보살피다
	approach	접근하다; 접근(법)		up to	~까지, ~의 책임인
	smoothly	매끄럽게, 순조롭게		inevitably	어쩔 수 없이, 불가피하게, 필연적으로
	raise	높이다, 올리다, 기르다, 제기하다; 인상		examine	검사[조사]하다, 진찰하다
	hand in	제출하다, 내다		transaction	거래, 매매, 처리
	come across	우연히 마주치다, 인상을 주다, 이해되다		slavery	노예 제도, 노예의 신분
20	resist	저항하다, 반대하다, 견디다		reside	살다, 거주하다, 존재하다, (~에) 속하다
	be capable of	~할 수 있다	22	firm	확고한, 고정된; 회사
	maxim	격언		concentrate on	~에 집중하다
	refuse	거부하다, 거절하다		A rather than B	B라기 보다는 A
	weakness	약점, 결점		restructure	재구성하다, 개편하다
	admit	인정[승인]하다, 허가하다		company	친구, 동료, 회사, 교제; 회사의
	damage	피해, 손상, 손해; 손해를 입히다		profitable	수익성이 있는, 유익한
	underestimate	과소평가하다, 경시하다; 과소평가		viable	성장할 수 있는
	capability	능력, 수완		term	기간, 용어, (-s) 조건, 관점; 말하다

Voca

	known as	~으로 알려진		diverse	다양한, 여러 가지의
	moral	도덕적인		consensus	의견 일치, 합의
	hazard	위험 (요소)		build up	강화[증강]하다, 기르다
	support	지지[지원]하다, 부양하다; 지지, 후원		particular	특정한, 개개의; 사항, 상세
	alter	바꾸다, 변경하다, 고치다		confidence	신뢰, 자신(감)
	rescue	구조하다, 구출하다; 구조, 구출		objectivity	객관성, 객관적 타당성
	get into	~에 흥미를 갖다, ~안으로 들어가다	24	tend to V	~하는 경향이 있다
	credit	공, 인정, 신용; 믿다, ~에게 돌리다		a series of	일련의
	crisis	위기, 중대 국면, 고비		psychologist	심리학자
	encourage	장려[격려]하다, 촉구하다		deadline	(마감) 기한, 최종 기한
	intervene	사이에 들다		be more likely to V	좀 더 ~할 가능성이 많다
	intended	의도된, 계획된		remote	외딴, 먼, 원격의, 희박한
	affect	~에 영향을 미치다, ~인 척하다; 정서		as a result	그 결과
	risky	위험한		timeframe	기간, 시간대
	decision making	의사 결정		view A as B	A를 B로 간주하다
23	diversity	다양(성)		imminent	임박한
	objective	목표, 목적, 객관적인		manageable	관리[처리]할 수 있는
	maintain	유지하다, 주장하다	25	emission	배출(물), 배출량, 발산
	aspire	열망[염원]하다, 동경하다		surpass	능가하다, 초월하다
	solution	해결(책), 용액		in terms of	~ 면에서, ~에 관하여
	ethnicity	민족적 배경		opposite	반대(되는 사람[것]); 반대의
	carry out	~을 수행하다, 실행하다	26	concord	일치, 화합, 조화
	pursue	추구하다, 쫓다		graduate	졸업하다; 대학원생, 졸업생
	vary	다르다, 바꾸다, 변하다		set up	설치하다, 마련하다, 시작하다
	perspective	관점, 시각, 전망, 경치, 원근법		poet	시인

Voca

	incredible	믿을 수 없는, 굉장한		continue to V	계속 ~하다
	source	원천, 근원, (-s) 출처, 정보원		cuddle	꼭 껴안다, 포옹하다; 포옹
	widely	널리, 크게		bounce	튀다, 뛰어오르다; 튀어오름
	lifetime	일생, 생애, 평생; 평생의		tickle	간질이다, 만족시키다; 간지럼
27	explore	탐구하다, 탐험하다		care about	~에 관심을 갖다, ~에 마음을 쓰다
	participation	참여, 참가		operate	작동하다, 운영하다, 수술하다
	workshop	작업장, 일터, 연수회		make the point	요점을 짚다, 요점을 말하다
	participate in	~에 참여[참가]하다	30	interrupt	방해하다, (잠깐) 중단시키다
	include	포함하다, 포괄하다		commercial	광고(방송); 상업적인
	material	재료, 물질; 물질의, 육체의, 중요한		remove	제거하다, 없애다, 옮기다
28	tasty	맛있는, 식욕을 돋우는		break up	부서지다, 부수다; 해체[해산]하다
	treat	대우하다, 다루다, 치료하다; 대접		annoying	성가신, 짜증스러운
	highlight	집중하다, 강조하다; 가장 중요한 부분		adaptation	각색, 개조, 적응
	performance	수행, 성과, 성적, 공연		in a row	연속해서, 나란히, 한 줄로
	entry	참가, 출품(작), 입구, 참가자		no longer	더 이상 ~아닌[하지 않는]
	necessary	필요한, 필연적인; (-s) 필수품		pleasurable	즐거운, 유쾌한, 만족을 주는
	show up	나타나다, 등장하다		adapt	조정하다, 적응시키다, 개작하다
29	built-in	내장된, 붙박이의		intersperse	흩뿌리다
	capacity	용량, 수용력, 능력		Brussels sprout	방울양배추
	prove	입증하다, ~으로 판명되다[드러나다]		disrupt	방해하다, 교란[붕괴]시키다; 혼란된, 분열된
	remarkable	놀랄 만한, 주목할 만한, 훌륭한		following	다음(의); 다음에 계속되는
	observation	관찰, 관측, 주시, 의견, 진술	31	serve	제공[기여]하다, 복무하다, 적합하다
	congenitally	선천적으로		practical	실용적인, 실제의
	deaf	귀머거리의, 귀가 먼		purpose	목적, 의도; 의도하다
	reinforce	강화하다, 보강하다		attraction	인력, 끌어당기는 힘, 매력

Voca

	supply	공급하다, 주다; 공급		delay	연기하다, 미루다; 지연, 지체
	arrange	정리[준비]하다, 배열[배치]하다, 각색하다		add to	~을 증가시키다, ~을 늘리다
	in order	차례차례, 알맞은, 적절한	33	instantaneously	즉각적으로, 당장, 즉석에서
	attractiveness	매력		glow	빛나다, 상기되다; 불빛, 홍조
	agreement	합의, 동의		physically	실제적으로, 신체적으로
	afterward	나중에, 그 후에		shin	정강이
	from scratch	처음부터		reach out	~에 접근하다, 손을 뻗다
	classified	분류된, 비밀의, 기밀 취급의		illuminate	밝게 하다
	psychology	심리, 심리학		bulb	구근, 전구
	phenomenon	현상, 사건, 비범한 인물 ((복수형 phenomena))		notion	개념, 생각, 관념
	deprived of	~가 없는, ~가 결핍된		nonsensical	무의미한, 터무니없는, 부조리한
	deem	생각하다, 여기다		entire	전체의, 완전한; 전부, 전체
	attractive	매력적인, 마음을 끄는		infinitely	무한히, 한없이, 대단히, 훨씬
32	invest	투자하다, (시간, 노력 등을) 들이다		vastness	광대함
	venture	모험, 모험적 행위; 위험을 무릅쓰고 하다		immense	엄청난, 막대한
	fallacy	그릇된 생각, 오류, 착오	34	capital	수도, 자본, 대문자; 자본의, 대문자의
	instinct	본능		consumption	소비, 소모
	prove to be ~	~임이 밝혀지다, 드러나다		fancy	공상, 좋아함; 공상하다; 화려한, 변덕스러운
	give up	포기하다, (정보 등을) 드러내다		at the same time	반면에, 동시에
	acknowledge	인정[승인]하다, 감사하다		admonish	훈계[질책]하다, 권고[충고]하다
	get back	돌아가다[오다], 물러가다, ~을 되찾다		neither A nor B	A도 B도 아니다
	avoid	피하다, 막다		agrarian	농업(농민)의
	bet	내기하다, 단언하다; 내기		reasonably	합리적으로, 타당하게, 적정하게
	rather than	~보다 오히려		soon after	~뒤에 곧
	lay	(물건을) 놓다, (알을) 낳다		harvest	수확(물); 수확하다

Voca

	sophisticated	고성능의, 정교한		pedestrian	보행자
	retirement	퇴직, 은퇴		plain	명백한, 평범한, 무늬가 없는; (-s) 평원
	divorce	이혼[분리]하다, 단절시키다; 이혼, 단절		collide	충돌하다, 상충하다
	flexibility	유연성, 융통성	37	employ	고용하다, 사용[이용]하다
35	manual	손의, 수동의; 소책자, 안내서		laboratory	실험실; 실험실의
	high-profile	세간의 이목을 끄는, 눈에 띄는		in the long run	결국에
	instruction	수업, 교육, (-s) 지시, 설명		crucial	필수적인, 결정적인, 아주 중요한
	for free	무료로		productive	생산적인, 다산의
	mere	단지 ~에 불과한, 단순한		tuition	수업, 교습, 수업료
	valuable	가치 있는, 귀중한, 값비싼; (-s) 귀중품	38	differ from	~와 다르다
	genetic	유전적인, 유전의, 유전학의		mass	질량, (큰) 덩어리, 집단; 많은, 대량의
	sequence	연속(물), 순서, 서열, 결과		replace	교체하다, 대체하다, 바꾸다
	interpretation	해석, 설명, 이해		obvious	분명한, 명백한
36	consume	소비하다, 섭취하다, 먹다		bidirectional	양방향의
	used to V	~하곤 했다, ~이었다[했다]		A as well as B	B뿐만 아니라 A도
	navigate	항해[조종]하다, 길을 찾다, 처리하다		exchange	교환하다, 환전하다; 교환, 환전
	gaze	응시하다, 바라보다; 응시		thoroughfare	통로
	guarantee	확실하게 하다, 보장하다; 보증(서)		commerce	상업, 무역, 통상
	figure	생각[계산]하다; 수치, 숫자, 인물, 모양		virtual	사실상의, 실질상의, 가상의
	attention	주의(력), 집중(력), 관심		order	명령[주문]하다, 정돈하다; 명령, 주문, 순서
	trick	속임수, 재주, 비결; 속임수의; 속이다		track	철로, 선로; 추적하다, 탐지하다
	give away	주다, 기부하다, 누설하다		corporate	회사의, 기업의, 법인의
	assure	확언하다, 보증하다		distribute	퍼뜨리다, 분배하다, 유통하다
	visual	시각의, 눈에 보이는		critique	평론[비평]하다, 비난하다
	prevalence	발병률, 널리 퍼짐, 유행		edit	편집하다, 교정[수정]하다

Voca

| ❶ voca | ❷ text | ❸ [/] | ❹ _____ | ❺ quiz 1 | ❻ quiz 2 | ❼ quiz 3 | ❽ quiz 4 | ❾ quiz 5 |

	or otherwise	혹은 그밖에, 그 반대이든		popularity	인기, 대중성
	modify	수정하다, 바꾸다		confused	혼란을 느끼는
39	pink slip	해고 통지서		physical	신체적인, 물리적인, 물질적인
	labor force	노동인구, 노동력		identical	동일한, 똑같은
	revolution	혁명, 큰 변화, 회전, 순환		subject	주제, 과목, 대상; 지배하다, 복종시키다
	workforce	전 종업원, 노동 인구, 총노동력		paradoxically	역설적으로
	live on	~을 먹고 살다, 주식으로 하다		resentment	분노, 적의
	automation	자동화		residence	거처, 거주, 주택
	eliminate	제거하다		involve	포함[수반]하다, 필요로 하다, 관련시키다
	all but	거의, ~외에 모두		focus on	~에 집중하다, 초점을 맞추다
	replace ~ with ...	~을 ...으로 대체하다		whereas	~에 반하여, 그런데, 그러나
	displaced	추방된, 쫓겨난, 난민의		individual	개인; 개인의, 개별적인, 독특한
	idle	한가한, 게으른		circumstance	상황, 정황, 환경
	entirely	완전히, 전적으로		resent	분개하다, 화를 내다
	manufacture	제조하다, 생산하다; 제조, 제품		bias	편견, 선입견; 편견[선입견]을 품게 하다
	occupation	직업, 업무, 점유, 이용	41-42	partial	부분적인, 편파적인, 불공평한
	appliance	가전제품, (가정용) 기구, 장치		minimize	최소화하다, 축소하다
	chemist	화학자, 약제사		seemingly	겉보기에는, 외견상으로
	build on	~을 발판으로 삼다, ~을 의지하다		consistent with	~와 일치하는
	previous	이전의, 사전의		justify	정당화하다, 옳음을 증명하다
	vast	광대한, 거대한, 막대한		on the one hand	한편으로는
	majority	가장 많은 수, 다수		sensible	분별력 있는, 의식하는, 상당한
40	spark	촉발시키다, 유발하다; 불꽃, 불똥		defend	방어[수비]하다, 옹호하다
	ownership	소유권, 회원권		conduct	~을 하다, 지휘하다, (전기 등을) 전도하다; 행동
	status	상태, 지위, 신분		analysis	분석 ((복수형 analyses))

| ❶ voca | ❷ text | ❸ [/] | ❹ _____ | ❺ quiz 1 | ❻ quiz 2 | ❼ quiz 3 | ❽ quiz 4 | ❾ quiz 5 |

prey	(동물의) 먹이, 희생자; 포식하다		respond to	~에 반응하다
cluster	무리를 이루다; 무리, 집단		hypothetical	가상적인
collectively	전체적으로, 집합적으로		dramatically	급격히, 극적으로, 연극으로
confirmation	증거, 확증		assess	(자질 등을) 재다, 평가[가늠]하다
nearly	거의, 대략, 간신히, 면밀하게		advantage	이익, 이점; 이롭게 하다
rely on	~에 의존[의지]하다	43-45	grab	집다, 붙잡다, 움켜잡다; 붙잡음
applicant	신청자, 지원자		attach	붙이다, 첨부하다, 애착을 갖게 하다
it turns out that	~인 것으로 드러나다		look up	찾아보다, 방문하다, 올려다보다
subconsciously	잠재 의식으로, 반 의식하에서		insist on -ing	~을 주장[고집]하다
make up	차지하다, 만들어내다, 화해하다		put together	~을 합치다, 조립하다, 한데 모으다
base on	~에 근거하다			
interaction	상호 작용			
evidence	증거, 징후			
phrase	구절, (문)구; 말로 표현하다			
confirm	확인[확증]하다, 공식화하다			
impression	인상, 감명, 흔적			
ambitious	야심 있는, 열망하는			
versus	대(對), ~에 대한, ~와 대비하여			
commit	저지르다, 맡기다, 전념[헌신]하다			
be prone to V	~하기 쉽다, ~하는 경향이 있다			
significant	상당한, 현저한, 중요한			
indicate	말하다, 나타내다, 표시하다			
candidate	후보자, 지원자			
structure	구조, 조직, 체계; 구성하다, 조직화하다			
obtain	얻다, 구하다, 획득하다, 행해지다			

Voca

18	resident				overestimate			
	take advantage of				accurately			
	parking lot				discern			
	plant				unlock			
	weed				potential			
	decoration			21	trappings			
	regard				be forced to V			
19	relay				in return			
	spot				suit			
	perform				depend on			
	make a mistake				attend			
	approach				up to			
	smoothly				inevitably			
	raise				examine			
	hand in				transaction			
	come across				slavery			
20	resist				reside			
	be capable of			22	firm			
	maxim				concentrate on			
	refuse				A rather than B			
	weakness				restructure			
	admit				company			
	damage				profitable			
	underestimate				viable			
	capability				term			

Voca

❶ voca	❷ text	❸ [/]	❹ _____	❺ quiz 1	❻ quiz 2	❼ quiz 3	❽ quiz 4	❾ quiz 5

	known as				diverse	
	moral				consensus	
	hazard				build up	
	support				particular	
	alter				confidence	
	rescue				objectivity	
	get into			24	tend to V	
	credit				a series of	
	crisis				psychologist	
	encourage				deadline	
	intervene				be more likely to V	
	intended				remote	
	affect				as a result	
	risky				timeframe	
	decision making				view A as B	
23	diversity				imminent	
	objective				manageable	
	maintain			25	emission	
	aspire				surpass	
	solution				in terms of	
	ethnicity				opposite	
	carry out			26	concord	
	pursue				qraduate	
	vary				set up	
	perspective				poet	

Voca

❶ voca	❷ text	❸ [/]	❹ _____	❺ quiz 1	❻ quiz 2	❼ quiz 3	❽ quiz 4	❾ quiz 5

	incredible			continue to V	
	source			cuddle	
	widely			bounce	
	lifetime			tickle	
27	explore			care about	
	participation			operate	
	workshop			make the point	
	participate in		30	interrupt	
	include			commercial	
	material			remove	
28	tasty			break up	
	treat			annoying	
	highlight			adaptation	
	performance			in a row	
	entry			no longer	
	necessary			pleasurable	
	show up			adapt	
29	built-in			intersperse	
	capacity			Brussels sprout	
	prove			disrupt	
	remarkable			following	
	observation		31	serve	
	congenitally			practical	
	deaf			purpose	
	reinforce			attraction	

	❶ voca	❷ text	❸ [/]	❹ _____	❺ quiz 1	❻ quiz 2	❼ quiz 3	❽ quiz 4	❾ quiz 5
	supply					delay			
	arrange					add to			
	in order				33	instantaneously			
	attractiveness					glow			
	agreement					physically			
	afterward					shin			
	from scratch					reach out			
	classified					illuminate			
	psychology					bulb			
	phenomenon					notion			
	deprived of					nonsensical			
	deem					entire			
	attractive					infinitely			
32	invest					vastness			
	venture					immense			
	fallacy				34	capital			
	instinct					consumption			
	prove to be ~					fancy			
	give up					at the same time			
	acknowledge					admonish			
	get back					neither A nor B			
	avoid					agrarian			
	bet					reasonably			
	rather than					soon after			
	lay					harvest			

Voca

	❶ voca	❷ text	❸ [/]	❹ _____	❺ quiz 1	❻ quiz 2	❼ quiz 3	❽ quiz 4	❾ quiz 5

	❶ voca	❺ quiz 1	❻ quiz 2
	sophisticated		pedestrian
	retirement		plain
	divorce		collide
	flexibility	37	employ
35	manual		laboratory
	high-profile		in the long run
	instruction		crucial
	for free		productive
	mere		tuition
	valuable	38	differ from
	genetic		mass
	sequence		replace
	interpretation		obvious
36	consume		bidirectional
	used to V		A as well as B
	navigate		exchange
	gaze		thoroughfare
	guarantee		commerce
	figure		virtual
	attention		order
	trick		track
	give away		corporate
	assure		distribute
	visual		critique
	prevalence		edit

❶ voca	❷ text	❸ [/]	❹ _____	❺ quiz 1	❻ quiz 2	❼ quiz 3	❽ quiz 4	❾ quiz 5
	or otherwise				popularity			
	modify				confused			
39	pink slip				physical			
	labor force				identical			
	revolution				subject			
	workforce				paradoxically			
	live on				resentment			
	automation				residence			
	eliminate				involve			
	all but				focus on			
	replace ~ with ...				whereas			
	displaced				individual			
	idle				circumstance			
	entirely				resent			
	manufacture				bias			
	occupation			41-42	partial			
	appliance				minimize			
	chemist				seemingly			
	build on				consistent with			
	previous				justify			
	vast				on the one hand			
	majority				sensible			
40	spark				defend			
	ownership				conduct			
	status				analysis			

Voca

❶ voca	❷ text	❸ [/]	❹ _____	❺ quiz 1	❻ quiz 2	❼ quiz 3	❽ quiz 4	❾ quiz 5
prey				respond to				
cluster				hypothetical				
collectively				dramatically				
confirmation				assess				
nearly				advantage				
rely on			43-45	grab				
applicant				attach				
it turns out that				look up				
subconsciously				insist on -ing				
make up				put together				
base on								
interaction								
evidence								
phrase								
confirm								
impression								
ambitious								
versus								
commit								
be prone to V								
significant								
indicate								
candidate								
structure								
obtain								

Voca

① voca	② text	③ [/]	④ ___	⑤ quiz 1	⑥ quiz 2	⑦ quiz 3	⑧ quiz 4	⑨ quiz 5
18	주민					과대평가하다; 과대평가		
	~을 활용[이용]하다					정확히, 정밀하게		
	주차장					식별[분별]하다, 인식[파악]하다		
	(묘목 등을) 심다; 식물, 공장					열다, ~을 밝히다, 누설하다		
	잡초; 풀을 뽑다, 제거하다					가능성이 있는, 잠재적인; 가능성, 잠재력		
	장식(품), 훈장	21				장식		
	간주[주목]하다, 관련있다; 관심, 존경, 관계					~하도록 강요받다		
19	전달[중계]하다, 교대시키다; 중계, 교대					대신에, 답례로		
	발견하다, 찾아내다; 장소, 반점					정장, 소송; 적합하다, (알)맞다		
	수행하다, 행동하다, 공연[연주]하다					~에 의존하다, ~에 달려 있다		
	실수하다					참석하다, 보살피다		
	접근하다; 접근(법)					~까지, ~의 책임인		
	매끄럽게, 순조롭게					어쩔 수 없이, 불가피하게, 필연적으로		
	높이다, 올리다, 기르다, 제기하다; 인상					검사[조사]하다, 진찰하다		
	제출하다, 내다					거래, 매매, 처리		
	우연히 마주치다, 인상을 주다, 이해되다					노예 제도, 노예의 신분		
20	저항하다, 반대하다, 견디다					살다, 거주하다, 존재하다, (~에) 속하다		
	~할 수 있다	22				확고한, 고정된; 회사		
	격언					~에 집중하다		
	거부하다, 거절하다					B라기 보다는 A		
	약점, 결점					재구성하다, 개편하다		
	인정[승인]하다, 허가하다					친구, 동료, 회사, 교제; 회사의		
	피해, 손상, 손해; 손해를 입히다					수익성이 있는, 유익한		
	과소평가하다, 경시하다; 과소평가					성장할 수 있는		
	능력, 수완					기간, 용어, (-s) 조건, 관점; 말하다		

Voca

❶ voca	❷ text	❸ [/]	❹ _____	❺ quiz 1	❻ quiz 2	❼ quiz 3	❽ quiz 4	❾ quiz 5
		~으로 알려진				다양한, 여러 가지의		
		도덕적인				의견 일치, 합의		
		위험 (요소)				강화[증강]하다, 기르다		
		지지[지원]하다, 부양하다; 지지, 후원				특정한, 개개의; 사항, 상세		
		바꾸다, 변경하다, 고치다				신뢰, 자신(감)		
		구조하다, 구출하다; 구조, 구출				객관성, 객관적 타당성		
		~에 흥미를 갖다, ~안으로 들어가다	24			~하는 경향이 있다		
		공, 인정, 신용; 믿다, ~에게 돌리다				일련의		
		위기, 중대 국면, 고비				심리학자		
		장려[격려]하다, 촉구하다				(마감) 기한, 최종 기한		
		사이에 들다				좀 더 ~할 가능성이 많다		
		의도된, 계획된				외딴, 먼, 원격의, 희박한		
		~에 영향을 미치다, ~인 척하다; 정서				그 결과		
		위험한				기간, 시간대		
		의사 결정				A를 B로 간주하다		
23		다양(성)				임박한		
		목표, 목적, 객관적인				관리[처리]할 수 있는		
		유지하다, 주장하다	25			배출(물), 배출량, 발산		
		열망[염원]하다, 동경하다				능가하다, 초월하다		
		해결(책), 용액				~ 면에서, ~에 관하여		
		민족적 배경				반대(되는 사람[것]); 반대의		
		~을 수행하다, 실행하다	26			일치, 화합, 조화		
		추구하다, 쫓다				졸업하다; 대학원생, 졸업생		
		다르다, 바꾸다, 변하다				설치하다, 마련하다, 시작하다		
		관점, 시각, 전망, 경치, 원근법				시인		

Voca

❶ voca	❷ text	❸ [/]	❹ _____	❺ quiz 1	❻ quiz 2	❼ quiz 3	❽ quiz 4	❾ quiz 5

text	뜻	text	뜻
	믿을 수 없는, 굉장한		계속 ~하다
	원천, 근원, (-s) 출처, 정보원		꼭 껴안다, 포옹하다; 포옹
	널리, 크게		튀다, 뛰어오르다; 튀어오름
	일생, 생애, 평생; 평생의		간질이다, 만족시키다; 간지럼
27	탐구하다, 탐험하다		~에 관심을 갖다, ~에 마음을 쓰다
	참여, 참가		작동하다, 운영하다, 수술하다
	작업장, 일터, 연수회		요점을 짚다, 요점을 말하다
	~에 참여[참가]하다	30	방해하다, (잠깐) 중단시키다
	포함하다, 포괄하다		광고(방송); 상업적인
	재료, 물질; 물질의, 육체의, 중요한		제거하다, 없애다, 옮기다
28	맛있는, 식욕을 돋우는		부서지다, 부수다; 해체[해산]하다
	대우하다, 다루다, 치료하다; 대접		성가신, 짜증스러운
	집중하다, 강조하다; 가장 중요한 부분		각색, 개조, 적응
	수행, 성과, 성적, 공연		연속해서, 나란히, 한 줄로
	참가, 출품(작), 입구, 참가자		더 이상 ~아닌[하지 않는]
	필요한, 필연적인; (-s) 필수품		즐거운, 유쾌한, 만족을 주는
	나타나다, 등장하다		조정하다, 적응시키다, 개작하다
29	내장된, 붙박이의		흩뿌리다
	용량, 수용력, 능력		방울양배추
	입증하다, ~으로 판명되다[드러나다]		방해하다, 교란[붕괴]시키다; 혼란된, 분열된
	놀랄 만한, 주목할 만한, 훌륭한		다음(의); 다음에 계속되는
	관찰, 관측, 주시, 의견, 진술	31	제공[기여]하다, 복무하다, 적합하다
	선천적으로		실용적인, 실제의
	귀머거리의, 귀가 먼		목적, 의도; 의도하다
	강화하다, 보강하다		인력, 끌어당기는 힘, 매력

❶ voca	❷ text	❸ [/]	❹ _____	❺ quiz 1	❻ quiz 2	❼ quiz 3	❽ quiz 4	❾ quiz 5
		공급하다, 주다; 공급						연기하다, 미루다; 지연, 지체
		정리[준비]하다, 배열[배치]하다, 각색하다						~을 증가시키다, ~을 늘리다
		차례차례, 알맞은, 적절한		33				즉각적으로, 당장, 즉석에서
		매력						빛나다, 상기되다; 불빛, 홍조
		합의, 동의						실제적으로, 신체적으로
		나중에, 그 후에						정강이
		처음부터						~에 접근하다, 손을 뻗다
		분류된, 비밀의, 기밀 취급의						밝게 하다
		심리, 심리학						구근, 전구
		현상, 사건, 비범한 인물 ((복수형 phenomena))						개념, 생각, 관념
		~가 없는, ~가 결핍된						무의미한, 터무니없는, 부조리한
		생각하다, 여기다						전체의, 완전한; 전부, 전체
		매력적인, 마음을 끄는						무한히, 한없이, 대단히, 훨씬
32		투자하다, (시간, 노력 등을) 들이다						광대함
		모험, 모험적 행위; 위험을 무릅쓰고 하다						엄청난, 막대한
		그릇된 생각, 오류, 착오		34				수도, 자본, 대문자; 자본의, 대문자의
		본능						소비, 소모
		~임이 밝혀지다, 드러나다						공상, 좋아함; 공상하다; 화려한, 변덕스러운
		포기하다, (정보 등을) 드러내다						반면에, 동시에
		인정[승인]하다, 감사하다						훈계[질책]하다, 권고[충고]하다
		돌아가다[오다], 물러가다, ~을 되찾다						A도 B도 아니다
		피하다, 막다						농입(농민)의
		내기하다, 단언하다; 내기						합리적으로, 타당하게, 적정하게
		~보다 오히려						~뒤에 곧
		(물건을) 놓다, (알을) 낳다						수확(물); 수확하다

Voca

❶ voca　❷ text　❸ [/]　❹ _____　❺ quiz 1　❻ quiz 2　❼ quiz 3　❽ quiz 4　❾ quiz 5

No.	뜻		뜻
	고성능의, 정교한		보행자
	퇴직, 은퇴		명백한, 평범한, 무늬가 없는; (-s) 평원
	이혼[분리]하다, 단절시키다; 이혼, 단절		충돌하다, 상충하다
	유연성, 융통성	37	고용하다, 사용[이용]하다
35	손의, 수동의; 소책자, 안내서		실험실; 실험실의
	세간의 이목을 끄는, 눈에 띄는		결국에
	수업, 교육, (-s) 지시, 설명		필수적인, 결정적인, 아주 중요한
	무료로		생산적인, 다산의
	단지 ~에 불과한, 단순한		수업, 교습, 수업료
	가치 있는, 귀중한, 값비싼; (-s) 귀중품	38	~와 다르다
	유전적인, 유전의, 유전학의		질량, (큰) 덩어리, 집단; 많은, 대량의
	연속(물), 순서, 서열, 결과		교체하다, 대체하다, 바꾸다
	해석, 설명, 이해		분명한, 명백한
36	소비하다, 섭취하다, 먹다		양방향의
	~하곤 했다, ~이었다[했다]		B뿐만 아니라 A도
	항해[조종]하다, 길을 찾다, 처리하다		교환하다, 환전하다; 교환, 환전
	응시하다, 바라보다; 응시		통로
	확실하게 하다, 보장하다; 보증(서)		상업, 무역, 통상
	생각[계산]하다; 수치, 숫자, 인물, 모양		사실상의, 실질상의, 가상의
	주의(력), 집중(력), 관심		명령[주문]하다, 정돈하다; 명령, 주문, 순서
	속임수, 재주, 비결; 속임수의; 속이다		철로, 선로; 추적하다, 탐지하다
	주다, 기부하다, 누설하다		회사의, 기업의, 법인의
	확언하다, 보증하다		퍼뜨리다, 분배하나, 유통하다
	시각의, 눈에 보이는		평론[비평]하다, 비난하다
	발병률, 널리 퍼짐, 유행		편집하다, 교정[수정]하다

❶ voca	❷ text	❸ [/]	❹ _____	❺ quiz 1	❻ quiz 2	❼ quiz 3	❽ quiz 4	❾ quiz 5

	혹은 그밖에, 그 반대이든			인기, 대중성
	수정하다, 바꾸다			혼란을 느끼는
39	해고 통지서			신체적인, 물리적인, 물질적인
	노동인구, 노동력			동일한, 똑같은
	혁명, 큰 변화, 회전, 순환			주제, 과목, 대상; 지배하다, 복종시키다
	전 종업원, 노동 인구, 총노동력			역설적으로
	~을 먹고 살다, 주식으로 하다			분노, 적의
	자동화			거처, 거주, 주택
	제거하다			포함[수반]하다, 필요로 하다, 관련시키다
	거의, ~외에 모두			~에 집중하다, 초점을 맞추다
	~을 ...으로 대체하다			~에 반하여, 그런데, 그러나
	추방된, 쫓겨난, 난민의			개인; 개인의, 개별적인, 독특한
	한가한, 게으른			상황, 정황, 환경
	완전히, 전적으로			분개하다, 화를 내다
	제조하다, 생산하다; 제조, 제품			편견, 선입견; 편견[선입견]을 품게 하다
	직업, 업무, 점유, 이용	41-42		부분적인, 편파적인, 불공평한
	가전제품, (가정용) 기구, 장치			최소화하다, 축소하다
	화학자, 약제사			겉보기에는, 외견상으로
	~을 발판으로 삼다, ~을 의지하다			~와 일치하는
	이전의, 사전의			정당화하다, 옳음을 증명하다
	광대한, 거대한, 막대한			한편으로는
	가장 많은 수, 다수			분별력 있는, 의식하는, 상당한
40	촉발시키다, 유발하다; 불꽃, 불똥			방어[수비]하다, 옹호하다
	소유권, 회원권			~을 하다, 지휘하다, (전기 등을) 전도하다; 행동
	상태, 지위, 신분			분석 ((복수형 analyses))

Voca

❶ voca	❷ text	❸ [/]	❹ _____	❺ quiz 1	❻ quiz 2	❼ quiz 3	❽ quiz 4	❾ quiz 5

	(동물의) 먹이, 희생자; 포식하다				~에 반응하다
	무리를 이루다; 무리, 집단				가상적인
	전체적으로, 집합적으로				급격히, 극적으로, 연극으로
	증거, 확증				(자질 등을) 재다, 평가[가늠]하다
	거의, 대략, 간신히, 면밀하게				이익, 이점; 이롭게 하다
	~에 의존[의지]하다	43-45			집다, 붙잡다, 움켜잡다; 붙잡음
	신청자, 지원자				붙이다, 첨부하다, 애착을 갖게 하다
	~인 것으로 드러나다				찾아보다, 방문하다, 올려다보다
	잠재 의식으로, 반 의식하에서				~을 주장[고집]하다
	차지하다, 만들어내다, 화해하다				~을 합치다, 조립하다, 한데 모으다
	~에 근거하다				
	상호 작용				
	증거, 징후				
	구절, (문)구; 말로 표현하다				
	확인[확증]하다, 공식화하다				
	인상, 감명, 흔적				
	야심 있는, 열망하는				
	대(對), ~에 대한, ~와 대비하여				
	저지르다, 맡기다, 전념[헌신]하다				
	~하기 쉽다, ~하는 경향이 있다				
	상당한, 현저한, 중요한				
	말하다, 나타내다, 표시하다				
	후보자, 지원자				
	구조, 조직, 체계; 구성하다, 조직화하다				
	얻다, 구하다, 획득하다, 행해지다				

2024 고2 6월 모의고사

18 목적

❶ Dear Residents,

주민들께,

❷ My name is Kari Patterson, and I'm the manager of the River View Apartments.

제 이름은 Kari Patterson이고, 저는 River View 아파트의 관리인입니다.

❸ It's time to take advantage of the sunny weather to make our community more beautiful.

우리의 커뮤니티를 더욱 아름답게 만들기 위해 화창한 날씨를 이용할 때입니다.

❹ On Saturday, July 13 at 9 a.m., residents will meet in the north parking lot.

7월 13일 토요일 오전 9시에, 주민들은 북쪽 주차장에서 만날 예정입니다.

❺ We will divide into teams to plant flowers and small trees, pull weeds, and put colorful decorations on the lawn.

우리는 팀을 나누어 꽃과 작은 나무를 심고, 잡초를 뽑고, 잔디밭에 다채로운 장식을 할 것입니다.

❻ Please join us for this year's Gardening Day, and remember no special skills or tools are required.

올해 정원 가꾸기 날에 우리와 함께 해 주시고, 특별한 기술이나 도구는 필요하지 않다는 것을 기억하세요.

❻ Last year, we had a great time working together, so come out and make this year's event even better!

작년에, 우리는 함께 일하며 즐거운 시간을 보냈으니, 오셔서 올해 행사도 더 멋지게 만들어 주세요!

❼ Warm regards, Kari Patterson
따뜻한 미음을 담아, Kari Patterson

19 심경

❶ It was the championship race.
결승전 경주였다.

❷ Emma was the final runner on her relay team.
Emma는 그녀의 계주 팀의 마지막 주자였다.

❸ She anxiously waited in her spot for her teammate to pass her the baton.
그녀는 그녀의 자리에서 팀 동료가 그녀에게 바통을 건네주기를 초조하게 기다렸다.

❹ Emma wasn't sure she could perform her role without making a mistake.
Emma는 그녀가 실수를 하지 않고 자신의 역할을 수행할 수 있을지 확신하지 못했다.

❺ Her hands shook as she thought, "What if I drop the baton?"
"만약 내가 바통을 떨어뜨리면 어떡하지?" 라고 생각하면서 그녀의 손이 떨렸다.

❻ She felt her heart rate increasing as her teammate approached.
그녀는 그녀의 팀 동료가 다가올수록 심박수가 증가하는 것을 느꼈다.

❼ But as she started running, she received the baton smoothly.
하지만 그녀가 달리기 시작했을 때, 그녀는 순조롭게 바통을 받았다.

❽ In the final 10 meters, she passed two other runners and crossed the finish line in first place!
마지막 10미터에서, 그녀는 두 명의 다른 주자를 제치고 나서 1위로 결승선을 통과했다!

❾ She raised her hands in the air, and a huge smile came across her face.
그녀는 두 손을 하늘로 치켜들고, 얼굴에 큰 미소를 지었다.

❿ As her teammates hugged her, she shouted, "We did it!"
팀 동료들이 그녀를 안아주자, 그녀는 "우리가 해냈어!"라고 소리쳤다.

⓫ All of her hard training had been worth it.
그녀의 모든 힘든 훈련이 그럴만한 가치가 있었다.

20 요지

❶ Most people resist the idea of a true self-estimate, probably because they fear it might mean downgrading some of their beliefs about who they are and what they're capable of.

대부분의 사람들은 그것(진정한 자기 평가)이 그들이 누구인지, 무엇을 할 수 있는지에 대한 믿음을 낮추는 것을 의미할지도 모른다고 두려워하기 때문에, 진정한 자기 평가에 대한 생각을 거부한다.

❷ As Goethe's maxim goes, it is a great failing "to see yourself as more than you are."

Goethe의 격언처럼, "너 자신을 현재의 너의 모습 이상으로 보는 것"은 큰 실수이다.

❸ How could you really be considered self-aware if you refuse to consider your weaknesses?

네가 너의 단점을 생각해 보기를 거부한다면 어떻게 너 자신을 인식하고 있다고 여겨질 수 있을까?

❹ Don't fear self-assessment because you're worried you might have to admit some things about yourself.

네가 너 자신에 대해 몇 가지를 인정해야 할지도 모른다는 걱정 때문에 자기를 평가하는 것을 두려워하지 마라.

❺ The second half of Goethe's maxim is important too.

Goethe 격언의 후반부도 역시 중요하다.

❻ He states that it is equally damaging to "value yourself at less than your true worth."

그는 "너의 진정한 가치보다 너 자신을 낮게 평가하는 것"도 똑같이 해롭다고 말한다.

❼ We underestimate our capabilities just as much and just as dangerously as we overestimate other abilities.

우리는 다른 능력들을 과대평가하는 것만큼 많이 그리고 위험하게 우리의 능력을 과소평가한다.

❽ Cultivate the ability to judge yourself accurately and honestly.

너 자신을 정확하게 그리고 정직하게 판단하는 능력을 길러라.

❾ Look inward to discern what you're capable of and what it will take to unlock that potential.

네가 할 수 있는 것과 너의 잠재력을 열기 위해 필요한 것을 파악하기 위해 내면을 들여다 봐라.

21 주장

❶ Take a look at some of the most powerful, rich, and famous people in the world. Ignore the
세계에서 가장 힘있고, 부유하며, 유명한 사람들 중 몇몇을 살펴봐라.

❷ Ignore the trappings of their success and what they're able to buy.
그들의 성공의 장식과 그들이 살 수 있는 것을 무시해라.

❸ Look instead at what they're forced to trade in return — look at what success has cost them.
대신 그들이 맞바꿔야 하는 것을 봐라 — 성공이 그들에게 치르게 한 것을 봐라.

❹ Mostly? Freedom. Their work demands they wear a suit.
대부분은? 자유이다. 그들의 업무는 그들이 정장을 입는 것을 요구한다.

❺ Their success depends on attending certain parties, kissing up to people they don't like.
그들의 성공은 특정 파티에 참석하여, 그들이 좋아하지 않는 사람들에게 아첨하는 것에 달려 있다.

❻ It will require — inevitably — realizing they are unable to say what they actually think.
그것은 요구할 것이다 — 필연적으로 — 그들이 실제로 생각하는 것을 말할 수 없다는 사실을 깨닫는 것을.

❼ Worse, it demands that they become a different type of person or do bad things.
더 나쁜 것은, 그것은 그들이 다른 유형의 사람이 되거나 부당한 일을 하도록 요구한다는 것이다.

❽ Sure, it might pay well — but they haven't truly examined the transaction.
물론, 그것은 많은 이익이 될지도 모른다 — 그러나 그들은 그 거래를 제대로 고찰한 적이 없다.

❾ As Seneca put it, "Slavery resides under marble and gold." Too many successful people are prisoners in jails of
their own making.
Seneca가 말했듯이, "대리석과 황금 아래에 노예 상태가 존재한다." 너무 많은 성공한 사람들은 그들이 스스로
만든 감옥의 죄수들이다.

❿ Is that what you want? Is that what you're working hard toward? Let's hope not.
그것이 당신이 원하는 것인가? 그깃이 당신이 목표로 하여 열심히 일하고 있는 것인가? 그렇지 않기를 바라자.

22 의미

❶ If a firm is going to be saved by the government, it might be easier to concentrate on lobbying the government for more money rather than taking the harder decision of restructuring the company to be able to be profitable and viable in the long term.

기업이 정부로부터 구제받으려면, 장기적으로 수익성이 나고 성장할 수 있도록 회사를 구조조정하는 어려운 결정을 내리기보다는 더 많은 돈을 받기 위해 정부에 로비하는 것에 집중하는 것이 더 쉬울지도 모른다.

❷ This is an example of something known as moral hazard — when government support alters the decisions firms take.

이것은 도덕적 해이라고 알려진 것의 한 예이다 — 정부의 지원이 기업이 내리는 결정을 바꿀 때.

❸ For example, if governments rescue banks who get into difficulty, as they did during the credit crisis of 2007-08, this could encourage banks to take greater risks in the future because they know there is a possibility that governments will intervene if they lose money.

예를 들어, 2007-08년 신용 위기 때 그들이 그랬던 것처럼, 만약 정부가 어려움에 처한 은행을 구제한다면, 이것은 은행이 앞으로 더 큰 위험을 감수하도록 조장하는데 그 이유는 그들이 손해를 보는 경우 정부가 개입할 가능성이 있다는 것을 그들이 알기 때문이다.

❹ Although the government rescue may be well intended, it can negatively affect the behavior of banks, encouraging risky and poor decision making.

정부의 구제는 좋은 의도일지라도, 그것은 은행의 행동에 부정적으로 영향을 미쳐, 위험하고 형편없는 의사 결정을 조장할 수 있다.

23 주제

❶ If there is little or no diversity of views, and all scientists see, think, and question the world in a similar way, then they will not, as a community, be as objective as they maintain they are, or at least aspire to be.
만약 견해의 다양성이 거의 없거나 전혀 없고, 모든 과학자들이 비슷한 방식으로 세상을 보고, 생각하고, 의문을 제기한다면, 그러면 그들은, 하나의 공동체로서, 자신들이 주장하는 것만큼, 혹은 적어도 그렇게 되기를 열망하는 것만큼, 객관적이지 않을 것이다.

❷ The solution is that there should be far greater diversity in the practice of science: in gender, ethnicity, and social and cultural backgrounds.
해결책은 과학의 실행에 있어 훨씬 더 많은 다양성이 있어야 한다는 것이다: 성별, 인종, 그리고 사회적 문화적 배경에서.

❸ Science works because it is carried out by people who pursue their curiosity about the natural world and test their and each other's ideas from as many varied perspectives and angles as possible.
과학은 그것이 자연 세계에 대한 호기심을 추구하고 가능한 한 다양한 관점과 각도에서 그들의 그리고 서로의 아이디어를 검증하는 사람들에 의해 수행되기 때문에 작동한다.

❹ When science is done by a diverse group of people, and if consensus builds up about a particular area of scientific knowledge, then we can have more confidence in its objectivity and truth.
과학이 다양한 집단의 사람들에 의해 행해질 때, 그리고 만약 과학지식의 특정 영역에 대한 의견 일치가 이루어진다면, 그러면 우리는 그것의 객관성과 진실성에 있어서 더 큰 자신감을 가질 수 있다.

24 제목

❶ We tend to break up time into units, such as weeks, months, and seasons; in a series of studies among farmers in India and students in North America, psychologists found that if a deadline is on the other side of a "break" — such as in the New Year — we're more likely to see it as remote, and, as a result, be less ready to jump into action.
우리는 시간을 주, 월, 계절과 같은 단위로 나누는 경향이 있다; 인도의 농부들과 북미의 학생들을 대상으로 한 일련의 연구에서, 심리학자들은 마감일이 "나뉨" — 새해와 같이 — 의 반대편에 있는 경우, 우리는 그것을 멀리 있는 것으로 여기고, 그 결과, 실행에 옮길 준비를 덜 할 가능성이 더 많다는 사실을 발견했다.

❷ What you need to do in that situation is find another way to think about the timeframe.
그러한 상황에서 당신이 해야 할 일은 그 시간 틀에 대해 생각하는 또 다른 방식을 찾는 것이다.

❸ For example, if it's November and the deadline is in January, it's better to tell yourself you have to get it done "this winter" rather than "next year."
예를 들어, 지금이 11월이고 마감일이 1월이라면, 네가 "내년"보다는 "이번 겨울"에 일을 끝내야 한다고 너 자신에게 말하는 것이 더 좋다.

❹ The best approach is to view deadlines as a challenge that you have to meet within a period that's imminent.
최고의 접근법은 마감일을 임박한 기간 내에 맞춰야 하는 도전으로 여기는 것이다.

❺ That way the stress is more manageable, and you have a better chance of starting — and therefore finishing — in good time.
그런 식으로 스트레스는 더 잘 관리될 수 있고, 적시에 작업을 시작 — 따라서 마무리 — 할 수 있는 가능성이 높아진다.

25 도표

❶ The graph above shows the amount of CO_2 emissions per person across selected Asian countries in 2010 and 2020.
위 그래프는 선택된 아시아 국가들의 2010년과 2020년 1인당 CO_2 배출량을 보여준다.

❷ All the countries except Uzbekistan had a greater amount of CO_2 emissions per person in 2020 than that in 2010. In 2010, the amount of CO_2 emissions per person of China was the largest among the five countries, followed by that of Mongolia.
우즈베키스탄을 제외한 모든 국가들은 2010년의 배출량보다 2020년의 1인당 CO_2 배출량이 더 많았다.

❸ In 2010, the amount of CO_2 emissions per person of China was the largest among the five countries, followed by that of Mongolia.
2010년에는, 중국의 1인당 CO_2 배출량이 5개국 중 가장 많았고, 몽골의 배출량이 그 뒤를 이었다.

❹ However, in 2020, Mongolia surpassed China in terms of the amount of CO_2 emissions per person.
그러나, 2020년에는, 1인당 CO_2 배출량에 있어서 몽골이 중국을 능가했다.

❺ In 2010, Uzbekistan produced a larger amount of CO_2 emissions per person than Vietnam, while the opposite was true in 2020.
2010년에는, 우즈베키스탄이 베트남보다 더 많은 1인당 CO_2 배출량을 만들어 냈지만, 2020년에는 그 반대였다.

❻ Among the five countries, India was the only one where the amount of CO_2 emissions per person was less than 2 tons in 2020.
5개국 중, 인도는 2020년에 1인당 CO_2 배출량이 2톤 미만인 유일한 국가였다.

26 일치

❶ Henry David Thoreau was born in Concord, Massachusetts in 1817. When he was 16, he entered Harvard College.
Henry David Thoreau는 1817년 Massachusetts주 Concord에서 태어났다.

❷ When he was 16, he entered Harvard College.
그가 16세 때, 그는 Harvard 대학에 입학했다.

❸ After graduating, Thoreau worked as a schoolteacher but he quit after two weeks.
졸업 후, Thoreau는 학교 교사로 일했지만 2주 후에 그만두었다.

❹ In June of 1838 he set up a school with his brother John.
1838년 6월에 그는 그의 형제인 John과 함께 학교를 세웠다.

❺ However, he had hopes of becoming a nature poet.
그러나, 그는 자연 시인이 되기를 희망했다.

❻ In 1845, he moved into a small self-built house near Walden Pond.
1845년, 그는 Walden 연못 근처에 직접 지은 작은 집으로 이사했다.

❼ At Walden, Thoreau did an incredible amount of reading.
Walden에서, Thoreau는 엄청난 양의 독서를 했다.

❽ The journal he wrote there became the source of his most famous book, Walden.
그가 그곳에서 쓴 저널이 그의 가장 유명한 저서인 Walden의 원천이 되었다.

❾ In his later life, Thoreau traveled to the Maine woods, to Cape Cod, and to Canada.
그의 인생 후반부에, Thoreau는 Maine 숲으로, Cape Cod로, 그리고 캐나다로 여행을 떠났다.

❿ At the age of 43, he ended his travels and returned to Concord.
43세의 나이에, 그는 그의 여행을 마치고 Concord로 돌아왔다.

⓫ Although his works were not widely read during his lifetime, he never stopped writing, and his works fill 20 volumes.
비록 그의 작품이 그의 일생 동안 널리 읽히지 않았지만, 그는 집필을 멈추지 않았고, 그의 작품은 20권에 달한다.

29 어법

❶ The built-in capacity for smiling is proven by the remarkable observation that babies who are congenitally both deaf and blind, who have never seen a human face, also start to smile at around 2 months.
미소 짓기에 대한 선천적인 능력은 선천적으로 청각 장애와 시각 장애가 있고, 사람 얼굴을 한 번도 본 적이 없는 아기들도, 약 2개월 즈음에 미소를 짓기 시작한다는 놀라운 관찰에 의해 증명된다.

❷ However, smiling in blind babies eventually disappears if nothing is done to reinforce it.
그러나, 시각장애를 가진 아기의 미소 짓기는 그것을 강화하기 위해 아무것도 행해지지 않으면 결국 사라진다.

❸ Without the right feedback, smiling dies out.
적절한 피드백이 없으면, 미소 짓기는 사라진다.

❹ But here's a fascinating fact: blind babies will continue to smile if they are cuddled, bounced, nudged, and tickled by an adult — anything to let them know that they are not alone and that someone cares about them.
하지만 여기에 흥미로운 사실이 있다: 만약 그들이 어른에 의해서 안기고, 흔들리고, 슬쩍 찔리고, 간지럽혀지면 — 그들이 혼자가 아니며 누군가 그들에게 관심을 갖고 있다는 것을 알게 하는 것 — 시각장애를 가진 아기들은 계속 미소를 지을 것이다.

❺ This social feedback encourages the baby to continue smiling.
이러한 사회적 피드백은 그 아기가 계속 미소를 지을 수 있도록 조장한다.

❻ In this way, early experience operates with our biology to establish social behaviors.
이런 방식으로, 초기 경험은 우리의 생리 작용과 함께 작용하여 사회적 행동을 형성한다.

❼ In fact, you don't need the cases of blind babies to make the point.
사실, 당신은 이를 설명하기 위해 시각장애를 가진 아기의 사례들을 필요로 하지 않는다.

❽ Babies with sight smile more at you when you look at them or, better still, smile back at them.
시력이 있는 아기들은 당신이 그들을 바라볼 때나, 더 나아가, 당신이 그들에게 미소를 지어줄 때, 당신에게 더 많이 미소 짓는다.

30 어휘

❶ Because people tend to adapt, interrupting positive things with negative ones can actually increase enjoyment.
사람들은 적응하는 경향이 있기 때문에, 긍정적인 것을 부정적인 것으로 방해하는 것이 실제로는 즐거움을 향상시킬 수 있다.

❷ Take commercials.
광고를 예로 들어 보자.

❸ Most people hate them, so removing them should make shows or other entertainment more enjoyable.
대부분의 사람들은 그것들을 싫어해서, 그것들을 제거하는 것이 쇼나 다른 오락물을 더 즐겁게 만들 수 있다.

❹ But the opposite is true.
하지만 그 반대가 사실이다.

❺ Shows are actually more enjoyable when they're broken up by annoying commercials.
쇼는 그것들이 성가신 광고들에 의해 중단될 때 실제로 더 즐거워진다.

❻ Because these less enjoyable moments break up adaptation to the positive experience of the show.
왜냐하면 이러한 덜 즐거운 순간들이 쇼의 긍정적인 경험에 대한 적응을 깨뜨리기 때문이다.

❼ Think about eating chocolate chips.
초콜릿 칩을 먹는 것을 생각해 보라.

❽ The first chip is delicious: sweet, melt-in-your-mouth goodness.
첫 번째 칩은 맛있다: 달콤하고, 입안에서 살살 녹는 좋은 맛.

❾ The second chip is also pretty good.
두 번째 칩도 꽤 맛있다.

❿ But by the fourth, fifth, or tenth chip in a row, the goodness is no longer as pleasurable.
하지만 네 번째, 다섯 번째, 혹은 열 번째 칩을 연속으로 먹으면 그 좋은 맛은 더 이상 즐겁지 않다.

⓫ We adapt. Interspersing positive experiences with less positive ones, however, can slow down adaptation.
우리는 적응한다. 그러나, 긍정적인 경험들에 덜 긍정적인 경험들을 간격을 두고 배치하는 것은 적응을 늦출 수 있다.

⓬ Eating a Brussels sprout between chocolate chips or viewing commercials between parts of TV shows disrupts the process.
초콜릿 칩 사이에 방울양배추를 먹거나 TV 쇼의 파트 사이에 광고를 보는 것은 이 과정을 방해한다.

⓭ The less positive moment makes the following positive one new again and thus more enjoyable.
덜 긍정적인 순간은 뒤에 오는 긍정적인 순간을 다시 새롭게 만들어서 더 즐겁게 만든다.

31 빈칸

❶ We collect stamps, coins, vintage cars even when they serve no practical purpose.
우리는 그것들이 실용적인 목적을 수행하지 않더라도 우표, 동전, 빈티지 자동차들을 수집한다.

❷ The post office doesn't accept the old stamps, the banks don't take old coins, and the vintage cars are no longer allowed on the road.
우체국은 오래된 우표를 받지 않고, 은행은 오래된 동전을 받지 않으며, 그리고 빈티지 자동차는 더 이상 도로에서 허용되지 않는다.

❸ These are all side issues; the attraction is that they are in short supply.
이런 것들은 모두 부수적인 문제이다; 매력은 그들이 부족한 공급에 있다는 것이다.

❹ In one study, students were asked to arrange ten posters in order of attractiveness — with the agreement that afterward they could keep one poster as a reward for their participation.
한 연구에서, 학생들은 포스터 10장을 매력도의 순서대로 배열하 도록 요청받았다 — 나중에 그들의 참여에 대한 보상으로 포스터 1장을 간직할 수 있다는 합의와 함께.

❺ Five minutes later, they were told that the poster with the third highest rating was no longer available.
5분 후, 그들은 세 번째 높은 평가의 포스터가 더 이상 이용 가능하지 않다는 것을 들었다.

❻ Then they were asked to judge all ten from scratch.
그런 다음 그들은 10개의 포스터를 모두 처음부터 평가하라고 요청을 받았다.

❼ The poster that was no longer available was suddenly classified as the most beautiful.
더 이상 이용할 수 없는 포스터가 갑자기 가장 아름다운 것으로 분류되었다.

❽ In psychology, this phenomenon is called reactance: when we are deprived of an option, we suddenly deem it more attractive.
심리학에서, 이러한 현상은 리액턴스라고 불린다: 우리가 선택지를 빼앗겼을 때, 우리는 그것을 갑자기 더 매력적으로 여긴다.

32 빈칸

❶ If we've invested in something that hasn't repaid us — be it money in a failing venture, or time in an unhappy relationship — we find it very difficult to walk away.
우리에게 보답해 주지 않는 것에 우리가 투자해 왔다면 — 실패한 사업에 투자한 돈이거나, 불행한 인간관계에 투자한 시간이던지 간에 — 우리는 벗어나기가 매우 어렵다는 것을 안다.

❷ This is the sunk cost fallacy.
이것은 매몰 비용 오류이다.

❸ Our instinct is to continue investing money or time as we hope that our investment will prove to be worthwhile in the end.
우리의 본능은 결국에는 우리의 투자가 가치 있는 것으로 입증될 것이라고 희망하면서 돈이나 시간에 투자를 계속 하는 것이다.

❹ Giving up would mean acknowledging that we've wasted something we can't get back, and that thought is so painful that we prefer to avoid it if we can.
포기한다는 것은 우리가 돌이킬 수 없는 무언가를 낭비해왔다고 인정하는 것을 의미하고, 그런 생각은 너무 고통스러워서 우리가 할 수 있다면 그것을 피하기를 선호한다.

❺ The problem, of course, is that if something really is a bad bet, then staying with it simply increases the amount we lose.
물론, 문제는 어떤 것이 정말 나쁜 투자라면, 그것을 계속하는 것은 우리가 잃는 총액을 증가시킬 뿐이라는 것이다.

❻ Rather than walk away from a bad five-year relationship, for example, we turn it into a bad 10-year relationship; rather than accept that we've lost a thousand dollars, we lay down another thousand and lose that too.
예를 들어, 5년의 나쁜 관계에서 벗어나기보다는 우리는 그것을 10년의 나쁜 관계로 바꾸고; 천 달러를 잃었다는 사실을 받아들이기보다는, 또 다른 천 달러를 내놓고 그것도 역시 잃는다.

❼ In the end, by delaying the pain of admitting our problem, we only add to it. Sometimes we just have to cut our losses.
결국, 우리의 문제를 인정하는 고통을 미룸으로써 우리는 그것에 보탤 뿐이다. 때때로 우리는 손실을 끊어야만 한다.

33 빈칸

❶ On our little world, light travels, for all practical purposes, instantaneously.
우리의 작은 세상에서, 실제로는 빛은 순간적으로 이동한다.

❷ If a light-bulb is glowing, then of course it's physically where we see it, shining away.
전구가 켜져 있다면, 당연히 그것은 우리가 보는 그 자리에서 빛을 내고 있다.

❸ We reach out our hand and touch it: It's there all right, and unpleasantly hot.
우리는 손을 뻗어 그것을 만진다: 그것은 바로 거기에 있고, 불쾌할 정도로 뜨겁다.

❹ If the filament fails, then the light goes out.
필라멘트가 나가면, 그때 빛은 꺼진다.

❺ We don't see it in the same place, glowing, illuminating the room years after the bulb breaks and it's removed from its socket.
전구가 망가져서 소켓에서 제거된 몇 년 후, 그 자리에 빛을 내고 방을 밝히고 있는 그것을 우리는 보지 못한다.

❻ The very notion seems nonsensical.
바로 그 개념은 말도 안 되는 것처럼 보인다.

❼ But if we're far enough away, an entire sun can go out and we'll continue to see it shining brightly; we won't learn of its death, it may be, for ages to come — in fact, for how long it takes light, which travels fast but not infinitely fast, to cross the intervening vastness.
하지만 우리가 충분히 멀리 떨어져 있다면, 항성 전체는 꺼질 수 있지만 우리는 그것이 밝게 빛나는 것을 계속 볼 것이다; 우리는 아마도 오랜 세월 동안 — 사실, 빠르지만 무한히 빠르지는 않게, 이동하는 빛이 그 사이에 낀 광대함을 가로지르는데 걸리는 시간 동안 그것의 소멸을 알지 못할 것이다.

❽ The immense distances to the stars and the galaxies mean that we see everything in space in the past.
별과 은하까지의 엄청난 거리는 우리가 우주 공간의 모든 것을 과거의 모습으로 보고 있다는 것을 의미한다.

34 빈칸

❶ Financial markets do more than take capital from the rich and lend it to everyone else.
금융 시장은 부자들로부터 자본을 받아 다른 모든 사람들에게 그것을 빌려주는 것 이상을 한다.

❷ They enable each of us to smooth consumption over our lifetimes, which is a fancy way of saying that we don't have to spend income at the same time we earn it.
그것들은 우리 각자가 평생에 걸쳐 소비를 원활하게 하도록 해주며, 그리고 이는 우리가 그것(소득)을 얻는 동시에 소득을 소비할 필요가 없다는 것을 말하는 멋진 방식이다.

❸ Shakespeare may have admonished us to be neither borrowers nor lenders; the fact is that most of us will be both at some point.
셰익스피어는 우리가 빌리는 사람도 빌려주는 사람도 되지 말라고 충고했을지도 모른다; 사실 우리 대부분은 어떤 때에는 둘 다 될 것이다.

❹ If we lived in an agrarian society, we would have to eat our crops reasonably soon after the harvest or find some way to store them.
만약 우리가 농경 사회에 산다면, 우리는 우리의 농작물을 수확 직후에 합리적으로 먹거나 또는 그것들을 저장할 어떤 방법을 찾아야 할 것이다.

❺ Financial markets are a more sophisticated way of managing the harvest.
금융 시장은 수확을 관리하는 더 정교한 방법이다.

❻ We can spend income now that we have not yet earned — as by borrowing for college or a home — or we can earn income now and spend it later, as by saving for retirement.
우리는 우리가 아직 벌지 않은 소득을 지금 소비할 수도 있고 — 대학이나 주택을 위해 빌리는 것처럼 — 혹은 우리는 은퇴를 위해 저축하는 것처럼, 지금 소득을 벌어서 나중에 그것을 소비할 수도 있다.

❼ The important point is that earning income has been divorced from spending it, allowing us much more flexibility in life.
중요한 점은 소득을 버는 것이 그것을 소비하는 것과 분리되어 있다는 것이고, 이는 우리에게 삶에서 훨씬 더 많은 유연성을 허용해준다.

35 무관

❶ As the old joke goes: "Software, free. User manual, $10,000."
다음과 같은 옛 농담처럼: "소프트웨어, 무료. 사용자 매뉴얼, 10,000달러."

❷ But it's no joke.
하지만 그것은 농담이 아니다.

❸ A couple of high-profile companies make their living selling instruction and paid support for free software.
세간의 이목을 끄는 몇몇 기업들은 무료 소프트웨어에 대한 지침과 유료 지원을 판매하면서 돈을 번다.

❹ The copy of code, being mere bits, is free.
단지 몇 비트일 뿐인 코드 사본은 무료이다.

❺ The lines of free code become valuable to you only through support and guidance.
무료 코드의 배열은 지원과 안내를 통해서만 당신에게 가치 있게 된다. 다가올 수십 년 안에 많은 의료 및 유전 정보가 이 경로를 따르게 될 것이다.

❻ A lot of medical and genetic information will go this route in the coming decades.
다가올 수십 년 안에 많은 의료 및 유전 정보가 이 경로를 따르게 될 것이다.

❼ Right now getting a full copy of all your DNA is very expensive ($10,000), but soon it won't be.
당신의 배열의 사본에 비용이 들지 않을 때, 그것이 의미하는 것, 당신이 그것에 관해 할 수 있는 것, 그리고 그것을 사용하는 방법에 관한 설명 — 당신의 유전자 매뉴얼 — 은 비싸질 것이다.

❼ The price is dropping so fast, it will be $100 soon, and then the next year insurance companies will offer to sequence you for free.
가격이 너무 빨리 떨어지고 있어, 곧 100달러가 될 것이고, 그 다음 해에는 보험 회사가 무료로 당신의 유전자 배열 순서를 밝혀줄 것을 제안할 것이다.

❽ When a copy of your sequence costs nothing, the interpretation of what it means, what you can do about it, and how to use it — the manual for your genes — will be expensive.
당신의 배열의 사본에 비용이 들지 않을 때, 그것이 의미하는 것, 당신이 그것에 관해 할 수 있는 것, 그리고 그것을 사용하는 방법에 관한 설명 — 당신의 유전자 매뉴얼 — 은 비싸질 것이다.

36 순서

❶ Brains are expensive in terms of energy.
에너지의 측면에서 뇌는 비용이 많이 든다.

❷ Twenty percent of the calories we consume are used to power the brain.
우리가 소비하는 칼로리의 20%는 뇌에 동력을 공급하는 데 사용된다.

❸ So brains try to operate in the most energy-efficient way possible, and that means processing only the minimum amount of information from our senses that we need to navigate the world.
따라서 뇌는 가능한 한 가장 에너지 효율적인 방식으로 작동하려고 애쓰며, 그것은 우리가 세상을 항해하는 데 필요로 하는 최소한의 양의 정보만을 우리 감각으로부터 처리하는 것을 의미한다.

❹ Neuroscientists weren't the first to discover that fixing your gaze on something is no guarantee of seeing it.
신경과학자들은 무언가에 당신의 시선을 고정하는 것이 그것을 본다는 보장이 없다는 사실을 발견한 최초가 아니었다.

❺ Magicians figured this out long ago.
마술사들은 오래 전에 이것을 알아냈다.

❻ By directing your attention, they perform tricks with their hands in full view.
당신의 주의를 끌어서, 그들은 다 보이는 데서 손으로 속임수를 행한다.

❼ Their actions should give away the game, but they can rest assured that your brain processes only small bits of the visual scene.
그들의 행동은 그 속임수를 드러내겠지만, 그들은 당신의 뇌가 시각적 장면의 오직 작은 부분들만을 처리한다는 것을 확신한 채로 있을 수 있다.

❽ This all helps to explain the prevalence of traffic accidents in which drivers hit pedestrians in plain view, or collide with cars directly in front of them. In many of these cases, the eyes are pointed in the right direction, but the brain isn't seeing what's really out there.
이 모든 것은 운전자가 명백한 시야에 있는 보행자들을 치거나, 바로 앞에 있는 차량들과 충돌하는 교통사고의 빈번함을 설명하는 데 도움이 된다. 많은 이러한 경우에서, 눈은 올바른 방향을 향하고 있지만, 뇌는 실제로 거기에 있는 것을 보고 있지 않다.

37 순서

❶ Buying a television is current consumption. It makes us happy today but does nothing to make us richer tomorrow.

텔레비전을 사는 것은 현재의 소비이다. 그것은 오늘 우리를 행복하게 하지만 내일 우리를 더 부유하게 만드는 데는 아무것도 하지 않는다.

❷ Yes, money spent on a television keeps workers employed at the television factory.

그렇다, 텔레비전에 소비되는 돈은 노동자들이 텔레비전 공장에 계속 고용되게 한다.

❸ But if the same money were invested, it would create jobs somewhere else, say for scientists in a laboratory or workers on a construction site, while also making us richer in the long run.

하지만 같은 돈이 투자된다면, 그것은 말하자면 실험실의 과학자들이나 건설 현장의 노동자들을 위한, 어딘가 다른 곳의 일자리를 창출하면서, 또한 장기적으로 우리를 더 부유하게 만들 것이다.

❹ Think about college as an example.

대학을 예로써 생각해 보자.

❺ Sending students to college creates jobs for professors.

학생들을 대학에 보내는 것은 교수들을 위한 일자리를 창출한다.

❻ Using the same money to buy fancy sports cars for high school graduates would create jobs for auto workers

같은 돈을 고등학교 졸업생에게 멋진 스포츠카를 사주는 데 쓰는 것은 자동차 노동자를 위한 일자리를 창출할 것이다.

❼ The crucial difference between these scenarios is that a college education makes a young person more productive for the rest of his or her life; a sports car does not.

이러한 시나리오들의 중대한 차이점은 대학 교육은 젊은이들이 그 또는 그녀의 남은 삶 동안 더 생산적이게 만들지만; 스포츠카는 그렇지 않다는 것이다.

❽ Thus, college tuition is an investment; buying a sports car is consumption.

따라서, 대학 등록금은 투자이다; 스포츠카를 구입하는 것은 소비이다.

38 삽입

❶ The Net differs from most of the mass media it replaces in an obvious and very important way: it's bidirectional.
인터넷은 그것이 대체하는 대부분의 대중 매체와 분명하고도 매우 중요한 방식으로 다르다: 그것은 두 방향으로 작용한다.

❷ We can send messages through the network as well as receive them, which has made the system all the more useful.
우리는 네트워크를 통해 메시지들을 받을 수 있을 뿐만 아니라 그것들을 보낼 수도 있는데, 이것은 그 시스템을 훨씬 더 유용하게 만들었다.

❸ The ability to exchange information online, to upload as well as download, has turned the Net into a thoroughfare for business and commerce.
온라인에서 정보를 교환하고, 다운로드할 뿐만 아니라 업로드하는 능력은, 인터넷을 비즈니스와 상거래를 위한 통로로 만들었다.

❹ With a few clicks, people can search virtual catalogues, place orders, track shipments, and update information in corporate databases.
몇 번의 클릭으로, 사람들은 가상 카탈로그를 검색하고, 주문을 하고, 배송을 추적하고, 그리고 기업의 데이터베이스에 정보를 업데이트할 수 있다.

❺ But the Net doesn't just connect us with businesses; it connects us with one another.
하지만 인터넷은 단지 우리를 기업과 연결하는 것만은 아니다; 그것은 우리를 서로서로 연결한다.

❻ It's a personal broadcasting medium as well as a commercial one.
그것은 상업용 매체일 뿐만 아니라 개인 방송 매체이다.

❼ Millions of people use it to distribute their own digital creations, in the form of blogs, videos, photos, songs, and podcasts, as well as to critique, edit, or otherwise modify the creations of others.
수백만 명의 사람들이 다른 사람들의 창작물을 비평하고, 편집하고, 또는 그렇지 않으면 수정하기 위해서뿐만 아니라, 블로그, 동영상, 사진, 노래, 그리고 팟캐스트의 형태로 자신의 디지털 창작물을 배포하기 위해서 그것을 사용한다.

39 삽입

❶ Imagine that seven out of ten working Americans got fired tomorrow. What would they all do?
미국인 직장인 10명 중 7명이 내일 해고된다고 상상해 보라. 그들은 모두 무엇을 할까?

❷ It's hard to believe you'd have an economy at all if you gave pink slips to more than half the labor force.
노동력의 절반 이상에게 해고 통지서를 보낸다면 경제가 유지될 것이라고 믿기 어려울 것이다.

❸ But that is what the industrial revolution did to the workforce of the early 19th century.
하지만 그것은 19세기 초 노동력에 산업혁명이 했던 것이다.

❹ Two hundred years ago, 70 percent of American workers lived on the farm.
200년 전, 미국 노동자의 70%가 농장에서 살았다.

❺ Today automation has eliminated all but 1 percent of their jobs, replacing them with machines. But the displaced workers did not sit idle.
오늘날 자동화는 1%를 제외한 모든 일자리를 제거하였고, 그것들을 기계로 대체하였다. 하지만 일자리를 잃은 노동자들은 한가롭게 앉아 있지 않았다.

❻ Instead, automation created hundreds of millions of jobs in entirely new fields.
그 대신, 자동화는 완전히 새로운 분야에서 수억 개의 일자리를 창출했다.

❼ Those who once farmed were now manning the factories that manufactured farm equipment, cars, and other industrial products.
한때 농사를 짓던 사람들은 이제 농기구, 자동차, 그리고 기타 산업 제품을 제조하는 공장에서 일하고 있다.

❽ Since then, wave upon wave of new occupations have arrived — appliance repair person, food chemist, photographer, web designer — each building on previous automation.
그 이후로, 가전제품 수리공, 식품 화학자, 사진작가, 웹 디자이너 등 이전의 자동화를 기반으로 한 새로운 직업이 계속해서 등장했다.

❾ Today, the vast majority of us are doing jobs that no farmer from the 1800s could have imagined.
오늘날, 우리 중 대다수는 1800년대의 농부들은 상상도 할 수 없었던 일을 하고 있다.

40 요약

❶ Many things spark envy : ownership, status, health, youth, talent, popularity, beauty.
많은 것들은 부러움을 불러일으킨다: 소유권, 지위, 건강, 젊음, 재능, 인기, 아름다움.

❷ It is often confused with jealousy because the physical reactions are identical.
이것은 신체적 반응이 동일하기 때문에 종종 질투와 혼동된다.

❸ The difference: the subject of envy is a thing (status, money, health etc.).
차이점: 부러움의 대상은 사물(지위, 돈, 건강 등)이다.

❹ The subject of jealousy is the behaviour of a third person.
질투의 대상은 제3자의 행동이다.

❺ Envy needs two people.
부러움은 두 사람을 필요로 한다.

❻ Jealousy, on the other hand, requires three: Peter is jealous of Sam because the beautiful girl next door rings him instead.
반면, 질투는 세 사람을 요구한다: Peter는 옆집의 예쁜 여자가 자기가 아니라 Sam에게 전화를 걸기 때문에 그를 질투한다.

❼ Paradoxically, with envy we direct resentments toward those who are most similar to us in age, career and residence.
역설적이게도, 부러움을 가질 때 우리는 나이, 경력, 거주지에 있어서 우리와 가장 비슷한 사람들에게 불쾌감을 향하게 한다.

❽ We don't envy businesspeople from the century before last.
우리는 지지난 세기의 사업가들을 부러워하지 않는다.

❾ We don't envy millionaires on the other side of the globe.
우리는 지구 반대편의 백만장자를 부러워하지 않는다.

❿ As a writer, I don't envy musicians, managers or dentists, but other writers.
작가로서, 나는 음악가, 매니저 또는 치과의사가 부럽지 않지만, 다른 작가들을 부러워한다.

⓫ As a CEO you envy other, bigger CEOs.
CEO로서 당신은 다른, 더 큰 CEO들을 부러워한다.

⓬ As a supermodel you envy more successful supermodels,
슈퍼 모델로서 당신은 더 성공한 슈퍼 모델들을 부러워한다.

⓭ Aristotle knew this: 'Potters envy potters.'
아리스토텔레스는 이를 알고 있었다: '도공은 도공을 부러워한다.'

41~42 제목, 어휘

❶ We have biases that support our biases!
우리는 우리의 편견을 뒷받침하는 편견을 가진다!

❷ If we're partial to one option — perhaps because it's more memorable, or framed to minimize loss, or seemingly consistent with a promising pattern — we tend to search for information that will justify choosing that option.
만약 우리가 한 가지 옵션에 편향된다면 — 그것이 아마도 더 잘 기억할만 하거나, 손실을 최소화하기 위해 짜맞춰졌거나, 혹은 유망한 패턴과 일치하는 것처럼 보이기 때문에 — 우리는 그 옵션을 선택한 것을 정당화할 정보를 찾는 경향이 있다.

❸ On the one hand, it's sensible to make choices that we can defend with data and a list of reasons.
한편으로는, 데이터와 이유들의 목록으로 방어할 수 있는 선택을 하는 것이 현명하다.

❹ On the other hand, if we're not careful, we're likely to conduct an imbalanced analysis, falling prey to a cluster of errors collectively known as "confirmation biases."
반면에, 만약 우리가 주의를 기울이지 않으면, 우리는 불균형한 분석을 수행할 가능성이 있어서, 총체적으로 "확증 편향"으로 알려져 있는 오류 덩어리의 희생양이 된다.

❺ For example, nearly all companies include classic "tell me about yourself" job interviews as part of the hiring process, and many rely on these interviews alone to evaluate applicants.
예를 들어, 거의 모든 기업이 채용 과정의 일부로 전통적인 "자기소개" 취업 면접을 실시하며, 많은 기업이 지원자를 평가하기 위해서 이러한 면접에만 의존한다.

❻ But it turns out that traditional interviews are actually one of the least useful tools for predicting an employee's future success.
하지만 전통적인 면접은 실제로 직원의 미래 성공을 예측하는 데 가장 유용하지 않은 도구 중 하나라는 것으로 판명된다.

❼ This is because interviewers often subconsciously make up their minds about interviewees based on their first few moments of interaction and spend the rest of the interview cherry-picking evidence and phrasing their questions to confirm that initial impression: "I see here you left a good position at your previous job.
이것은 면접관들이 종종 잠재의식적으로 처음 몇 순간의 상호작용을 바탕으로 면접 대상자에 대한 결정을 내리고, 그 첫인상을 확인하기 위해 증거를 고르고 질문을 만드는 데 면접의 나머지 시간을 보내기 때문이다

❽ You must be pretty ambitious, right?" versus "You must not have been very committed, huh?"
"당신은 이전 직장에서 좋은 직책을 두고 나오신 게 보이네요. 틀림없이 야망이 꽤 크시겠어요, 그렇죠?" 대 "당신은 그다지 헌신적이지 않았음에 틀림없네요, 그렇죠?"

❾ This means that interviewers can be prone to overlooking significant information that would clearly indicate whether this candidate was actually the best person to hire.

이것은 면접관이 이 지원자가 실제로 채용하기에 가장 좋은 사람인지 여부를 명확하게 보여줄 수 있는 중요한 정보를 간과하기 쉽다는 것을 의미한다.

❿ More structured approaches, like obtaining samples of a candidate's work or asking how he would respond to difficult hypothetical situations, are dramatically better at assessing future success, with a nearly threefold advantage over traditional interviews.

지원자의 업무 샘플을 확보하거나 가정된 어려운 상황에 어떻게 그가 대응할지 묻는 것과 같은 보다 구조화된 접근 방식은, 전통적인 면접보다, 거의 세 배의 이점으로 미래의 성공을 평가하는 데 훨씬 더 낫다.

43~45 순서, 지칭, 세부 내용

❶ On Saturday morning, Todd and his 5-year-old daughter Ava walked out of the store with the groceries they had just purchased.
토요일 아침에, Todd와 그의 다섯 살짜리 딸 Ava는 그들이 방금 구입한 식료품을 가지고 가게에서 걸어 나왔다.

❷ As they pushed their grocery cart through the parking lot, they saw a red car pulling into the space next to their pick-up truck.
그들이 주차장에서 식료품 카트를 밀면서 갈 때, 그들은 빨간 차 한 대가 그들의 픽업 트럭 옆 공간으로 들어오는 것을 보았다.

❸ A young man named Greg was driving.
Greg라는 이름의 한 젊은 남자가 운전을 하고 있었다.

❹ "That's a cool car," Ava said to her dad.
"저것은 멋진 차네요."라고 Ava가 그녀의 아빠에게 말했다.

❺ He agreed and looked at Greg, who finished parking and opened his door.
그는 동의했고 Greg를 보았는데, 그는 주차를 마치고 그의 문을 열었다.

❻ As Todd finished loading his groceries, Greg's door remained open.
Todd가 그의 식료품을 싣는 것을 끝냈을 때, Greg의 문은 열린 채로 있었다.

❼ Todd noticed Greg didn't get out of his car.
Todd는 Greg가 그의 차에서 내리지 않은 것을 알아차렸다.

❽ But he was pulling something from his car.
그러나 그는 그의 차에서 무엇인가를 꺼내고 있었다.

❾ He put a metal frame on the ground beside his door.
그는 그의 문 옆 바닥에 금속 프레임을 두었다.

❿ Remaining in the driver's seat, he then reached back into his car to grab something else.
운전석에 머무른 채, 그는 무엇인가 다른 것을 잡기 위해 그의 차 안 뒤쪽으로 손을 뻗었다.

⓫ Todd realized what he was doing and considered whether he should try to help him.
Todd는 그가 무엇을 하고 있는지를 깨닫고 그가 그를 도와야 할지를 생각했다.

⓬ After a moment, he decided to approach Greg. By this time, Greg had already pulled one thin wheel out of his car and attached it to the frame.
잠시 후, 그는 Greg에게 다가가기로 결심했다. 그때 쯤, Greg는 이미 그의 차에서 얇은 바퀴 하나를 꺼내었고 그것을 프레임에 끼웠다.

⓭ He was now pulling a second wheel out when he looked up and saw Todd standing near him.
그가 고개를 들어 그의 근처에 서 있는 Todd를 보았을 때 그는 이제 두 번째 바퀴를 꺼내는 중이었다.

⓮ Todd said, "Hi there! Have a great weekend!" Greg seemed a bit surprised, but replied by wishing him a great weekend too.
Todd는 "안녕하세요! 주말 잘 보내세요!"라고 말했다. Greg는 약간 놀란 것처럼 보였지만, 그에게도 좋은 주말을 보내라고 답했다.

⓯ Then Greg added, "Thanks for letting me have my independence." "Of course," Todd said.
그러자 Greg는 "내가 독립성을 가질 수 있게 해줘서 고맙습니다."라고 덧붙였다. "물론이죠."라고 Todd가 말했다.

⓰ After Todd and Ava climbed into their truck, Ava became curious. So she asked why he didn't offer to help the man with his wheelchair.
Todd와 Ava가 그들의 트럭에 올라탄 후에, Ava는 호기심이 생겼다. 그래서 그녀는 왜 그가 그 남자에게 휠체어에 대해 도움을 제공하지 않았는지를 물었다.

⓱ Todd said, "Why do you insist on brushing your teeth without my help?" She answered, "Because I know how to!"
Todd는 "왜 너는 내 도움 없이 너의 이를 닦으려고 고집하니?"라고 말했다. 그녀는 "왜냐하면 제가 어떻게 하는지를 알기 때문이죠!"라고 답했다.

⓲ He said, "And the man knows how to put together his wheelchair."
그는 "그리고 그 남자는 그의 휠체어를 어떻게 조립하는지 알고 있어."라고 말했다.

⓳ Ava understood that sometimes the best way to help someone is to not help at all.
Ava는 때때로 누군가를 돕는 가장 좋은 방법은 전혀 도와주지 않는 것임을 이해했다.

18.

Dear Residents,

My name is Kari Patterson, and I'm the manager of the River View Apartments. It's time to take advantage of the sunny weather [**making / to make**]1) our community more beautiful. On Saturday, July 13 at 9 a.m., residents will [**be met / meet**]2) in the north parking lot. We will divide into teams to plant flowers and small trees, pull weeds, and [**put / putting**]3) colorful decorations on the lawn. Please join us for this year's Gardening Day, and [**remember / to remember**]4) no special skills or tools are required. Last year, we had a great time working together, so come out and [**make / making**]5) this year's event even better!

Warm regards, / Kari Patterson

주민들게, 제 이름은 Kari Patterson이고, 저는 River View 아파트의 관리인입니다. 우리의 커뮤니티를 더욱 아름답게 만들기 위해 화창한 날씨를 이용할 때입니다. 7월 13일 토요일 오전 9시에, 주민들은 북쪽 주차장에서 만날 예정입니다. 우리는 팀을 나누어 꽃과 작은 나무를 심고, 잡초를 뽑고, 잔디밭에 다채로운 장식을 할 것입니다. 올해 정원가꾸기 날에 우리와 함께 해 주시고, 특별한 기술이나 도구는 필요하지 않다는 것을 기억하세요. 작년에, 우리는 함께 일하며 즐거운 시간을 보냈으니, 오셔서 올해 행사도 더 멋지게 만들어 주세요!

따뜻한 마음을 담아, Kari Patterson

19.

It was the championship race. Emma was the final runner on her relay team. She anxiously waited in her spot for her teammate [**pass / to pass**]6) her the baton. Emma wasn't sure she could perform her role without [**make / making**]7) a mistake. Her hands shook as she thought, "What if I drop the baton?" She felt her heart rate increasing as her teammate approached. But as she started running, she received the baton [**smooth / smoothly**]8). In the final 10 meters, she passed two [**another / other**]9) runners and [**crossed / crossing**]10) the finish line in first place! She raised her hands in the air, and a huge smile came across her face. As her teammates hugged her, she shouted, "We did it!" All of her hard training had been worth it.

결승전 경주였다. Emma는 그녀의 계주 팀의 마지막 주자였다. 그녀는 그녀의 자리에서 팀 동료가 그녀에게 바통을 건네주기를 초조하게 기다렸다. Emma는 그녀가 실수를 하지 않고 자신의 역할을 수행할 수 있을지 확신하지 못했다. "만약 내가 바통을 떨어뜨리면 어떡하지?" 라고 생각하면서 그녀의 손이 떨렸다. 그녀는 그녀의 팀 동료가 다가올수록 심박수가 증가하는 것을 느꼈다. 하지만 그녀가 달리기 시작했을 때, 그녀는 순조롭게 바통을 받았다. 마지막 10미터에서, 그녀는 두 명의 다른 주자를 제치고 나서 1위로 결승선을 통과했다! 그녀는 두 손을 하늘로 치켜들고, 얼굴에 큰 미소를 지었다. 팀 동료들이 그녀를 안아주자, 그녀는 "우리가 해냈어!"라고 소리쳤다. 그녀의 모든 힘든 훈련이 그럴만한 가치가 있었다.

20.

Most people resist the idea of a true self-estimate, probably [**because / because of**]11) they fear it might mean downgrading some of their beliefs about who they are and [**what / which**]12) they're capable of. As Goethe's maxim goes, it is a great failing "to see [**you / yourself**]13) as more than you are." How could you really [**be considered / consider**]14) self-aware if you refuse to consider your weaknesses? Don't fear self-assessment [**because / because of**]15) you're worried you might have to admit some things about yourself. The second half of Goethe's maxim is important too. He states that it is equally [**damaged / damaging**]16) to "value yourself at less than your true worth." We underestimate our capabilities just as much and just as dangerously as we overestimate [**another / other**]17) abilities. Cultivate the ability to judge yourself [**accurate / accurately**]18) and [**honest / honestly**]19). Look inward to discern what you're capable of and [**that / what**]20) it will take to unlock that potential.

대부분의 사람들은 그것(진정한 자기 평가)이 그들이 누구인지, 무엇을 할 수 있는지에 대한 믿음을 낮추는 것을 의미할지도 모른다고 두려워하기 때문에, 진정한 자기 평가에 대한 생각을 거부한다. Goethe의 격언처럼, "너 자신을 현재의 너의 모습 이상으로 보는 것"은 큰 실수이다. 네가 너의 단점을 생각해 보기를 거부한다면 어떻게 너 자신을 인식하고 있다고 여겨질 수 있을까? 네가 너 자신에 대해 몇 가지를 인정해야 할지도 모른다는 걱정 때문에 자기를 평가하는 것을 두려워하지 마라. Goethe 격언의 후반부도 역시 중요하다. 그는 "너의 진정한 가치보다 너 자신을 낮게 평가하는 것"도 똑같이 해롭다고 말한다. 우리는 다른 능력들을 과대평가 하는 것만큼 많이 그리고 위험하게 우리의 능력을 과소평가한다. 너 자신을 정확하게 그리고 정직하게 판단하는 능력을 길러라. 네가 할 수 있는 것과 너의 잠재력을 열기 위해 필요한 것을 파악하기 위해 내면을 들여다 봐라.

21.

[**Take / Taking**]21) a look at some of the most powerful, rich, and famous people in the world. Ignore the trappings of their success and [**that / what**]22) they're able to buy. Look instead at [**that / what**]23) they're forced [**to trade / trading**]24) in return — look at what success has cost [**them / themselves**]25). Mostly? Freedom. Their work demands they wear a suit. Their success depends on [**attending / to attend**]26) certain parties, kissing up to people they don't like. It will [**acquire / require**]27) — inevitably — realizing they are unable to say [**that / what**]28) they actually think. Worse, it demands [**what / that**]29) they become a different type of person or do bad things. Sure, it might pay well — but they haven't truly [**examined / examining**]30) the transaction. As Seneca put it, "Slavery [**reside / resides**]31) under marble and gold." Too many [**successful / successive**]32) people are prisoners in jails of their own making. Is that what you want? Is that what you're working hard toward? Let's hope not.

세계에서 가장 힘있고, 부유하며, 유명한 사람들 중 몇몇을 살펴봐라. 그들의 성공의 장식과 그들이 살 수 있는 것을 무시해라. 대신 그들이 맞바꿔야 하는 것을 봐라 — 성공이 그들에게 치르게 한 것을 봐라. 대부분은? 자유이다. 그들의 업무는 그들이 정장을 입는 것을 요구한다. 그들의 성공은 특정 파티에 참석하여, 그들이 좋아하지 않는 사람들에게 아첨하는 것에 달려 있다. 그것은 요구할 것이다 — 필연적으로 — 그들이 실제로 생각하는 것을 말할 수 없다는 사실을 깨닫는 것을. 더 나쁜 것은, 그것은 그들이 다른 유형의 사람이 되거나 부당한 일을 하도록 요구한다는 것이다. 물론, 그것은 많은 이익이 될지도 모른다 — 그러나 그들은 그 거래를 제대로 고찰한 적이 없다. Seneca가 말했듯이, "대리석과 황금 아래에 노예 상태가 존재한다." 너무 많은 성공한 사람들은 그들이 스스로 만든 감옥의 죄수들이다. 그것이 당신이 원하는 것인가? 그것이 당신이 목표로 하여 열심히 일하고 있는 것인가? 그렇지 않기를 바라자.

22.

If a firm is going to [**be saved / save**]33) by the government, it might be easier to concentrate on [**lobby / lobbying**]34) the government for more money rather than taking the harder decision of [**restructure / restructuring**]35) the company to be able to be profitable and viable in the long term. This is an example of something known as [**moral / mortal**]36) hazard — when government support alters the decisions firms [**take / taken**]37). For example, if governments rescue banks who get into difficulty, as they [**did / were**]38) during the credit crisis of 2007-08, this could encourage banks [**take / to take**]39) greater risks in the future because they know there is a possibility that governments will [**interfere / intervene**]40) if they lose money. Although the government rescue may be well intended, it can [**negatively / positively**]41) affect the behavior of banks, [**discouraging / encouraging**]42) risky and poor decision making.

기업이 정부로부터 구제받으려면, 장기적으로 수익성이 나고 성장할 수 있도록 회사를 구조조정하는 어려운 결정을 내리기보다는 더 많은 돈을 받기 위해 정부에 로비하는 것에 집중하는 것이 더 쉬울지도 모른다. 이것은 도덕적 해이라고 알려진 것의 한 예이다 — 정부의 지원이 기업이 내리는 결정을 바꿀 때. 예를 들어, 2007-08년 신용 위기 때 그들이 그랬던 것처럼, 만약 정부가 어려움에 처한 은행을 구제한다면, 이것은 은행이 앞으로 더 큰 위험을 감수하도록 조장하는데 그 이유는 그들이 손해를 보는 경우 정부가 개입할 가능성이 있다는 것을 그들이 알기 때문이다. 정부의 구제는 좋은 의도일지라도, 그것은 은행의 행동에 부정적으로 영향을 미쳐, 위험하고 형편없는 의사 결정을 조장할 수 있다.

23.

If there is [**few / little**]43) or no diversity of views, and all scientists see, think, and question the world in a similar way, then they will not, as a community, be as [**objective / subjective**]44) as they maintain they are, or at least [**aspire / inspire**]45) to be. The solution is that there should be far [**great / greater**]46) diversity in the practice of science: in gender, ethnicity, and social and cultural backgrounds. Science works because it [**carried out / is carried out**]47) by people who pursue their curiosity about the natural world and [**test / testing**]48) their and each other's ideas from as many [**varied / varying**]49) perspectives and angles as possible. When science is done by a diverse group of people, and if consensus [**build / builds**]50) up about a particular area of scientific knowledge, then we can have more confidence in its [**objectivity / subjectivity**]51) and truth.

만약 견해의 다양성이 거의 없거나 전혀 없고, 모든 과학자들이 비슷한 방식으로 세상을 보고, 생각하고, 의문을 제기한다면, 그러면 그들은, 하나의 공동체로서, 자신들이 주장하는 것만큼, 혹은 적어도 그렇게 되기를 열망하는 것만큼, 객관적이지 않을 것이다. 해결책은 과학의 실행에 있어 훨씬 더 많은 다양성이 있어야 한다는 것이다: 성별, 인종, 그리고 사회적 문화적 배경에서. 과학은 그것이 자연 세계에 대한 호기심을 추구하고 가능한 한 다양한 관점과 각도에서 그들의 그리고 서로의 아이디어를 검증하는 사람들에 의해 수행되기 때문에 작동한다. 과학이 다양한 집단의 사람들에 의해 행해질 때, 그리고 만약 과학지식의 특정 영역에 대한 의견 일치가 이루어진다면, 그러면 우리는 그것의 객관성과 진실성에 있어서 더 큰 자신감을 가질 수 있다.

24.

We tend to [**break / breaking**]52) up time into units, such as weeks, months, and seasons; in a series of studies among farmers in India and students in North America, psychologists found [**that / what**]53) if a deadline is on the other side of a "break" — such as in the New Year — we're [**less / more**]54) likely to see it as remote, and, as a result, be [**less / more**]55) ready to jump into action. [**That / What**]56) you need to do in that situation is find [**another / the other**]57) way to think about the timeframe. For example, if it's November and the deadline is in January, it's better to tell yourself you have to get it done "this winter" rather than "next year." The best approach is to view deadlines as a challenge that you have to [**be met / meet**]58) within a period that's [**eminent / imminent**]59). That way the stress is more manageable, and you have a better chance of [**start / starting**]60) — and therefore [**finish / finishing**]61) — in good time.

우리는 시간을 주, 월, 계절과 같은 단위로 나누는 경향이 있다; 인도의 농부들과 북미의 학생들을 대상으로 한 일련의 연구에서, 심리학자들은 마감일이 "나뉨" — 새해와 같이 — 의 반대편에 있는 경우, 우리는 그것을 멀리 있는 것으로 여기고, 그 결과, 실행에 옮길 준비를 덜 할 가능성이 더 많다는 사실을 발견했다. 그러한 상황에서 당신이 해야 할 일은 그 시간 틀에 대해 생각하는 또 다른 방식을 찾는 것이다. 예를 들어, 지금이 11월이고 마감일이 1월이라면, 네가 "내년"보다는 "이번 겨울"에 일을 끝내야 한다고 너 자신에게 말하는 것이 더 좋다. 최고의 접근법은 마감일을 임박한 기간 내에 맞춰야 하는 도전으로 여기는 것이다. 그런 식으로 스트레스는 더 잘 관리될 수 있고, 적시에 작업을 시작 — 따라서 마무리 — 할 수 있는 가능성이 높아진다.

25.

The graph above shows the amount of CO₂ emissions per person across [**selected** / **selecting**]⁶²⁾ Asian countries in 2010 and 2020. All the countries except Uzbekistan had a greater amount of CO₂ emissions per person in 2020 than that in 2010. In 2010, the amount of CO₂ emissions per person of China was the largest among the five countries, [**followed** / **following**]⁶³⁾ by that of Mongolia. However, in 2020, Mongolia [**surpassed** / **surpassing**]⁶⁴⁾ China in terms of the amount of CO₂ emissions per person. In 2010, Uzbekistan produced a larger amount of CO₂ emissions per person than Vietnam, while the [**opposite** / **same**]⁶⁵⁾ was true in 2020. Among the five countries, India was the only one [**where** / **which**]⁶⁶⁾ the amount of CO₂ emissions per person was less than 2 tons in 2020.

위 그래프는 선택된 아시아 국가들의 2010년과 2020년 1인당 CO₂ 배출량을 보여준다. 우즈베키스탄을 제외한 모든 국가들은 2010년의 배출량보다 2020년의 1인당 CO₂ 배출량이 더 많았다. 2010년에는, 중국의 1인당 CO₂ 배출량이 5개국 중 가장 많았고, 몽골의 배출량이 그 뒤를 이었다. 그러나, 2020년에는, 1인당 CO₂ 배출량에 있어서 몽골이 중국을 능가했다. 2010년에는, 우즈베키스탄이 베트남보다 더 많은 1인당 CO₂ 배출량을 만들어 냈지만, 2020년에는 그 반대였다. 5개국 중, 인도는 2020년에 1인당 CO₂ 배출량이 2톤 미만인 유일한 국가였다.

26.

Henry David Thoreau [**born** / **was born**]⁶⁷⁾ in Concord, Massachusetts in 1817. When he was 16, he entered Harvard College. After graduating, Thoreau worked as a schoolteacher but he quit after two weeks. In June of 1838 he set up a school with his brother John. However, he had hopes of [**become** / **becoming**]⁶⁸⁾ a nature poet. In 1845, he moved into a small self-built house [**near** / **nearly**]⁶⁹⁾ Walden Pond. At Walden, Thoreau did an incredible amount of reading. The journal he wrote there became the source of his most famous book, Walden. In his later life, Thoreau traveled to the Maine woods, to Cape Cod, and to Canada. At the age of 43, he ended his travels and [**returned** / **returning**]⁷⁰⁾ to Concord. Although his works were not widely read [**during** / **while**]⁷¹⁾ his lifetime, he never stopped [**to write** / **writing**]⁷²⁾, and his works fill 20 volumes.

Henry David Thoreau는 1817년 Massachusetts주 Concord에서 태어났다. 그가 16세 때, 그는 Harvard 대학에 입학했다. 졸업 후, Thoreau는 학교 교사로 일했지만 2주 후에 그만두었다. 1838년 6월에 그는 그의 형제인 John과 함께 학교를 세웠다. 그러나, 그는 자연 시인이 되기를 희망했다. 1845년, 그는 Walden 연못 근처에 직접 지은 작은 집으로 이사했다. Walden에서, Thoreau는 엄청난 양의 독서를 했다. 그가 그곳에서 쓴 저널이 그의 가장 유명한 저서인 Walden의 원천이 되었다. 그의 인생 후반부에, Thoreau는 Maine 숲으로, Cape Cod로, 그리고 캐나다로 여행을 떠났다. 43세의 나이에, 그는 그의 여행을 마치고 Concord로 돌아왔다. 비록 그의 작품이 그의 일생 동안 널리 읽히지 않았지만, 그는 집필을 멈추지 않았고, 그의 작품은 20권에 달한다.

29.

The built-in capacity for smiling [**is proven** / **proven**]⁷³⁾ by the remarkable observation [**that** / **what**]⁷⁴⁾ babies who are congenitally both deaf and blind, who have never seen a human face, also start to smile at around 2 months. However, smiling in blind babies eventually [**disappear** / **disappears**]⁷⁵⁾ if nothing is done to reinforce [**them** / **it**]⁷⁶⁾. Without the right feedback, smiling dies out. But here's a fascinating fact: blind babies will continue to smile if they [**x** / **are**]⁷⁷⁾ cuddled, bounced, nudged, and tickled by an adult — anything to let them [**know** / **to know**]⁷⁸⁾ that they are not alone and that someone cares about them. This social feedback [**encourage** / **encourages**]⁷⁹⁾ the baby to continue smiling. In this way, early experience operates with our biology to establish [**asocial** / **social**]⁸⁰⁾ behaviors. In fact, you don't need the cases of blind babies to make the point. Babies [**with** / **without**]⁸¹⁾ sight smile more at you when you look at them or, better still, smile back at them.

미소 짓기에 대한 선천적인 능력은 선천적으로 청각 장애와 시각 장애가 있고, 사람 얼굴을 한 번도 본 적이 없는 아기들도, 약 2개월 즈음에 미소를 짓기 시작한다는 놀라운 관찰에 의해 증명된다. 그러나, 시각장애를 가진 아기의 미소 짓기는 그것을 강화하기 위해 아무것도 행해지지 않으면 결국 사라진다. 적절한 피드백이 없으면, 미소 짓기는 사라진다. 하지만 여기에 흥미로운 사실이 있다: 만약 그들이 어른에 의해서 안기고, 흔들리고, 슬쩍 찔리고, 간지럽혀지면 — 그들이 혼자가 아니며 누군가 그들에게 관심을 갖고 있다는 것을 알게 하는 것 — 시각장애를 가진 아기들은 계속 미소를 지을 것이다. 이러한 사회적 피드백은 그 아기가 계속 미소를 지을 수 있도록 조장한다. 이런 방식으로, 초기 경험은 우리의 생리 작용과 함께 작용하여 사회적 행동을 형성한다. 사실, 당신은 이를 설명하기 위해 시각장애를 가진 아기의 사례들을 필요로 하지 않는다. 시력이 있는 아기들은 당신이 그들을 바라볼 때나, 더 나아가, 당신이 그들에게 미소를 지어줄 때, 당신에게 더 많이 미소 짓는다.

30.

Because people tend to adapt, interrupting [**negative / positive**][82] things with [**negative / positive**][83] ones can actually increase enjoyment. Take commercials. Most people hate [**it / them**][84], so removing them should make shows or other entertainment [**less / more**][85] enjoyable. But the opposite is [**false / true**][86]. Shows are actually more enjoyable when they're broken up by [**annoyed / annoying**][87] commercials. Because these [**less / more**][88] enjoyable moments [**add / break**][89] up adaptation to the positive experience of the show. Think about eating chocolate chips. The first chip is delicious: sweet, melt-in-your-mouth goodness. The second chip is also pretty good. But by the fourth, fifth, or tenth chip in a row, the goodness is no longer as [**pleasurable / pleasure**][90]. We adapt. Interspersing positive experiences with [**less / more**][91] positive ones, however, can slow down adaptation. Eating a Brussels sprout between chocolate chips or viewing commercials between parts of TV shows [**disrupt / disrupts**][92] the process. The less positive moment makes the following positive one new again and thus [**less / more**][93] enjoyable.

사람들은 적응하는 경향이 있기 때문에, 긍정적인 것을 부정적인 것으로 방해하는 것이 실제로는 즐거움을 향상시킬 수 있다. 광고를 예로 들어 보자. 대부분의 사람들은 그것들을 싫어해서, 그것들을 제거하는 것이 쇼나 다른 오락물을 더 즐겁게 만들 수 있다. 하지만 그 반대가 사실이다. 쇼는 그것들이 성가신 광고들에 의해 중단될 때 실제로 더 즐거워진다. 왜냐하면 이러한 덜 즐거운 순간들이 쇼의 긍정적인 경험에 대한 적응을 깨뜨리기 때문이다. 초콜릿 칩을 먹는 것을 생각해 보라. 첫 번째 칩은 맛있다: 달콤하고, 입안에서 살살 녹는 좋은 맛. 두 번째 칩도 꽤 맛있다. 하지만 네 번째, 다섯 번째, 혹은 열 번째 칩을 연속으로 먹으면 그 좋은 맛은 더 이상 즐겁지 않다. 우리는 적응한다. 그러나, 긍정적인 경험들에 덜 긍정적인 경험들을 간격을 두고 배치하는 것은 적응을 늦출 수 있다. 초콜릿 칩 사이에 방울양배추를 먹거나 TV 쇼의 파트 사이에 광고를 보는 것은 이 과정을 방해한다. 덜 긍정적인 순간은 뒤에 오는 긍정적인 순간을 다시 새롭게 만들어서 더 즐겁게 만든다.

31.

We collect stamps, coins, vintage cars even when they serve no [**economic / practical**][94] purpose. The post office doesn't accept the old stamps, the banks don't take old coins, and the vintage cars are no longer [**allowed / allowing**][95] on the road. These are all side issues; the attraction is [**that / what**][96] they are in short supply. In one study, students [**asked / were asked**][97] to arrange ten posters in order of attractiveness — with the agreement that afterward they could keep one poster as a [**award / reward**][98] for their participation. Five minutes later, they [**told / were told**][99] that the poster with the third highest rating was no longer available. Then they [**asked / were asked**][100] to judge all ten from scratch. The poster that was no longer available was suddenly [**classified / classifying**][101] as the most beautiful. In psychology, this phenomenon [**called / is called**][102] reactance: when we are deprived of an option, we [**accidentally / suddenly**][103] deem it [**less / more**][104] attractive.

우리는 그것들이 실용적인 목적을 수행하지 않더라도 우표, 동전, 빈티지 자동차들을 수집한다. 우체국은 오래된 우표를 받지 않고, 은행은 오래된 동전을 받지 않으며, 그리고 빈티지 자동차는 더 이상 도로에서 허용되지 않는다. 이런 것들은 모두 부수적인 문제이다; 매력은 그들이 부족한 공급에 있다는 것이다. 한 연구에서, 학생들은 포스터 10장을 매력도의 순서대로 배열하 도록 요청받았다 — 나중에 그들의 참여에 대한 보상으로 포스터 1장을 간직할 수 있다는 합의와 함께. 5분 후, 그들은 세 번째 높은 평가의 포스터가 더 이상 이용 가능하지 않다는 것을 들었다. 그런 다음 그들은 10개의 포스터를 모두 처음부터 평가하라고 요청을 받았다. 더 이상 이용할 수 없는 포스터가 갑자기 가장 아름다운 것으로 분류되었다. 심리학에서, 이러한 현상은 리액턴스라고 불린다: 우리가 선택지를 빼앗겼을 때, 우리는 그것을 갑자기 더 매력적으로 여긴다.

32.

If we've invested in something [**that / what**]105) hasn't repaid us — be it money in a failing venture, or time in an unhappy relationship — we find it very difficult [**to walk / walk**]106) away. This is the sunk cost fallacy. Our [**instinct / reason**]107) is to continue investing money or time as we hope that our investment will [**approve / prove**]108) to be worthwhile in the end. Giving up would mean [**acknowledging / disagreeing**]109) that we've wasted something we can't get back, and that thought is so painful that we prefer to [**avoid / face**]110) it if we can. The problem, of course, is that if something really is a bad bet, then staying with [**it / them**]111) simply increases the amount we lose. Rather than walk away [**from / to**]112) a bad five-year relationship, for example, we turn it into a bad 10-year relationship; rather than accept that we've lost a thousand dollars, we lay down [**another / the other**]113) thousand and lose that too. In the end, by [**delaying / hurrying**]114) the pain of admitting our problem, we only add to it. Sometimes we just have to cut our losses.

우리에게 보답해 주지 않는 것에 우리가 투자해 왔다면 — 실패한 사업에 투자한 돈이거나, 불행한 인간관계에 투자한 시간이던지 간에 — 우리는 벗어나기가 매우 어렵다는 것을 안다. 이것은 매몰 비용 오류이다. 우리의 본능은 결국에는 우리의 투자가 가치 있는 것으로 입증될 것이라고 희망하면서 돈이나 시간에 투자를 계속 하는 것이다. 포기한다는 것은 우리가 돌이킬 수 없는 무언가를 낭비해왔다고 인정하는 것을 의미하고, 그런 생각은 너무 고통스러워서 우리가 할 수 있다면 그것을 피하기를 선호한다. 물론, 문제는 어떤 것이 정말 나쁜 투자라면, 그것을 계속하는 것은 우리가 잃는 총액을 증가시킬 뿐이라는 것이다. 예를 들어, 5년의 나쁜 관계에서 벗어나기보다는 우리는 그것을 10년의 나쁜 관계로 바꾸고; 천 달러를 잃었다는 사실을 받아들이기보다는, 또 다른 천 달러를 내놓고 그것도 역시 잃는다. 결국, 우리의 문제를 인정하는 고통을 미룸으로써 우리는 그것에 보탤 뿐이다. 때때로 우리는 손실을 끊어야만 한다.

33.

On our little world, light travels, for all practical purposes, instantaneously. If a light-bulb is glowing, then of course it's physically [**where / when**]115) we see it, shining away. We reach out our hand and [**touch / touched**]116) it: It's there all right, and [**unpleasant / unpleasantly**]117) hot. If the filament fails, then the light goes out. We don't see it in the same place, glowing, illuminating the room years after the bulb breaks and it's [**removed / removing**]118) from its socket. The very notion seems [**logical / nonsensical**]119). But if we're [**enough far / far enough**]120) away, an entire sun can go out and we'll continue to see it shining brightly; we won't learn of its death, it may be, for ages to come — in fact, for how long it takes light, [**that / which**]121) travels fast but not infinitely fast, to cross the intervening vastness. The [**immense / immerse**]122) distances to the stars and the galaxies mean that we see [**everything / nothing**]123) in space in the past.

우리의 작은 세상에서, 실제로는 빛은 순간적으로 이동한다. 전구가 켜져 있다면, 당연히 그것은 우리가 보는 그 자리에서 빛을 내고 있다. 우리는 손을 뻗어 그것을 만진다: 그것은 바로 거기에 있고, 불쾌할 정도로 뜨겁다. 필라멘트가 나가면, 그때 빛은 꺼신다. 전구가 망가져서 소켓에서 제거된 몇 년 후, 그 자리에 빛을 내고 방을 밝히고 있는 그것을 우리는 보지 못한다. 바로 그 개념은 말도 안 되는 것처럼 보인다. 하지만 우리가 충분히 멀리 떨어져 있다면, 항성 전체는 꺼질 수 있지만 우리는 그것이 밝게 빛나는 것을 계속 볼 것이다; 우리는 아마도 오랜 세월 동안 — 사실, 빠르지만 무한히 빠르지는 않게, 이동하는 빛이 그 사이에 낀 광대함을 가로지르는데 걸리는 시간 동안 그것의 소멸을 알지 못할 것이다. 별과 은하까지의 엄청난 거리는 우리가 우주 공간의 모든 것을 과거의 모습으로 보고 있다는 것을 의미한다.

34.

Financial markets do more than take capital from the rich and lend [it / them]124) to everyone else. They enable each of us [smooth / to smooth]125) consumption over our lifetimes, which is a fancy way of saying that we [x / don't]126) have to spend income at the same time we earn it. Shakespeare may have admonished us to be [either / neither]127) borrowers nor lenders; the fact is that most of us will be both at some point. If we [live / lived]128) in an agrarian society, we would have to eat our crops [reasonable / reasonably]129) soon after the harvest or find some way to store [it / them]130). Financial markets are a [less / more]131) sophisticated way of managing the harvest. We can spend income now that we have not yet earned — as by borrowing for college or a home — or we can earn income now and spend [it / them]132) later, as by saving for retirement. The important point is [that / what]133) earning income has been divorced from spending it, [allowed / allowing]134) us much more flexibility in life.

금융 시장은 부자들로부터 자본을 받아 다른 모든 사람들에게 그것을 빌려주는 것 이상을 한다. 그것들은 우리 각자가 평생에 걸쳐 소비를 원활하게 하도록 해주며, 그리고 이는 우리가 그것(소득)을 얻는 동시에 소득을 소비할 필요가 없다는 것을 말하는 멋진 방식이다. 셰익스피어는 우리가 빌리는 사람도 빌려주는 사람도 되지 말라고 충고했을지도 모른다; 사실 우리 대부분은 어떤 때에는 둘 다 될 것이다. 만약 우리가 농경 사회에 산다면, 우리는 우리의 농작물을 수확 직후에 합리적으로 먹거나 또는 그것들을 저장할 어떤 방법을 찾아야 할 것이다. 금융 시장은 수확을 관리하는 더 정교한 방법이다. 우리는 우리가 아직 벌지 않은 소득을 지금 소비할 수도 있고 — 대학이나 주택을 위해 빌리는 것처럼 — 혹은 우리는 은퇴를 위해 저축하는 것처럼, 지금 소득을 벌어서 나중에 그것을 소비할 수도 있다. 중요한 점은 소득을 버는 것이 그것을 소비하는 것과 분리되어 있다는 것이고, 이는 우리에게 삶에서 훨씬 더 많은 유연성을 허용해준다.

35.

As the old joke goes: "Software, free. User manual, $10,000." But it's no joke. A couple of high-profile companies make their living selling instruction and [paid / paying]135) support for free software. The copy of code, being [mere / merely]136) bits, is free. The lines of free code [become / becomes]137) valuable to you only through support and guidance. A lot of medical and genetic information will go this route in the coming decades. Right now [get / getting]138) a full copy of all your DNA is very expensive ($10,000), but soon it won't be. The price is [dropped / dropping]139) so fast, it will be $100 soon, and then the next year insurance companies will offer to sequence you for free. When a copy of your sequence costs [nothing / something]140), the interpretation of what it means, what you can do about it, and how to use it — the manual for your genes — will be [expensive / inexpensive]141).

다음과 같은 옛 농담처럼: "소프트웨어, 무료. 사용자 매뉴얼, 10,000달러." 하지만 그것은 농담이 아니다. 세간의 이목을 끄는 몇몇 기업들은 무료 소프트웨어에 대한 지침과 유료 지원을 판매하면서 돈을 번다. 단지 몇 비트일 뿐인 코드 사본은 무료이다. 무료 코드의 배열은 지원과 안내를 통해서만 당신에게 가치 있게 된다. 다가올 수십 년 안에 많은 의료 및 유전 정보가 이 경로를 따르게 될 것이다. 지금은 당신의 모든 DNA의 전체 사본을 얻는 것이 매우 비싸지만 (10,000달러), 곧 그렇지 않게 될 것이다. 가격이 너무 빨리 떨어지고 있어, 곧 100달러가 될 것이고, 그 다음 해에는 보험 회사가 무료로 당신의 유전자 배열 순서를 밝혀줄 것을 제안할 것이다. 당신의 배열의 사본에 비용이 들지 않을 때, 그것이 의미하는 것, 당신이 그것에 관해 할 수 있는 것, 그리고 그것을 사용하는 방법에 관한 설명 — 당신의 유전자 매뉴얼 — 은 비싸질 것이다.

36.

Brains are expensive in terms of energy. Twenty percent of the calories we consume [are / is]142) used to power the brain. So brains try [operating / to operate]143) in the most energy-efficient way possible, and that means processing only the [maximum / minimum]144) amount of information from our senses that we need to [navigate / navigating]145) the world. Neuroscientists weren't the first to discover [that / what]146) fixing your gaze on something is no guarantee of seeing it. Magicians figured [**out this / this out**]¹⁴⁷⁾ long ago. By directing your attention, they perform tricks with their hands in full view. Their actions should give away the game, but they can rest [**assured / reassured**]¹⁴⁸⁾ that your brain processes only small bits of the visual scene. This all helps to explain the prevalence of traffic accidents [**which / in which**]¹⁴⁹⁾ drivers hit pedestrians in plain view, or collide with cars [**direct / directly**]¹⁵⁰⁾ in front of them. In many of these cases, the eyes are pointed in the right direction, but the brain isn't seeing [**that's / what's**]¹⁵¹⁾ really out there.

에너지의 측면에서 뇌는 비용이 많이 든다. 우리가 소비하는 칼로리의 20%는 뇌에 동력을 공급하는 데 사용된다. 따라서 뇌는 가능한 한 가장 에너지 효율적인 방식으로 작동하려고 애쓰며, 그것은 우리가 세상을 항해하는 데 필요로 하는 최소한의 양의 정보만을 우리 감각으로부터 처리하는 것을 의미한다. 신경과학자들은 무언가에 당신의 시선을 고정하는 것이 그것을 본다는 보장이 없다는 사실을 발견한 최초가 아니었다. 마술사들은 오래전에 이것을 알아냈다. 당신의 주의를 끌어서, 그들은 다 보이는 데서 손으로 속임수를 행한다. 그들의 행동은 그 속임수를 드러내겠지만, 그들은 당신의 뇌가 시각적 장면의 오직 작은 부분들만을 처리한다는 것을 확신한 채로 있을 수 있다. 이 모든 것은 운전자가 명백한 시야에 있는 보행자들을 치거나, 바로 앞에 있는 차량들과 충돌하는 교통사고의 빈번함을 설명하는 데 도움이 된다. 많은 이러한 경우에서, 눈은 올바른 방향을 향하고 있지만, 뇌는 실제로 거기에 있는 것을 보고 있지 않다.

37.

Buying a television is [**current / currently**]¹⁵²⁾ consumption. It makes us happy today but does nothing to make us richer tomorrow. Yes, money spent on a television keeps workers [**employed / employing**]¹⁵³⁾ at the television factory. But if the same money [**invested / were invested,**]¹⁵⁴⁾ it would create jobs somewhere else, say for scientists in a laboratory or workers on a construction site, while also [**make / making**]¹⁵⁵⁾ us richer in the long run. Think about college as an example. Sending students to college [**create / creates**]¹⁵⁶⁾ jobs for professors. Using the same money to buy fancy sports cars for high school graduates would create jobs for auto workers. The [**crucial / minor**]¹⁵⁷⁾ difference between these scenarios is that a college education makes a young person [**less / more**]¹⁵⁸⁾ productive for the rest of his or her life; a sports car does not. Thus, college [**intuition / tuition**]¹⁵⁹⁾ is an investment; buying a sports car is consumption.

텔레비전을 사는 것은 현재의 소비이다. 그것은 오늘 우리를 행복하게 하지만 내일 우리를 더 부유하게 만드는 데는 아무것도 하지 않는다. 그렇다, 텔레비전에 소비되는 돈은 노동자들이 텔레비전 공장에 계속 고용되게 한다. 하지만 같은 돈이 투자된다면, 그것은 말하자면 실험실의 과학자들이나 건설 현장의 노동자들을 위한, 어딘가 다른 곳의 일자리를 창출하면서, 또한 장기적으로 우리를 더 부유하게 만들 것이다. 대학을 예로써 생각해 보자. 학생들을 대학에 보내는 것은 교수들을 위한 일자리를 창출한다. 같은 돈을 고등학교 졸업생에게 멋진 스포츠카를 사주는 데 쓰는 것은 자동차 노동자를 위한 일자리를 창출할 것이다. 이러한 시나리오들의 중대한 사이점은 내학 교육은 젊은이늘이 그 또는 그녀의 남은 삶 동안 더 생산적이게 만들지만; 스포츠카는 그렇지 않다는 것이다. 따라서, 대학 등록금은 투자이다; 스포츠카를 구입하는 것은 소비이다.

38.

The Net differs from most of the mass media it replaces in an [**obvious / obviously**]¹⁶⁰⁾ and very important way: it's [**bidirectional / indirectional**]¹⁶¹⁾. We can send messages through the network as well as [**receive / receiving**]¹⁶²⁾ them, [**that / which**]¹⁶³⁾ has made the system all the more useful. The ability to [**change / exchange**]¹⁶⁴⁾ information online, to upload as well as download, has turned the Net into a thoroughfare for business and commerce. With [**few / a few**]¹⁶⁵⁾ clicks, people can search virtual catalogues, place orders, track shipments, and [**update / updating**]¹⁶⁶⁾ information in corporate databases. But the Net doesn't just connect us with businesses; it connects us with one another. It's a [**interpersonal / personal**]¹⁶⁷⁾ broadcasting medium as well as a commercial one. Millions of people use [**it / them**]¹⁶⁸⁾ to distribute their own digital creations, in the form of blogs, videos, photos, songs, and podcasts, as well as to critique, edit, or otherwise [**modify / modifying**]¹⁶⁹⁾ the creations of others.

인터넷은 그것이 대체하는 대부분의 대중 매체와 분명하고도 매우 중요한 방식으로 다르다: 그것은 두 방향으로 작용한다. 우리는 네트워크를 통해 메시지들을 받을 수 있을 뿐만 아니라 그것들을 보낼 수도 있는데, 이것은 그 시스템을 훨씬 더 유용하게 만들었다. 온라인에서 정보를 교환하고, 다운로드할 뿐만 아니라 업로드하는 능력은, 인터넷을 비즈니스와 상거래를 위한 통로로 만들었다. 몇 번의 클릭으로, 사람들은 가상 카탈로그를 검색하고, 주문을 하고, 배송을 추적하고, 그리고 기업의 데이터베이스에 정보를 업데이트할 수 있다. 하지만 인터넷은 단지 우리를 기업과 연결하는 것만은 아니다; 그것은 우리를 서로서로 연결한다. 그것은 상업용 매체일 뿐만 아니라 개인 방송 매체이다. 수백만 명의 사람들이 다른 사람들의 창작물을 비평하고, 편집하고, 또는 그렇지 않으면 수정하기 위해서뿐만 아니라, 블로그, 동영상, 사진, 노래, 그리고 팟캐스트의 형태로 자신의 디지털 창작물을 배포하기 위해서 그것을 사용한다.

39.

Imagine that seven out of ten working Americans [**fired / got fired**]170) tomorrow. What would they all do? It's hard to believe you'd have an economy at all if you gave pink slips to more than half the labor force. But that is [**what / which**]171) the industrial revolution [**did / had**]172) to the workforce of the early 19th century. Two hundred years ago, 70 percent of American workers lived on the farm. Today automation [**eliminated / has eliminated**]173) all but 1 percent of their jobs, [**replaced / replacing**]174) them with machines. But the [**displaced / displacing**]175) workers did not sit idle. Instead, automation created hundreds of millions of jobs in [**entire / entirely**]176) new fields. Those who once farmed were now manning the factories [**that / where**]177) manufactured farm equipment, cars, and other industrial products. Since then, wave upon wave of new occupations have arrived — appliance repair person, food chemist, photographer, web designer — each building on previous automation. Today, the vast majority of us are doing jobs that no farmer from the 1800s could [**x / have**]178) imagined.

미국인 직장인 10명 중 7명이 내일 해고된다고 상상해 보라. 그들은 모두 무엇을 할까? 노동력의 절반 이상에게 해고 통지서를 보낸다면 경제가 유지될 것이라고 믿기 어려울 것이다. 하지만 그것은 19세기 초 노동력에 산업혁명이 했던 것이다. 200년 전, 미국 노동자의 70%가 농장에서 살았다. 오늘날 자동화는 1%를 제외한 모든 일자리를 제거하였고, 그것들을 기계로 대체하였다. 하지만 일자리를 잃은 노동자들은 한가롭게 앉아있지 않았다. 그 대신, 자동화는 완전히 새로운 분야에서 수억 개의 일자리를 창출했다. 한때 농사를 짓던 사람들은 이제 농기구, 자동차, 그리고 기타 산업 제품을 제조하는 공장에서 일하고 있다. 그 이후로, 가전제품 수리공, 식품 화학자, 사진작가, 웹 디자이너 등 이전의 자동화를 기반으로 한 새로운 직업이 계속해서 등장했다. 오늘날, 우리 중 대다수는 1800년대의 농부들은 상상도 할 수 없었던 일을 하고 있다.

40.

Many things spark envy : ownership, status, health, youth, talent, popularity, beauty. It is often [**confused / confusing**]179) with jealousy because the physical reactions are identical. The difference: the subject of envy is a thing (status, money, health etc.). The subject of jealousy is the behaviour of a third person. Envy [**need / needs**]180) two people. Jealousy, on the other hand, [**acquires / requires**]181) three: Peter is jealous of Sam [**because / because of**]182) the beautiful girl next door rings him instead. Paradoxically, with envy we direct resentments toward those who are most [**different / similar**]183) to us in age, career and residence. We don't envy businesspeople from the century before last. We don't envy millionaires on [**another / the other**]184) side of the globe. As a writer, I don't envy musicians, managers or dentists, but [**another / other**]185) writers. As a CEO you envy other, bigger CEOs. As a supermodel you envy more [**successful / successive**]186) supermodels. Aristotle knew this: 'Potters envy potters.'

많은 것들은 부러움을 불러일으킨다: 소유권, 지위, 건강, 젊음, 재능, 인기, 아름다움. 이것은 신체적 반응이 동일하기 때문에 종종 질투와 혼동된다. 차이점: 부러움의 대상은 사물(지위, 돈, 건강 등)이다. 질투의 대상은 제3자의 행동이다. 부러움은 두 사람을 필요로 한다. 반면, 질투는 세 사람을 요구한다: Peter는 옆집의 예쁜 여자가 자기가 아니라 Sam에게 전화를 걸기 때문에 그를 질투한다. 역설적이게도, 부러움을 가질 때 우리는 나이, 경력, 거주지에 있어서 우리와 가장 비슷한 사람들에게 불쾌감을 향하게 한다. 우리는 지지난 세기의 사업가들을 부러워하지 않는다. 우리는 지구 반대편의 백만장자를 부러워하지 않는다. 작가로서, 나는 음악가, 매니저 또는 치과의사가 부럽지 않지만, 다른 작가들을 부러워한다. CEO로서 당신은 다른, 더 큰 CEO들을 부러워한다. 슈퍼 모델로서 당신은 더 성공한 슈퍼 모델들을 부러워한다. 아리스토텔레스는 이를 알고 있었다: '도공은 도공을 부러워한다.'

41~42.

We have biases that support our biases! If we're [**impartial / partial**]187) to one option — perhaps [**because / because of**]188) it's more memorable, or framed to minimize loss, or seemingly consistent with a promising pattern — we tend to search for information [**that / what**]189) will justify choosing that option. On the one hand, it's [**sensible / sensitive**]190) to make choices that we can defend with data and a list of reasons. On the other hand, if we're not careful, we're likely to conduct an [**balanced / imbalanced**]191) analysis, falling prey to a cluster of errors collectively known as "confirmation biases." For example, [**near / nearly**]192) all companies include classic "tell me about yourself" job interviews as part of the hiring process, and many rely on these interviews alone to evaluate applicants. But it turns out that traditional interviews are actually one of the least useful [**tool / tools**]193) for predicting an employee's future success. This is [**because / why**]194) interviewers often subconsciously make up their minds about interviewees based on their first few moments of interaction and spend the rest of the interview cherry-picking evidence and [**phrase / phrasing**]195) their questions to [**confirm / conform**]196) that initial impression: "I see here you left a good position at your previous job. You must be pretty ambitious, right?" versus "You must not have been very committed, huh?" This means that interviewers can be prone to [**noticing / overlooking**]197) significant information that would clearly indicate whether this candidate was actually the best person to hire. More structured approaches, like obtaining samples of a candidate's work or [**ask / asking**]198) how he would respond to difficult hypothetical situations, [**are / is**]199) dramatically better at assessing future success, with a nearly threefold advantage over traditional interviews.

우리는 우리의 편견을 뒷받침하는 편견을 가진다! 만약 우리가 한 가지 옵션에 편향된다면 — 그것이 아마도 더 잘 기억할만 하거나, 손실을 최소화하기 위해 짜맞춰졌거나, 혹은 유망한 패턴과 일치하는 것처럼 보이기 때문에 — 우리는 그 옵션을 선택한 것을 정당화할 정보를 찾는 경향이 있다. 한편으로는, 데이터와 이유들의 목록으로 방어할 수 있는 선택을 하는 것이 현명하다. 반면에, 만약 우리가 주의를 기울이지 않으면, 우리는 불균형한 분석을 수행할 가능성이 있어서, 총체적으로 "확증 편향"으로 알려져 있는 오류 덩어리의 희생양이 된다. 예를 들어, 거의 모든 기업이 채용 과정의 일부로 전통적인 "자기소개" 취업 면접을 실시하며, 많은 기업이 지원자를 평가하기 위해서 이러한 면접에만 의존한다. 하지만 전통적인 면접은 실제로 직원의 미래 성공을 예측하는 데 가장 유용하지 않은 도구 중 하나라는 것으로 판명된다. 이것은 면접관들이 종종 잠재의식적으로 처음 몇 순간의 상호작용을 바탕으로 면접 대상자에 대한 결정을 내리고, 그 첫인상을 확인하기 위해 증거를 고르고 질문을 만드는 데 면접의 나머지 시간을 보내기 때문이다: "당신은 이전 직장에서 좋은 직책을 두고 나오신 게 보이네요. 틀림없이 야망이 꽤 크시겠어요, 그렇죠?" 대 "당신은 그다지 헌신적이지 않았음에 틀림없네요, 그렇죠?" 이것은 면접관이 이 지원자가 실제로 채용하기에 가장 좋은 사람인지 여부를 명확하게 보여줄 수 있는 중요한 정보를 간과하기 쉽다는 것을 의미한다. 지원자의 업무 샘플을 확보하거나 가정된 어려운 상황에 어떻게 그가 대응할지 묻는 것과 같은 보다 구조화된 접근 방식은, 전통적인 면접보다, 거의 세 배의 이점으로 미래의 성공을 평가하는 데 훨씬 더 낫다.

43~45.

On Saturday morning, Todd and his 5-year-old daughter Ava walked out of the store with the groceries they [**had / have**]²⁰⁰⁾ just purchased. As they pushed their grocery cart through the parking lot, they saw a red car pulling into the space next to their pick-up truck. A young man named Greg was driving. "That's a cool car," Ava said to her dad. He agreed and looked at Greg, who finished parking and [**opened / opening**]²⁰¹⁾ his door. As Todd finished loading his groceries, Greg's door remained open. Todd noticed Greg didn't get out of his car. But he was pulling something from his car. He put a metal frame on the ground [**beside / besides**]²⁰²⁾ his door. Remaining in the driver's seat, he then reached back into his car to grab something else. Todd realized [**that / what**]²⁰³⁾ he was doing and considered whether he should try to help him. After a moment, he decided to [**approach / approaching**]²⁰⁴⁾ Greg. By this time, Greg had already pulled one thin wheel out of his car and attached [**it / them**]²⁰⁵⁾ to the frame. He was now [**pulled / pulling**]²⁰⁶⁾ a second wheel out when he looked up and saw Todd standing near him. Todd said, "Hi there! Have a great weekend!" Greg seemed a bit surprised, but [**replied / replying**]²⁰⁷⁾ by wishing him a great weekend too. Then Greg added, "Thanks for letting me [**have / to have**]²⁰⁸⁾ my independence." "Of course," Todd said. After Todd and Ava climbed into their truck, Ava became [**curious / curiously**]²⁰⁹⁾. So she asked why he didn't offer to help the man with his wheelchair. Todd said, "Why do you insist on [**brush / brushing**]²¹⁰⁾ your teeth without my help?" She answered, "Because I know how to!" He said, "And the man knows how to put together his wheelchair." Ava understood that sometimes the best way to help someone is to not help at all.

토요일 아침에, Todd와 그의 다섯 살짜리 딸 Ava는 그들이 방금 구입한 식료품을 가지고 가게에서 걸어 나왔다. 그들이 주차장에서 식료품 카트를 밀면서 갈 때, 그들은 빨간 차 한 대가 그들의 픽업 트럭 옆 공간으로 들어오는 것을 보았다. Greg라는 이름의 한 젊은 남자가 운전을 하고 있었다. "저것은 멋진 차네요."라고 Ava가 그녀의 아빠에게 말했다. 그는 동의했고 Greg를 보았는데, 그는 주차를 마치고 그의 문을 열었다. Todd가 그의 식료품을 싣는 것을 끝냈을 때, Greg의 문은 열린 채로 있었다. Todd는 Greg가 그의 차에서 내리지 않은 것을 알아차렸다. 그러나 그는 그의 차에서 무엇인가를 꺼내고 있었다. 그는 그의 문 옆 바닥에 금속 프레임을 두었다. 운전석에 머무른 채, 그는 무엇인가 다른 것을 잡기 위해 그의 차 안 뒤쪽으로 손을 뻗었다. Todd는 그가 무엇을 하고 있는지를 깨닫고 그가 그를 도와야 할지를 생각했다. 잠시 후, 그는 Greg에게 다가가기로 결심했다. 그때 쯤, Greg는 이미 그의 차에서 얇은 바퀴 하나를 꺼내었고 그것을 프레임에 끼웠다. 그가 고개를 들어 그의 근처에 서 있는 Todd를 보았을 때 그는 이제 두 번째 바퀴를 꺼내는 중이었다. Todd는 "안녕하세요! 주말 잘 보내세요!"라고 말했다. Greg는 약간 놀란 것처럼 보였지만, 그에게도 좋은 주말을 보내라고 답했다. 그러자 Greg는 "내가 독립성을 가질 수 있게 해줘서 고맙습니다."라고 덧붙였다. "물론이죠."라고 Todd가 말했다. Todd와 Ava가 그들의 트럭에 올라탄 후에, Ava는 호기심이 생겼다. 그래서 그녀는 왜 그가 그 남자에게 휠체어에 대해 도움을 제공하지 않았는지를 물었다. Todd는 "왜 너는 내 도움 없이 너의 이를 닦으려고 고집하니?"라고 말했다. 그녀는 "왜냐하면 제가 어떻게 하는지를 알기 때문이죠!"라고 답했다. 그는 "그리고 그 남자는 그의 휠체어를 어떻게 조립하는지 알고 있어."라고 말했다. Ava는 때때로 누군가를 돕는 가장 좋은 방법은 전혀 도와주지 않는 것임을 이해했다.

18.

Dear Residents, / My name is Kari Patterson, and I'm the manager of the River View Apartments. It's time to take advantage of the sunny weather [**making / to make**]1) our community more beautiful. On Saturday, July 13 at 9 a.m., residents will [**be met / meet**]2) in the north parking lot. We will divide into teams to plant flowers and small trees, pull weeds, and [**put / putting**]3) colorful decorations on the lawn. Please join us for this year's Gardening Day, and [**remember / to remember**]4) no special skills or tools are required. Last year, we had a great time working together, so come out and [**make / making**]5) this year's event even better! Warm regards, / Kari Patterson

19.

It was the championship race. Emma was the final runner on her relay team. She anxiously waited in her spot for her teammate [**pass / to pass**]6) her the baton. Emma wasn't sure she could perform her role without [**make / making**]7) a mistake. Her hands shook as she thought, "What if I drop the baton?" She felt her heart rate increasing as her teammate approached. But as she started running, she received the baton [**smooth / smoothly**]8). In the final 10 meters, she passed two [**another / other**]9) runners and [**crossed / crossing**]10) the finish line in first place! She raised her hands in the air, and a huge smile came across her face. As her teammates hugged her, she shouted, "We did it!" All of her hard training had been worth it.

20.

Most people resist the idea of a true self-estimate, probably [**because / because of**]11) they fear it might mean downgrading some of their beliefs about who they are and [**what / which**]12) they're capable of. As Goethe's maxim goes, it is a great failing "to see [**you / yourself**]13) as more than you are." How could you really [**be considered / consider**]14) self-aware if you refuse to consider your weaknesses? Don't fear self-assessment [**because / because of**]15) you're worried you might have to admit some things about yourself. The second half of Goethe's maxim is important too. He states that it is equally [**damaged / damaging**]16) to "value yourself at less than your true worth." We underestimate our capabilities just as much and just as dangerously as we overestimate [**another / other**]17) abilities. Cultivate the ability to judge yourself [**accurate / accurately**]18) and [**honest / honestly**]19). Look inward to discern what you're capable of and [**that / what**]20) it will take to unlock that potential.

21.

[**Take / Taking**]21) a look at some of the most powerful, rich, and famous people in the world. Ignore the trappings of their success and [**that / what**]22) they're able to buy. Look instead at [**that / what**]23) they're forced [**to trade / trading**]24) in return — look at what success has cost [**them / themselves**]25). Mostly? Freedom. Their work demands they wear a suit. Their success depends on [**attending / to attend**]26) certain parties, kissing up to people they don't like. It will [**acquire / require**]27) — inevitably — realizing they are unable to say [**that / what**]28) they actually think. Worse, it demands [**what / that**]29) they become a different type of person or do bad things. Sure, it might pay well — but they haven't truly [**examined / examining**]30) the transaction. As Seneca put it, "Slavery [**reside / resides**]31) under marble and gold." Too many [**successful / successive**]32) people are prisoners in jails of their own making. Is that what you want? Is that what you're working hard toward? Let's hope not.

22.

If a firm is going to [**be saved / save**]³³⁾ by the government, it might be easier to concentrate on [**lobby / lobbying**]³⁴⁾ the government for more money rather than taking the harder decision of [**restructure / restructuring**]³⁵⁾ the company to be able to be profitable and viable in the long term. This is an example of something known as [**moral / mortal**]³⁶⁾ hazard — when government support alters the decisions firms [**take / taken**]³⁷⁾. For example, if governments rescue banks who get into difficulty, as they [**did / were**]³⁸⁾ during the credit crisis of 2007-08, this could encourage banks [**take / to take**]³⁹⁾ greater risks in the future because they know there is a possibility that governments will [**interfere / intervene**]⁴⁰⁾ if they lose money. Although the government rescue may be well intended, it can [**negatively / positively**]⁴¹⁾ affect the behavior of banks, [**discouraging / encouraging**]⁴²⁾ risky and poor decision making.

23.

If there is [**few / little**]⁴³⁾ or no diversity of views, and all scientists see, think, and question the world in a similar way, then they will not, as a community, be as [**objective / subjective**]⁴⁴⁾ as they maintain they are, or at least [**aspire / inspire**]⁴⁵⁾ to be. The solution is that there should be far [**great / greater**]⁴⁶⁾ diversity in the practice of science: in gender, ethnicity, and social and cultural backgrounds. Science works because it [**carried out / is carried out**]⁴⁷⁾ by people who pursue their curiosity about the natural world and [**test / testing**]⁴⁸⁾ their and each other's ideas from as many [**varied / varying**]⁴⁹⁾ perspectives and angles as possible. When science is done by a diverse group of people, and if consensus [**build / builds**]⁵⁰⁾ up about a particular area of scientific knowledge, then we can have more confidence in its [**objectivity / subjectivity**]⁵¹⁾ and truth.

24.

We tend to [**break / breaking**]⁵²⁾ up time into units, such as weeks, months, and seasons; in a series of studies among farmers in India and students in North America, psychologists found [**that / what**]⁵³⁾ if a deadline is on the other side of a "break" — such as in the New Year — we're [**less / more**]⁵⁴⁾ likely to see it as remote, and, as a result, be [**less / more**]⁵⁵⁾ ready to jump into action. [**That / What**]⁵⁶⁾ you need to do in that situation is find [**another / the other**]⁵⁷⁾ way to think about the timeframe. For example, if it's November and the deadline is in January, it's better to tell yourself you have to get it done "this winter" rather than "next year." The best approach is to view deadlines as a challenge that you have to [**be met / meet**]⁵⁸⁾ within a period that's [**eminent / imminent**]⁵⁹⁾. That way the stress is more manageable, and you have a better chance of [**start / starting**]⁶⁰⁾ — and therefore [**finish / finishing**]⁶¹⁾ — in good time.

25.

The graph above shows the amount of CO_2 emissions per person across [**selected / selecting**]⁶²⁾ Asian countries in 2010 and 2020. All the countries except Uzbekistan had a greater amount of CO_2 emissions per person in 2020 than that in 2010. In 2010, the amount of CO_2 emissions per person of China was the largest among the five countries, [**followed / following**]⁶³⁾ by that of Mongolia. However, in 2020, Mongolia [**surpassed / surpassing**]⁶⁴⁾ China in terms of the amount of CO_2 emissions per person. In 2010, Uzbekistan produced a larger amount of CO_2 emissions per person than Vietnam, while the [**opposite / same**]⁶⁵⁾ was true in 2020. Among the five countries, India was the only one [**where / which**]⁶⁶⁾ the amount of CO_2 emissions per person was less than 2 tons in 2020.

26.

Henry David Thoreau [**born / was born**]⁶⁷⁾ in Concord, Massachusetts in 1817. When he was 16, he entered Harvard College. After graduating, Thoreau worked as a schoolteacher but he quit after two weeks. In June of 1838 he set up a school with his brother John. However, he had hopes of [**become / becoming**]⁶⁸⁾ a nature poet. In 1845, he moved into a small self-built house [**near / nearly**]⁶⁹⁾ Walden Pond. At Walden, Thoreau did an incredible amount of reading. The journal he wrote there became the source of his most famous book, Walden. In his later life, Thoreau traveled to the Maine woods, to Cape Cod, and to Canada. At the age of 43, he ended his travels and [**returned / returning**]⁷⁰⁾ to Concord. Although his works were not widely read [**during / while**]⁷¹⁾ his lifetime, he never stopped [**to write / writing**]⁷²⁾, and his works fill 20 volumes.

29.

The built-in capacity for smiling [**is proven / proven**]⁷³⁾ by the remarkable observation [**that / what**]⁷⁴⁾ babies who are congenitally both deaf and blind, who have never seen a human face, also start to smile at around 2 months. However, smiling in blind babies eventually [**disappear / disappears**]⁷⁵⁾ if nothing is done to reinforce [**them / it**]⁷⁶⁾. Without the right feedback, smiling dies out. But here's a fascinating fact: blind babies will continue to smile if they [**x / are**]⁷⁷⁾ cuddled, bounced, nudged, and tickled by an adult — anything to let them [**know / to know**]⁷⁸⁾ that they are not alone and that someone cares about them. This social feedback [**encourage / encourages**]⁷⁹⁾ the baby to continue smiling. In this way, early experience operates with our biology to establish [**asocial / social**]⁸⁰⁾ behaviors. In fact, you don't need the cases of blind babies to make the point. Babies [**with / without**]⁸¹⁾ sight smile more at you when you look at them or, better still, smile back at them.

30.

Because people tend to adapt, interrupting [**negative / positive**]⁸²⁾ things with [**negative / positive**]⁸³⁾ ones can actually increase enjoyment. Take commercials. Most people hate [**it / them**]⁸⁴⁾, so removing them should make shows or other entertainment [**less / more**]⁸⁵⁾ enjoyable. But the opposite is [**false / true**]⁸⁶⁾. Shows are actually more enjoyable when they're broken up by [**annoyed / annoying**]⁸⁷⁾ commercials. Because these [**less / more**]⁸⁸⁾ enjoyable moments [**add / break**]⁸⁹⁾ up adaptation to the positive experience of the show. Think about eating chocolate chips. The first chip is delicious: sweet, melt-in-your-mouth goodness. The second chip is also pretty good. But by the fourth, fifth, or tenth chip in a row, the goodness is no longer as [**pleasurable / pleasure**]⁹⁰⁾. We adapt. Interspersing positive experiences with [**less / more**]⁹¹⁾ positive ones, however, can slow down adaptation. Eating a Brussels sprout between chocolate chips or viewing commercials between parts of TV shows [**disrupt / disrupts**]⁹²⁾ the process. The less positive moment makes the following positive one new again and thus [**less / more**]⁹³⁾ enjoyable.

31.

We collect stamps, coins, vintage cars even when they serve no [**economic / practical**]⁹⁴⁾ purpose. The post office doesn't accept the old stamps, the banks don't take old coins, and the vintage cars are no longer [**allowed / allowing**]⁹⁵⁾ on the road. These are all side issues; the attraction is [**that / what**]⁹⁶⁾ they are in short supply. In one study, students [**asked / were asked**]⁹⁷⁾ to arrange ten posters in order of attractiveness — with the agreement that afterward they could keep one poster as a [**award / reward**]⁹⁸⁾ for their participation. Five minutes later, they [**told / were told**]⁹⁹⁾ that the poster with the third highest rating was no longer available. Then they [**asked / were asked**]¹⁰⁰⁾ to judge all ten from scratch. The poster that was no longer available was suddenly [**classified / classifying**]¹⁰¹⁾ as the most beautiful. In psychology, this phenomenon [**called / is called**]¹⁰²⁾ reactance: when we are deprived of an option, we [**accidentally / suddenly**]¹⁰³⁾ deem it [**less / more**]¹⁰⁴⁾ attractive.

32.

If we've invested in something **[that / what]**105) hasn't repaid us — be it money in a failing venture, or time in an unhappy relationship — we find it very difficult **[to walk / walk]**106) away. This is the sunk cost fallacy. Our **[instinct / reason]**107) is to continue investing money or time as we hope that our investment will **[approve / prove]**108) to be worthwhile in the end. Giving up would mean **[acknowledging / disagreeing]**109) that we've wasted something we can't get back, and that thought is so painful that we prefer to **[avoid / face]**110) it if we can. The problem, of course, is that if something really is a bad bet, then staying with **[it / them]**111) simply increases the amount we lose. Rather than walk away **[from / to]**112) a bad five-year relationship, for example, we turn it into a bad 10-year relationship; rather than accept that we've lost a thousand dollars, we lay down **[another / the other]**113) thousand and lose that too. In the end, by **[delaying / hurrying]**114) the pain of admitting our problem, we only add to it. Sometimes we just have to cut our losses.

33.

On our little world, light travels, for all practical purposes, instantaneously. If a light-bulb is glowing, then of course it's physically **[where / when]**115) we see it, shining away. We reach out our hand and **[touch / touched]**116) it: It's there all right, and **[unpleasant / unpleasantly]**117) hot. If the filament fails, then the light goes out. We don't see it in the same place, glowing, illuminating the room years after the bulb breaks and it's **[removed / removing]**118) from its socket. The very notion seems **[logical / nonsensical]**119). But if we're **[enough far / far enough]**120) away, an entire sun can go out and we'll continue to see it shining brightly; we won't learn of its death, it may be, for ages to come — in fact, for how long it takes light, **[that / which]**121) travels fast but not infinitely fast, to cross the intervening vastness. The **[immense / immerse]**122) distances to the stars and the galaxies mean that we see **[everything / nothing]**123) in space in the past.

34.

Financial markets do more than take capital from the rich and lend **[it / them]**124) to everyone else. They enable each of us **[smooth / to smooth]**125) consumption over our lifetimes, which is a fancy way of saying that we **[x / don't]**126) have to spend income at the same time we earn it. Shakespeare may have admonished us to be **[either / neither]**127) borrowers nor lenders; the fact is that most of us will be both at some point. If we **[live / lived]**128) in an agrarian society, we would have to eat our crops **[reasonable / reasonably]**129) soon after the harvest or find some way to store **[it / them]**130). Financial markets are a **[less / more]**131) sophisticated way of managing the harvest. We can spend income now that we have not yet earned — as by borrowing for college or a home — or we can earn income now and spend **[it / them]**132) later, as by saving for retirement. The important point is **[that / what]**133) earning income has been divorced from spending it, **[allowed / allowing]**134) us much more flexibility in life.

35.

As the old joke goes: "Software, free. User manual, $10,000." But it's no joke. A couple of high-profile companies make their living selling instruction and **[paid / paying]**135) support for free software. The copy of code, being **[mere / merely]**136) bits, is free. The lines of free code **[become / becomes]**137) valuable to you only through support and guidance. A lot of medical and genetic information will go this route in the coming decades. Right now **[get / getting]**138) a full copy of all your DNA is very expensive ($10,000), but soon it won't be. The price is **[dropped / dropping]**139) so fast, it will be $100 soon, and then the next year insurance companies will offer to sequence you for free. When a copy of your sequence costs **[nothing / something]**140), the interpretation of what it means, what you can do about it, and how to use it — the manual for your genes — will be **[expensive / inexpensive]**141).

36.

Brains are expensive in terms of energy. Twenty percent of the calories we consume [**are / is**]142) used to power the brain. So brains try [**operating / to operate**]143) in the most energy-efficient way possible, and that means processing only the [**maximum / minimum**]144) amount of information from our senses that we need to [**navigate / navigating**]145) the world. Neuroscientists weren't the first to discover [**that / what**]146) fixing your gaze on something is no guarantee of seeing it. Magicians figured [**out this / this out**]147) long ago. By directing your attention, they perform tricks with their hands in full view. Their actions should give away the game, but they can rest [**assured / reassured**]148) that your brain processes only small bits of the visual scene. This all helps to explain the prevalence of traffic accidents [**which / in which**]149) drivers hit pedestrians in plain view, or collide with cars [**direct / directly**]150) in front of them. In many of these cases, the eyes are pointed in the right direction, but the brain isn't seeing [**that's / what's**]151) really out there.

37.

Buying a television is [**current / currently**]152) consumption. It makes us happy today but does nothing to make us richer tomorrow. Yes, money spent on a television keeps workers [**employed / employing**]153) at the television factory. But if the same money [**invested / were invested,**]154) it would create jobs somewhere else, say for scientists in a laboratory or workers on a construction site, while also [**make / making**]155) us richer in the long run. Think about college as an example. Sending students to college [**create / creates**]156) jobs for professors. Using the same money to buy fancy sports cars for high school graduates would create jobs for auto workers. The [**crucial / minor**]157) difference between these scenarios is that a college education makes a young person [**less / more**]158) productive for the rest of his or her life; a sports car does not. Thus, college [**intuition / tuition**]159) is an investment; buying a sports car is consumption.

38.

The Net differs from most of the mass media it replaces in an [**obvious / obviously**]160) and very important way: it's [**bidirectional / indirectional**]161). We can send messages through the network as well as [**receive / receiving**]162) them, [**that / which**]163) has made the system all the more useful. The ability to [**change / exchange**]164) information online, to upload as well as download, has turned the Net into a thoroughfare for business and commerce. With [**few / a few**]165) clicks, people can search virtual catalogues, place orders, track shipments, and [**update / updating**]166) information in corporate databases. But the Net doesn't just connect us with businesses; it connects us with one another. It's a [**interpersonal / personal**]167) broadcasting medium as well as a commercial one. Millions of people use [**it / them**]168) to distribute their own digital creations, in the form of blogs, videos, photos, songs, and podcasts, as well as to critique, edit, or otherwise [**modify / modifying**]169) the creations of others.

39.

Imagine that seven out of ten working Americans [**fired / got fired**]170) tomorrow. What would they all do? It's hard to believe you'd have an economy at all if you gave pink slips to more than half the labor force. But that is [**what / which**]171) the industrial revolution [**did / had**]172) to the workforce of the early 19th century. Two hundred years ago, 70 percent of American workers lived on the farm. Today automation [**eliminated / has eliminated**]173) all but 1 percent of their jobs, [**replaced / replacing**]174) them with machines. But the [**displaced / displacing**]175) workers did not sit idle. Instead, automation created hundreds of millions of jobs in [**entire / entirely**]176) new fields. Those who once farmed were now manning the factories [**that / where**]177) manufactured farm equipment, cars, and other industrial products. Since then, wave upon wave of new occupations have arrived — appliance repair person, food chemist, photographer, web designer — each building on previous automation. Today, the vast majority of us are doing jobs that no farmer from the 1800s could [**x / have**]178) imagined.

40.

Many things spark envy : ownership, status, health, youth, talent, popularity, beauty. It is often [**confused /**
confusing]179) with jealousy because the physical reactions are identical. The difference: the subject of envy is
a thing (status, money, health etc.). The subject of jealousy is the behaviour of a third person. Envy [**need /**
needs]180) two people. Jealousy, on the other hand, [**acquires / requires**]181) three: Peter is jealous of Sam [
because / because of]182) the beautiful girl next door rings him instead. Paradoxically, with envy we direct
resentments toward those who are most [**different / similar**]183) to us in age, career and residence. We don't
envy businesspeople from the century before last. We don't envy millionaires on [**another / the other**]184) side
of the globe. As a writer, I don't envy musicians, managers or dentists, but [**another / other**]185) writers. As a
CEO you envy other, bigger CEOs. As a supermodel you envy more [**successful / successive**]186) supermodels.
Aristotle knew this: 'Potters envy potters.'

41~42.

We have biases that support our biases! If we're [**impartial / partial**]187) to one option — perhaps [**because /**
because of]188) it's more memorable, or framed to minimize loss, or seemingly consistent with a promising
pattern — we tend to search for information [**that / what**]189) will justify choosing that option. On the one
hand, it's [**sensible / sensitive**]190) to make choices that we can defend with data and a list of reasons. On the
other hand, if we're not careful, we're likely to conduct an [**balanced / imbalanced**]191) analysis, falling prey to
a cluster of errors collectively known as "confirmation biases." For example, [**near / nearly**]192) all companies
include classic "tell me about yourself" job interviews as part of the hiring process, and many rely on these
interviews alone to evaluate applicants. But it turns out that traditional interviews are actually one of the least
useful [**tool / tools**]193) for predicting an employee's future success. This is [**because / why**]194) interviewers
often subconsciously make up their minds about interviewees based on their first few moments of interaction
and spend the rest of the interview cherry-picking evidence and [**phrase / phrasing**]195) their questions to [
confirm / conform]196) that initial impression: "I see here you left a good position at your previous job. You
must be pretty ambitious, right?" versus "You must not have been very committed, huh?" This means that
interviewers can be prone to [**noticing / overlooking**]197) significant information that would clearly indicate
whether this candidate was actually the best person to hire. More structured approaches, like obtaining
samples of a candidate's work or [**ask / asking**]198) how he would respond to difficult hypothetical situations,
[**are / is**]199) dramatically better at assessing future success, with a nearly threefold advantage over traditional
interviews.

43~45.

On Saturday morning, Todd and his 5-year-old daughter Ava walked out of the store with the groceries they [**had / have**]200) just purchased. As they pushed their grocery cart through the parking lot, they saw a red car pulling into the space next to their pick-up truck. A young man named Greg was driving. "That's a cool car," Ava said to her dad. He agreed and looked at Greg, who finished parking and [**opened / opening**]201) his door. As Todd finished loading his groceries, Greg's door remained open. Todd noticed Greg didn't get out of his car. But he was pulling something from his car. He put a metal frame on the ground [**beside / besides**]202) his door. Remaining in the driver's seat, he then reached back into his car to grab something else. Todd realized [**that / what**]203) he was doing and considered whether he should try to help him. After a moment, he decided to [**approach / approaching**]204) Greg. By this time, Greg had already pulled one thin wheel out of his car and attached [**it / them**]205) to the frame. He was now [**pulled / pulling**]206) a second wheel out when he looked up and saw Todd standing near him. Todd said, "Hi there! Have a great weekend!" Greg seemed a bit surprised, but [**replied / replying**]207) by wishing him a great weekend too. Then Greg added, "Thanks for letting me [**have / to have**]208) my independence." "Of course," Todd said. After Todd and Ava climbed into their truck, Ava became [**curious / curiously**]209). So she asked why he didn't offer to help the man with his wheelchair. Todd said, "Why do you insist on [**brush / brushing**]210) your teeth without my help?" She answered, "Because I know how to!" He said, "And the man knows how to put together his wheelchair." Ava understood that sometimes the best way to help someone is to not help at all.

2024 고2 6월 모의고사 　　❶ 회차 : 　　점 / 300점

❶ voca　❷ text　❸ [/]　④ _____　❺ quiz 1　❻ quiz 2　❼ quiz 3　❽ quiz 4　❾ quiz 5

18.

Dear Residents,

My name is Kari Patterson, and I'm the manager of the River View Apartments. It's time to take **a_____**
_1) of the sunny weather to make our community more beautiful. On Saturday, July 13 at 9 a.m., **r_____**
_2) will meet in the north parking lot. We will divide into teams to plant flowers and small trees, pull weeds, and put colorful decorations on the lawn. Please join us for this year's Gardening Day, and remember no special skills or tools are **r_____3)** . Last year, we had a great time working together, so come out and make this year's event even better!

Warm regards, / Kari Patterson

주민들게, / 제 이름은 Kari Patterson이고, 저는 River View 아파트의 관리인입니다. 우리의 커뮤니티를 더욱 아름답게 만들기 위해 화창한 날씨를 이용할 때입니다. 7월 13일 토요일 오전 9시에, 주민들은 북쪽 주차장에서 만날 예정입니다. 우리는 팀을 나누어 꽃과 작은 나무를 심고, 잡초를 뽑고, 잔디밭에 다채로운 장식을 할 것입니다. 올해 정원가꾸기 날에 우리와 함께 해 주시고, 특별한 기술이나 도구는 필요하지 않다는 것을 기억하세요. 작년에, 우리는 함께 일하며 즐거운 시간을 보냈으니, 오셔서 올해 행사도 더 멋지게 만들어 주세요! / 따뜻한 마음을 담아, Kari Patterson

19.

It was the championship race. Emma was the final runner on her relay team. She **a_____4)** waited in her spot for her teammate to pass her the **b_____5)** . Emma wasn't sure she could **p_____6)** her role without making a mistake. Her hands shook as she thought, "What if I drop the baton?" She felt her heart rate increasing as her teammate **a_____7)** . But as she started running, she received the baton smoothly. In the final 10 meters, she passed two other runners and crossed the finish line in first place! She raised her hands in the air, and a huge smile came across her face. As her teammates hugged her, she shouted, "We did it!" All of her hard training had been **w_____8)** it.

결승전 경주였다. Emma는 그녀의 계주 팀의 마지막 주자였다. 그녀는 그녀의 자리에서 팀 동료가 그녀에게 바통을 건네주기를 초조하게 기다렸다. Emma는 그녀가 실수를 하지 않고 자신의 역할을 수행할 수 있을지 확신하지 못했다. "만약 내가 바통을 떨어뜨리면 어떡하지?" 라고 생각하면서 그녀의 손이 떨렸다. 그녀는 그녀의 팀 동료가 다가올수록 심박수가 증가하는 것을 느꼈다. 하지만 그녀가 달리기 시작했을 때, 그녀는 순조롭게 바통을 받았다. 마지막 10미터에서, 그녀는 두 명의 다른 주자를 제치고 나서 1위로 결승선을 통과했다! 그녀는 두 손을 하늘로 치켜들고, 얼굴에 큰 미소를 지었다. 팀 동료들이 그녀를 안아주자, 그녀는 "우리가 해냈어!"라고 소리쳤다. 그녀의 모든 힘든 훈련이 그럴만한 가치가 있었다.

20.

Most people resist the idea of a true **s_____9)** , probably because they fear it might mean **d_____10)** some of their **b_____11)** about who they are and what they're capable of. As Goethe's maxim goes, it is a great failing "to see yourself as more than you are." How could you really be considered **s_____12)** if you refuse to consider your **w_____13)** ? Don't fear **s_____14)** because you're worried you might have to admit some things about yourself. The second half of Goethe's **m_____15)** is important too. He states that it is equally **d_____16)** to "value yourself at l_____17) than your true worth." We **u_____18)** our capabilities just as much and just as dangerously as we **o_____19)** other abilities. **C_____20)** the ability to **j_____21)** yourself accurately and honestly. Look inward to **d_____22)** what you're capable of and what it will take to unlock that **p_____23)** .

대부분의 사람들은 그것(진정한 자기 평가)이 그들이 누구인지, 무엇을 할 수 있는지에 대한 믿음을 낮추는 것을 의미할지도 모른다고 두려워하기 때문에, 진정한 자기 평가에 대한 생각을 거부한다. Goethe의 격언처럼, "너 자신을 현재의 너의 모습 이상으로 보는 것"은 큰 실수이다. 네가 너의 단점을 생각해 보기를 거부한다면 어떻게 너 자신을 인식하고 있다고 여겨질 수 있을까? 네가 너 자신에 대해 몇 가지를 인정해야 할지도 모른다는 걱정 때문에 자기를 평가하는 것을 두려워하지 마라. Goethe 격언의 후반부도 역시 중요하다. 그는 "너의 진정한 가치보다 너 자신을 낮게 평가하는 것"도 똑같이 해롭다고 말한다. 우리는 다른 능력들을 과대평가 하는 것만큼 많이 그리고 위험하게 우리의 능력을 과소평가한다. 너 자신을 정확하게 그리고 정직하게 판단하는 능력을 길러라. 네가 할 수 있는 것과 너의 잠재력을 열기 위해 필요한 것을 파악하기 위해 내면을 들여다 봐라.

21.

Take a look at some of the **m_____ 24)** powerful, rich, and famous people in the world. Ignore the **t_____ 25)** of their success and what they're able to buy. Look instead at what they're **f_____ 26)** to trade in return — look at what success has **c_____ 27)** them. **M_____ 28)** Freedom. Their work **d_____ 29)** they wear a suit. Their success depends on **a_____ 30)** certain parties, kissing up to people they don't like. It will require — **i_____ 31)** — realizing they are unable to say what they actually think. **W_____ 32)** it demands that they become a different type of person or do bad things. Sure, it might **p_____ 33)** well — but they haven't truly **e_____ 34)** the transaction. As Seneca put it, "Slavery **r_____ 35)** under marble and gold." Too many successful people are prisoners in jails of their own making. Is that what you want? Is that what you're working hard toward? Let's hope not.

세계에서 가장 힘있고, 부유하며, 유명한 사람들 중 몇몇을 살펴봐라. 그들의 성공의 장식과 그들이 살 수 있는 것을 무시해라. 대신 그들이 맞바꿔야 하는 것을 봐라 — 성공이 그들에게 치르게 한 것을 봐라. 대부분은? 자유이다. 그들의 업무는 그들이 정장을 입는 것을 요구한다. 그들의 성공은 특정 파티에 참석하여, 그들이 좋아하지 않는 사람들에게 아첨하는 것에 달려 있다. 그것은 요구할 것이다 — 필연적으로 — 그들이 실제로 생각하는 것을 말할 수 없다는 사실을 깨닫는 것을. 더 나쁜 것은, 그것은 그들이 다른 유형의 사람이 되거나 부당한 일을 하도록 요구한다는 것이다. 물론, 그것은 많은 이익이 될지도 모른다 — 그러나 그들은 그 거래를 제대로 고찰한 적이 없다. Seneca가 말했듯이, "대리석과 황금 아래에 노예 상태가 존재한다." 너무 많은 성공한 사람들은 그들이 스스로 만든 감옥의 죄수들이다. 그것이 당신이 원하는 것인가? 그것이 당신이 목표로 하여 열심히 일하고 있는 것인가? 그렇지 않기를 바라자.

22.

If a firm is going to be **s_____ 36)** by the government, it might be **e_____ 37)** to concentrate on lobbying the government for more money rather than taking the harder decision of **r_____ 38)** the company to be able to be **p_____ 39)** and **v_____ 40)** in the long term. This is an example of something known as moral hazard — when government support **a_____ 41)** the decisions firms **t_____ 42)** . For example, if governments rescue banks who get into difficulty, as they did during the credit crisis of 2007-08, this could encourage banks to take greater risks in the future because they know there is a **p_____ 43)** that governments will **i_____ 44)** if they lose money. Although the government rescue may be well **i_____ 45)** it can negatively affect the behavior of banks, encouraging **r_____ 46)** and poor decision making.

기업이 정부로부터 구제받으려면, 장기적으로 수익성이 나고 성장할 수 있도록 회사를 구조조정하는 어려운 결정을 내리기보다는 더 많은 돈을 빌기 위해 정부에 로비하는 것에 집중하는 것이 더 쉬울지도 모른다. 이것은 도덕적 해이라고 알려진 것의 한 예이다 — 정부의 지원이 기업이 내리는 결정을 바꿀 때. 예를 들어, 2007-08년 신용 위기 때 그들이 그랬던 것처럼, 만약 정부가 어려움에 처한 은행을 구제한다면, 이것은 은행이 앞으로 더 큰 위험을 감수하도록 조장하는데 그 이유는 그들이 손해를 보는 경우 정부가 개입할 가능성이 있다는 것을 그들이 알기 때문이다. 정부의 구제는 좋은 의도일지라도, 그것은 은행의 행동에 부정적으로 영향을 미쳐, 위험하고 형편없는 의사 결정을 조장할 수 있다.

23.

If there is little or no d_____47) of views, and all scientists see, think, and question the world in a similar way, then they will not, as a community, be as o_____48) as they maintain they are, or at l_____49) aspire to be. The solution is that there should be far greater d_____50) in the practice of science: in gender, e_____51) and social and cultural backgrounds. Science works because it is c_____52) out by people who pursue their curiosity about the natural world and test their and each other's ideas from as many v_____53) perspectives and a_____54) as possible. When science is d_____55) by a diverse group of people, and if c_____56) builds up about a particular area of scientific knowledge, then we can have more confidence in its o_____57) and truth.

만약 견해의 다양성이 거의 없거나 전혀 없고, 모든 과학자들이 비슷한 방식으로 세상을 보고, 생각하고, 의문을 제기한다면, 그러면 그들은, 하나의 공동체로서, 자신들이 주장하는 것만큼, 혹은 적어도 그렇게 되기를 열망하는 것만큼, 객관적이지 않을 것이다. 해결책은 과학의 실행에 있어 훨씬 더 많은 다양성이 있어야 한다는 것이다: 성별, 인종, 그리고 사회적 문화적 배경에서. 과학은 그것이 자연 세계에 대한 호기심을 추구하고 가능한 한 다양한 관점과 각도에서 그들의 그리고 서로의 아이디어를 검증하는 사람들에 의해 수행되기 때문에 작동한다. 과학이 다양한 집단의 사람들에 의해 행해질 때, 그리고 만약 과학지식의 특정 영역에 대한 의견 일치가 이루어진다면, 그러면 우리는 그것의 객관성과 진실성에 있어서 더 큰 자신감을 가질 수 있다.

24.

We tend to break up time into units, such as weeks, months, and seasons; in a series of studies a_____58) farmers in India and students in North America, p_____59) found that if a d_____60) is on the other side of a "break" — such as in the New Year — we're more l_____61) to see it as remote, and, as a result, be l_____62) ready to jump into action. What you need to do in that situation is find another way to think about the t_____63) . For example, if it's November and the deadline is in January, it's better to tell yourself you have to get it d_____64) "this winter" rather than "next year." The best a_____65) is to v_____66) deadlines as a challenge that you have to meet within a p_____67) that's i_____68) . That way the stress is more m_____69) and you have a better chance of starting — and therefore finishing — in good time.

우리는 시간을 주, 월, 계절과 같은 단위로 나누는 경향이 있다; 인도의 농부들과 북미의 학생들을 대상으로 한 일련의 연구에서, 심리학자들은 마감일이 "나뉨" — 새해와 같이 — 의 반대편에 있는 경우, 우리는 그것을 멀리 있는 것으로 여기고, 그 결과, 실행에 옮길 준비를 덜 할 가능성이 더 많다는 사실을 발견했다. 그러한 상황에서 당신이 해야 할 일은 그 시간 틀에 대해 생각하는 또 다른 방식을 찾는 것이다. 예를 들어, 지금이 11월이고 마감일이 1월이라면, 네가 "내년"보다는 "이번 겨울"에 일을 끝내야 한다고 너 자신에게 말하는 것이 더 좋다. 최고의 접근법은 마감일을 임박한 기간 내에 맞춰야 하는 도전으로 여기는 것이다. 그런 식으로 스트레스는 더 잘 관리될 수 있고, 적시에 작업을 시작 — 따라서 마무리 — 할 수 있는 가능성이 높아진다.

25.

The graph a_____70) shows the amount of CO₂ e_____71) per person a_____72) selected Asian countries in 2010 and 2020. All the countries except Uzbekistan had a g_____73) amount of CO₂ emissions per person in 2020 than that in 2010. In 2010, the amount of CO₂ emissions per person of China was the l_____74) among the five countries, followed by that of Mongolia. However, in 2020, Mongolia s_____75) China in terms of the amount of CO₂ emissions per person In 2010, Uzbekistan produced a l_____76) amount of CO₂ emissions per person than Vietnam, while the o_____77) was true in 2020. Among the five countries, India was the only one where the amount of CO₂ emissions per person was l_____78) than 2 tons in 2020.

위 그래프는 선택된 아시아 국가들의 2010년과 2020년 1인당 CO_2 배출량을 보여준다. 우즈베키스탄을 제외한 모든 국가들은 2010년의 배출량보다 2020년의 1인당 CO_2 배출량이 더 많았다. 2010년에는, 중국의 1인당 CO_2 배출량이 5개국 중 가장 많았고, 몽골의 배출량이 그 뒤를 이었다. 그러나, 2020년에는, 1인당 CO_2 배출량에 있어서 몽골이 중국을 능가했다. 2010년에는, 우즈베키스탄이 베트남보다 더 많은 1인당 CO_2 배출량을 만들어 냈지만, 2020년에는 그 반대였다. 5개국 중, 인도는 2020년에 1인당 CO_2 배출량이 2톤 미만인 유일한 국가였다.

26.

Henry David Thoreau was born in Concord, Massachusetts in 1817. When he was 16, he entered Harvard College. After g_____79) Thoreau w_____80) as a schoolteacher but he q_____81) after two weeks. In June of 1838 he set up a school with his brother John. However, he had hopes of becoming a nature p_____82) . In 1845, he m_____83) into a small self-built house near Walden Pond. At Walden, Thoreau did an incredible amount of r_____84) . The journal he w_____85) there became the source of his most famous book, Walden. In his l_____86) life, Thoreau t_____87) to the Maine woods, to Cape Cod, and to Canada. At the age of 43, he e_____88) his travels and r_____89) to Concord. Although his works were not w_____90) read during his lifetime, he never s_____91) writing, and his works f_____92) 20 volumes.

Henry David Thoreau는 1817년 Massachusetts주 Concord에서 태어났다. 그가 16세 때, 그는 Harvard 대학에 입학했다. 졸업 후, Thoreau는 학교 교사로 일했지만 2주 후에 그만두었다. 1838년 6월에 그는 그의 형제인 John과 함께 학교를 세웠다. 그러나, 그는 자연 시인이 되기를 희망했다. 1845년, 그는 Walden 연못 근처에 직접 지은 작은 집으로 이사했다. Walden에서, Thoreau는 엄청난 양의 독서를 했다. 그가 그곳에서 쓴 저널이 그의 가장 유명한 저서인 Walden의 원천이 되었다. 그의 인생 후반부에, Thoreau는 Maine 숲으로, Cape Cod로, 그리고 캐나다로 여행을 떠났다. 43세의 나이에, 그는 그의 여행을 마치고 Concord로 돌아왔다. 비록 그의 작품이 그의 일생 동안 널리 읽히지 않았지만, 그는 집필을 멈추지 않았고, 그의 작품은 20권에 달한다.

29.

The built-in c_____93) for smiling is p_____94) by the r_____95) observation that babies who are c_____96) both deaf and blind, who have never seen a human face, also start to smile at a_____97) 2 months. However, s_____98) in blind babies eventually disappears if n_____99) is done to reinforce it. Without the right feedback, smiling dies out. But here's a f_____100) fact: blind babies will continue to smile if they are cuddled, bounced, nudged, and tickled by an adult — anything to l_____101) them know that they are not alone and that someone cares about them. This social feedback encourages the baby to continue s_____102) In this way, early experience o_____103) with our b_____104) to establish social behaviors. In fact, you don't need the cases of blind babies to make the point. Babies with sight smile more at you when you look at them or, b_____105) still, smile back at them.

미소 짓기에 대한 선천적인 능력은 선천적으로 청각 장애와 시각 장애가 있고, 사람 얼굴을 한 번도 본 적이 없는 아기들도, 약 2개월 즈음에 미소를 짓기 시작한다는 놀라운 관찰에 의해 증명된다. 그러나, 시각장애를 가진 아기의 미소 짓기는 그것을 강화하기 위해 아무것도 행해지지 않으면 결국 사라진다. 적절한 피드백이 없으면, 미소 짓기는 사라진다. 하지만 여기에 흥미로운 사실이 있다; 만약 그들이 어른에 의해서 아기고, 흔들리고, 슬쩍 찔리고, 간지럽혀지면 — 그들이 혼자가 아니며 누군가 그들에게 관심을 갖고 있다는 것을 알게 하는 것 — 시각장애를 가진 아기들은 계속 미소를 지을 것이다. 이러한 사회적 피드백은 그 아기가 계속 미소를 지을 수 있도록 조장한다. 이런 방식으로, 초기 경험은 우리의 생리 작용과 함께 작용하여 사회적 행동을 형성한다. 사실, 당신은 이를 설명하기 위해 시각장애를 가진 아기의 사례들을 필요로 하지 않는다. 시력이 있는 아기들은 당신이 그들을 바라볼 때나, 더 나아가, 당신이 그들에게 미소를 지어줄 때, 당신에게 더 많이 미소 짓는다.

30.

Because people tend to a_____ 106) , interrupting positive things with negative ones can actually increase enjoyment. Take c_____ 107) . Most people hate them, so r_____ 108) them should make shows or other entertainment more enjoyable. But the o_____ 109) is true. Shows are actually more enjoyable when they're b_____ 110) up by a_____ 111) commercials. Because these l_____ 112) enjoyable moments break up adaptation to the positive experience of the show. Think about eating chocolate chips. The first chip is delicious: sweet, melt-in-your-mouth goodness. The second chip is also pretty good. But by the fourth, fifth, or tenth chip in a row, the goodness is no l_____ 113) as p_____ 114) . We adapt. I_____ 115) positive experiences with l_____ 116) positive ones, however, can slow down adaptation. Eating a Brussels sprout between chocolate chips or viewing commercials between parts of TV shows d_____ 117) the process. The less positive moment makes the f_____ 118) positive one new again and t_____ 119) more enjoyable.

사람들은 적응하는 경향이 있기 때문에, 긍정적인 것을 부정적인 것으로 방해하는 것이 실제로는 즐거움을 향상시킬 수 있다. 광고를 예로 들어 보자. 대부분의 사람들은 그것들을 싫어해서, 그것들을 제거하는 것이 쇼나 다른 오락물을 더 즐겁게 만들 수 있다. 하지만 그 반대가 사실이다. 쇼는 그것들이 성가신 광고들에 의해 중단될 때 실제로 더 즐거워진다. 왜냐하면 이러한 덜 즐거운 순간들이 쇼의 긍정적인 경험에 대한 적응을 깨뜨리기 때문이다. 초콜릿 칩을 먹는 것을 생각해 보라. 첫 번째 칩은 맛있다: 달콤하고, 입안에서 살살 녹는 좋은 맛. 두 번째 칩도 꽤 맛있다. 하지만 네 번째, 다섯 번째, 혹은 열 번째 칩을 연속으로 먹으면 그 좋은 맛은 더 이상 즐겁지 않다. 우리는 적응한다. 그러나, 긍정적인 경험들에 덜 긍정적인 경험들을 간격을 두고 배치하는 것은 적응을 늦출 수 있다. 초콜릿 칩 사이에 방울양배추를 먹거나 TV 쇼의 파트 사이에 광고를 보는 것은 이 과정을 방해한다. 덜 긍정적인 순간은 뒤에 오는 긍정적인 순간을 다시 새롭게 만들어서 더 즐겁게 만든다.

31.

We collect stamps, coins, vintage cars e_____ 120) when they s_____ 121) no practical purpose. The post office doesn't a_____ 122) the old stamps, the banks don't take old coins, and the vintage cars are no longer a_____ 123) on the road. These are all s_____ 124) issues; the attraction is that they are in short s_____ 125) In one study, students were asked to a_____ 126) ten posters in order of a_____ 127) — with the agreement that afterward they could keep one poster as a reward for their participation. Five minutes later, they were told that the poster with the third h_____ 128) rating was no longer available. Then they were asked to judge all ten from s_____ 129) . The poster that was no longer available was suddenly c_____ 130) as the most beautiful. In p_____ 131) , this p_____ 132) is called reactance: when we are d_____ 133) of an option, we suddenly d_____ 134) it more attractive.

우리는 그것들이 실용적인 목적을 수행하지 않더라도 우표, 동전, 빈티지 자동차들을 수집한다. 우체국은 오래된 우표를 받지 않고, 은행은 오래된 동전을 받지 않으며, 그리고 빈티지 자동차는 더 이상 도로에서 허용되지 않는다. 이런 것들은 모두 부수적인 문제이다; 매력은 그들이 부족한 공급에 있다는 것이다. 한 연구에서, 학생들은 포스터 10장을 매력도의 순서대로 배열하도록 요청받았다 — 나중에 그들의 참여에 대한 보상으로 포스터 1장을 간직할 수 있다는 합의와 함께. 5분 후, 그들은 세 번째 높은 평가의 포스터가 더 이상 이용 가능하지 않다는 것을 들었다. 그런 다음 그들은 10개의 포스터를 모두 처음부터 평가하라고 요청을 받았다. 더 이상 이용할 수 없는 포스터가 갑자기 가장 아름다운 것으로 분류되었다. 심리학에서, 이러한 현상은 리액턴스라고 불린다: 우리가 선택지를 빼앗겼을 때, 우리는 그것을 갑자기 더 매력적으로 여긴다.

32.

If we've i_____135) in something that hasn't repaid us — be it money in a f_____136) venture, or time in an unhappy relationship — we find it very difficult to walk away. This is the s_____137) cost fallacy. Our instinct is to continue i_____138) money or time as we hope that our investment will p_____139) to be w_____140) in the end. G_____141) up would mean a_____142) that we've wasted something we can't get back, and that thought is so painful that we p_____143) to avoid it if we can. The problem, of course, is that if something really is a bad b_____144) then staying with it simply increases the amount we lose. Rather than walk away from a bad five-year relationship, for example, we turn it into a bad 10-year relationship; rather than accept that we've l_____145) a thousand dollars, we l_____146) down another thousand and lose that too. In the end, by d_____147) the pain of a_____148) our problem, we only add to it. Sometimes we just have to cut our losses.

우리에게 보답해 주지 않는 것에 우리가 투자해 왔다면 — 실패한 사업에 투자한 돈이거나, 불행한 인간관계에 투자한 시간이던지 간에 — 우리는 벗어나기가 매우 어렵다는 것을 안다. 이것은 매몰 비용 오류이다. 우리의 본능은 결국에는 우리의 투자가 가치 있는 것으로 입증될 것이라고 희망하면서 돈이나 시간에 투자를 계속 하는 것이다. 포기한다는 것은 우리가 돌이킬 수 없는 무언가를 낭비해왔다고 인정하는 것을 의미하고, 그런 생각은 너무 고통스러워서 우리가 할 수 있다면 그것을 피하기를 선호한다. 물론, 문제는 어떤 것이 정말 나쁜 투자라면, 그것을 계속하는 것은 우리가 잃는 총액을 증가시킬 뿐이라는 것이다. 예를 들어, 5년의 나쁜 관계에서 벗어나기보다는 우리는 그것을 10년의 나쁜 관계로 바꾸고; 천 달러를 잃었다는 사실을 받아들이기보다는, 또 다른 천 달러를 내놓고 그것도 역시 잃는다. 결국, 우리의 문제를 인정하는 고통을 미룸으로써 우리는 그것에 보탤 뿐이다. 때때로 우리는 손실을 끊어야만 한다.

33.

On our little world, light t_____149) , for all practical purposes, i_____150) . If a light-bulb is glowing, then of course it's physically where we see it, shining away. We r_____151) out our hand and touch it: It's there all right, and u_____152) hot. If the f_____153) fails, then the light goes out. We don't see it in the same place, glowing, illuminating the room years after the bulb b_____154) and it's r_____155) from its socket. The very notion seems n_____156) . But if we're far enough away, an entire sun can go out and we'll continue to see it shining brightly; we w_____157) learn of its death, it may be, for ages to come — in fact, for how long it takes light, which travels fast but not i_____158) fast, to cross the i_____159) v_____160) The i_____161) distances to the stars and the galaxies mean that we see everything in space in the past.

우리의 작은 세상에서, 실제로는 빛은 순간적으로 이동한다. 전구가 켜져 있다면, 당연히 그것은 우리가 보는 그 자리에서 빛을 내고 있다. 우리는 손을 뻗어 그것을 만진다: 그것은 바로 거기에 있고, 불쾌할 정도로 뜨겁다. 필라멘트가 나가면, 그 때 빛은 꺼진다. 전구가 망가져서 소켓에서 제거된 몇 년 후, 그 자리에 빛을 내고 방을 밝히고 있는 그것을 우리는 보지 못한다. 바로 그 개념은 말도 안 되는 것처럼 보인다 하지만 우리가 충분히 멀리 떨어져 있다면, 항성 전체는 꺼질 수 있지만 우리는 그것이 밝게 빛나는 것을 계속 볼 것이다; 우리는 아마도 오랜 세월 동안 — 사실, 빠르지만 무한히 빠르지는 않게, 이동하는 빛이 그 사이에 낀 광대함을 가로지르는데 걸리는 시간 동안 그것의 소멸을 알지 못할 것이다. 별과 은하까지의 엄청난 거리는 우리가 우주 공간의 모든 것을 과거의 모습으로 보고 있다는 것을 의미한다.

34.

Financial markets do more than take capital from the rich and l_____162) it to everyone else. They enable each of us to s_____163) consumption o_____164) our lifetimes, which is a fancy way of saying that we don't have to spend income at the same time we e_____165) it. Shakespeare may have a_____166) us to be n_____167) borrowers nor lenders; the fact is that most of us will be both at some point. If we lived in an a_____168) society, we would have to eat our crops r_____169) soon after the harvest or find some way to s_____170) them. Financial markets are a more s_____171) way of managing the harvest. We can spend income now that we have not yet earned — as by borrowing for college or a home — or we can earn income now and spend it later, as by saving for r_____172) . The important point is that earning income has been d_____173) from spending it, allowing us much more f_____174) in life.

금융 시장은 부자들로부터 자본을 받아 다른 모든 사람들에게 그것을 빌려주는 것 이상을 한다. 그것들은 우리 각자가 평생에 걸쳐 소비를 원활하게 하도록 해주며, 그리고 이는 우리가 그것(소득)을 얻는 동시에 소득을 소비할 필요가 없다는 것을 말하는 멋진 방식이다. 셰익스피어는 우리가 빌리는 사람도 빌려주는 사람도 되지 말라고 충고했을지도 모른다; 사실 우리 대부분은 어떤 때에는 둘 다 될 것이다. 만약 우리가 농경 사회에 산다면, 우리는 우리의 농작물을 수확 직후에 합리적으로 먹거나 또는 그것들을 저장할 어떤 방법을 찾아야 할 것이다. 금융 시장은 수확을 관리하는 더 정교한 방법이다. 우리는 우리가 아직 벌지 않은 소득을 지금 소비할 수도 있고 — 대학이나 주택을 위해 빌리는 것처럼 — 혹은 우리는 은퇴를 위해 저축하는 것처럼, 지금 소득을 벌어서 나중에 그것을 소비할 수도 있다. 중요한 점은 소득을 버는 것이 그것을 소비하는 것과 분리되어 있다는 것이고, 이는 우리에게 삶에서 훨씬 더 많은 유연성을 허용해준다.

35.

As the old joke goes: "Software, free. User manual, $10,000." But it's no joke. A c_____175) of high-p_____176) companies make their living selling instruction and p_____177) support for free software. The copy of code, being m_____178) bits, is free. The lines of free code become v_____179) to you only through support and guidance. A lot of medical and g_____180) information will go this route in the c_____181) decades. Right now getting a full copy of all your DNA is very expensive ($10,000), but soon it won't be. The price is d_____182) so fast, it will be $100 soon, and then the next year i_____183) companies will offer to s_____184) you for free. When a copy of your sequence costs nothing, the i_____185) of what it means, what you can do about it, and how to use it — the manual for your genes — will be expensive.

다음과 같은 옛 농담처럼: "소프트웨어, 무료. 사용자 매뉴얼, 10,000달러." 하지만 그것은 농담이 아니다. 세간의 이목을 끄는 몇몇 기업들은 무료 소프트웨어에 대한 지침과 유료 지원을 판매하면서 돈을 번다. 단지 몇 비트일 뿐인 코드 사본은 무료이다. 무료 코드의 배열은 지원과 안내를 통해서만 당신에게 가치 있게 된다. 다가올 수십 년 안에 많은 의료 및 유전 정보가 이 경로를 따르게 될 것이다. 지금은 당신의 모든 DNA의 전체 사본을 얻는 것이 매우 비싸지만 (10,000달러), 곧 그렇지 않게 될 것이다. 가격이 너무 빨리 떨어지고 있어, 곧 100달러가 될 것이고, 그 다음 해에는 보험 회사가 무료로 당신의 유전자 배열 순서를 밝혀줄 것을 제안할 것이다. 당신의 배열의 사본에 비용이 들지 않을 때, 그것이 의미하는 것, 당신이 그것에 관해 할 수 있는 것, 그리고 그것을 사용하는 방법에 관한 설명 — 당신의 유전자 매뉴얼 — 은 비싸질 것이다.

36.

Brains are expensive in t_____186) of energy. Twenty percent of the calories we c_____187) are used to power the brain. So brains try to o_____188) in the most energy-e_____189) way possible, and that means p_____190) only the m_____191) amount of information from our senses that we need to n_____192) the world. Neuroscientists weren't the first to discover that fixing your g_____193) on something is no guarantee of seeing it. Magicians f_____194) this out long ago. By directing your attention, they perform tricks with their hands in full view. Their actions should give away the game, but they can rest a_____195) that your brain processes only small bits of the v_____196) scene. This all helps to explain the p_____197) of traffic accidents in which drivers hit p_____198) in plain view, or collide with cars directly in front of them. In many of these cases, the eyes are p_____199) in the right direction, but the brain isn't s_____200) what's really out there.

에너지의 측면에서 뇌는 비용이 많이 든다. 우리가 소비하는 칼로리의 20%는 뇌에 동력을 공급하는 데 사용된다. 따라서 뇌는 가능한 한 가장 에너지 효율적인 방식으로 작동하려고 애쓰며, 그것은 우리가 세상을 항해하는 데 필요로 하는 최소한의 양의 정보만을 우리 감각으로부터 처리하는 것을 의미한다. 신경과학자들은 무언가에 당신의 시선을 고정하는 것이 그것을 본다는 보장이 없다는 사실을 발견한 최초가 아니었다. 마술사들은 오래 전에 이것을 알아냈다. 당신의 주의를 끌어서, 그들은 다 보이는 데서 손으로 속임수를 행한다. 그들의 행동은 그 속임수를 드러내겠지만, 그들은 당신의 뇌가 시각적 장면의 오직 작은 부분들만을 처리한다는 것을 확신한 채로 있을 수 있다. 이 모든 것은 운전자가 명백한 시야에 있는 보행자들을 치거나, 바로 앞에 있는 차량들과 충돌하는 교통사고의 빈번함을 설명하는 데 도움이 된다. 많은 이러한 경우에서, 눈은 올바른 방향을 향하고 있지만, 뇌는 실제로 거기에 있는 것을 보고 있지 않다.

37.

Buying a television is current consumption. It makes us happy today but does nothing to make us r_____201) tomorrow. Yes, money spent on a television k_____202) workers e_____203) at the television factory. But if the same money were i_____204), it would create jobs somewhere else, say for scientists in a l_____205) or workers on a c_____206) site, while also m_____207) us r_____208) in the long run. Think about college as an example. S_____209) students to college creates jobs for professors. Using the same money to buy fancy sports cars for high school graduates would c_____210) jobs for auto workers. The c_____211) difference between these s_____212) is that a college education m_____213) a young person more p_____214) for the rest of his or her life; a sports car does not. Thus, college tuition is an i_____215) ; buying a sports car is c_____216).

텔레비전을 사는 것은 현재의 소비이다. 그것은 오늘 우리를 행복하게 하지만 내일 우리를 더 부유하게 만드는 데는 아무 것도 하지 않는다. 그렇다, 텔레비전에 소비되는 돈은 노동자들이 텔레비전 공장에 계속 고용되게 한다. 하지만 같은 돈이 투자된다면, 그것은 말하자면 실험실의 과학자들이나 건설 현장의 노동자들을 위한, 어딘가 다른 곳의 일자리를 창출하면서, 또한 장기적으로 우리를 더 부유하게 만들 것이다. 대학을 예로써 생각해 보자. 학생들을 대학에 보내는 것은 교수들을 위한 일자리를 창출한다. 같은 돈을 고등학교 졸업생에게 멋진 스포츠카를 사주는 데 쓰는 것은 자동차 노동자를 위한 일자리를 창출할 것이다. 이러한 시나리오들의 중대한 차이점은 대학 교육은 젊은이들이 그 또는 그녀의 남은 삶 동안 더 생산적이게 만들지만; 스포츠카는 그렇지 않다는 것이다. 따라서, 대학 등록금은 투자이다; 스포츠카를 구입하는 것은 소비이다.

38.

The Net d_____217) from most of the mass media it r_____218) in an obvious and very important way: it's b_____219). We can send messages through the network as well as receive them, which has made the system all the m_____220) useful. The ability to exchange information online, to upload as w_____221) as download, has t_____222) the Net into a t_____223) for business and c_____224). With a few clicks, people can s_____225) virtual catalogues, place orders, track shipments, and update information in c_____226) databases. But the Net doesn't just c_____227) us with businesses; it c_____228) us with one another. It's a personal b_____229) medium as well as a c_____230) one. Millions of people use it to d_____231) their own digital creations, in the form of blogs, videos, photos, songs, and podcasts, as well as to critique, edit, or otherwise m_____232) the creations of others.

인터넷은 그것이 대체하는 대부분의 대중 매체와 분명하고도 매우 중요한 방식으로 다르다: 그것은 두 방향으로 작용한다. 우리는 네트워크를 통해 메시지들을 받을 수 있을 뿐만 아니라 그것들을 보낼 수도 있는데, 이것은 그 시스템을 훨씬 더 유용하게 만들었다. 온라인에서 정보를 교환하고, 다운로드할 뿐만 아니라 업로드하는 능력은, 인터넷을 비즈니스와 상거래를 위한 통로로 만들었다. 몇 번의 클릭으로, 사람들은 가상 카탈로그를 검색하고, 주문을 하고, 배송을 추적하고, 그리고 기업의 데이터베이스에 정보를 업데이트할 수 있다. 하지만 인터넷은 단지 우리를 기업과 연결하는 것만은 아니다; 그것은 우리를 서로서로 연결한다. 그것은 상업용 매체일 뿐만 아니라 개인 방송 매체이다. 수백만 명의 사람들이 다른 사람들의 창작물을 비평하고, 편집하고, 또는 그렇지 않으면 수정하기 위해서뿐만 아니라, 블로그, 동영상, 사진, 노래, 그리고 팟캐스트의 형태로 자신의 디지털 창작물을 배포하기 위해서 그것을 사용한다.

39.

Imagine that seven out of ten working Americans got f_____233) tomorrow. What would they all do? It's hard to believe you'd have an e_____234) at all if you gave pink slips to more than half the l_____235) force. But that is what the industrial r_____236) did to the w_____237) of the early 19th century. Two hundred years ago, 70 percent of American workers lived on the farm. Today a_____238) has e_____239) all but 1 percent of their jobs, r_____240) them with machines. But the d_____241) workers did not sit idle. Instead, a_____242) created hundreds of millions of jobs in e_____243) new fields. Those who once farmed were now m_____244) the factories that manufactured farm equipment, cars, and other industrial products. Since then, wave upon wave of new occupations have a_____245) — a_____246) repair person, food chemist, photographer, web designer — each b_____247) on previous automation. Today, the v_____248) majority of us are doing jobs that no farmer from the 1800s could have imagined.

미국인 직장인 10명 중 7명이 내일 해고된다고 상상해 보라. 그들은 모두 무엇을 할까? 노동력의 절반 이상에게 해고 통지서를 보낸다면 경제가 유지될 것이라고 믿기 어려울 것이다. 하지만 그것은 19세기 초 노동력에 산업혁명이 했던 것이다. 200년 전, 미국 노동자의 70%가 농장에서 살았다. 오늘날 자동화는 1%를 제외한 모든 일자리를 제거하였고, 그것들을 기계로 대체하였다. 하지만 일자리를 잃은 노동자들은 한가롭게 앉아있지 않았다. 그 대신, 자동화는 완전히 새로운 분야에서 수억 개의 일자리를 창출했다. 한때 농사를 짓던 사람들은 이제 농기구, 자동차, 그리고 기타 산업 제품을 제조하는 공장에서 일하고 있다. 그 이후로, 가전제품 수리공, 식품 화학자, 사진작가, 웹 디자이너 등 이전의 자동화를 기반으로 한 새로운 직업이 계속해서 등장했다. 오늘날, 우리 중 대다수는 1800년대의 농부들은 상상도 할 수 없었던 일을 하고 있다.

40.

Many things spark envy : ownership, status, health, youth, talent, popularity, beauty. It is often **c**_____ _249) with jealousy because the physical reactions are **i**_____250) . The **d**_____251) : the subject of envy is a thing (status, money, health etc.). The subject of jealousy is the behaviour of a third person. Envy needs two people. Jealousy, on the other hand, **r**_____252) three: Peter is jealous of Sam because the beautiful girl next door rings him **i**_____253) . **P**_____254) , with envy we direct **r**_____255) toward those who are **m**_____256) similar to us in age, career and **r**_____257) . We don't envy businesspeople from the **c**_____258) before **l**_____259) . We don't envy millionaires on the other **s**_____260) of the globe. As a writer, I don't envy musicians, managers or dentists, but other writers. As a CEO you envy other, bigger CEOs. As a supermodel you envy more **s**_____261) supermodels. Aristotle knew this: 'Potters envy potters.'

많은 것들은 부러움을 불러일으킨다: 소유권, 지위, 건강, 젊음, 재능, 인기, 아름다움. 이것은 신체적 반응이 동일하기 때문에 종종 질투와 혼동된다. 차이점: 부러움의 대상은 사물(지위, 돈, 건강 등)이다. 질투의 대상은 제3자의 행동이다. 부러움은 두 사람을 필요로 한다. 반면, 질투는 세 사람을 요구한다: Peter는 옆집의 예쁜 여자가 자기가 아니라 Sam에게 전화를 걸기 때문에 그를 질투한다. 역설적이게도, 부러움을 가질 때 우리는 나이, 경력, 거주지에 있어서 우리와 가장 비슷한 사람들에게 불쾌감을 향하게 한다. 우리는 지지난 세기의 사업가들을 부러워하지 않는다. 우리는 지구 반대편의 백만장자를 부러워하지 않는다. 작가로서, 나는 음악가, 매니저 또는 치과의사가 부럽지 않지만, 다른 작가들을 부러워한다. CEO로서 당신은 다른, 더 큰 CEO들을 부러워한다. 슈퍼 모델로서 당신은 더 성공한 슈퍼 모델들을 부러워한다. 아리스토텔레스는 이를 알고 있었다: '도공은 도공을 부러워한다.'

41~42.

We have **b**_____262) that support our **b**_____263) ! If we're **p**_____264) to one option — perhaps because it's more **m**_____265) , or framed to **m**_____266) loss, or seemingly **c**_____267) with a promising pattern — we tend to search for information that will justify **c**_____ _268) that option. On the one hand, it's **s**_____269) to make choices that we can defend with data and a list of reasons. On the other hand, if we're not careful, we're likely to conduct an **i**_____270) analysis, falling prey to a cluster of errors collectively known as "confirmation biases."

For example, nearly all companies include classic "tell me about yourself" job interviews as part of the **h**_____271) process, and many **r**_____272) on these interviews alone to evaluate **a**_____273) . But it turns out that traditional interviews are actually one of the least useful tools for predicting an employee's future success. This is because interviewers often **s**_____274) make up their minds about interviewees based on their first few moments of **i**_____275) and spend the **r**_____276) of the interview cherry-picking evidence and **p**_____277) their questions to confirm that **i**_____278) impression: "I see here you left a good position at your previous job. You must be pretty ambitious, right?" versus "You must not have been very committed, huh?" This means that interviewers can be **p**_____279) to overlooking **s**_____280) information that would clearly **i**_____281) whether this candidate was actually the best person to hire. More structured approaches, like **o**_____282) samples of a candidate's work or asking how he would respond to difficult **h**_____283) situations, are dramatically better at **a**_____284) future success, with a nearly **t**_____285) advantage over traditional interviews.

우리는 우리의 편견을 뒷받침하는 편견을 가진다! 만약 우리가 한 가지 옵션에 편향된다면 — 그것이 아마도 더 잘 기억할 만 하거나, 손실을 최소화하기 위해 짜맞춰졌거나, 혹은 유망한 패턴과 일치하는 것처럼 보이기 때문에 — 우리는 그 옵션을 선택한 것을 정당화할 정보를 찾는 경향이 있다. 한편으로는, 데이터와 이유들의 목록으로 방어할 수 있는 선택을 하는 것이 현명하다. 반면에, 만약 우리가 주의를 기울이지 않으면, 우리는 불균형한 분석을 수행할 가능성이 있어서, 총체적으로 "확증 편향"으로 알려져 있는 오류 덩어리의 희생양이 된다. 예를 들어, 거의 모든 기업이 채용 과정의 일부로 전통적인 "자기소개" 취업 면접을 실시하며, 많은 기업이 지원자를 평가하기 위해서 이러한 면접에만 의존한다. 하지만 전통적인 면접은 실제로 직원의 미래 성공을 예측하는 데 가장 유용하지 않은 도구 중 하나라는 것으로 판명된다. 이것은 면접관들이 종종 잠재의식적으로 처음 몇 순간의 상호작용을 바탕으로 면접 대상자에 대한 결정을 내리고, 그 첫인상을 확인하기 위해 증거를 고르고 질문을 만드는 데 면접의 나머지 시간을 보내기 때문이다: "당신은 이전 직장에서 좋은 직책을 두고 나오신 게 보이네요. 틀림없이 야망이 꽤 크시겠어요, 그렇죠?" 대 "당신은 그다지 헌신적이지 않았음에 틀림없네요, 그렇죠?" 이것은 면접관이 이 지원자가 실제로 채용하기에 가장 좋은 사람인지 여부를 명확하게 보여줄 수 있는 중요한 정보를 간과하기 쉽다는 것을 의미한다. 지원자의 업무 샘플을 확보하거나 가정된 어려운 상황에 어떻게 그가 대응할지 묻는 것과 같은 보다 구조화된 접근 방식은, 전통적인 면접보다, 거의 세 배의 이점으로 미래의 성공을 평가하는 데 훨씬 더 낫다.

43~45.

On Saturday morning, Todd and his 5-year-old daughter Ava w_____286) out of the store with the groceries they had just purchased. As they pushed their grocery cart through the parking lot, they saw a red car p_____287) into the space next to their pick-up truck. A young man named Greg was driving. "That's a cool car," Ava said to her dad. He a_____288) and looked at Greg, who finished parking and opened his door. As Todd finished l_____289) his groceries, Greg's door r_____290) open. Todd noticed Greg didn't get out of his car. But he was pulling something from his car. He put a metal frame on the ground b_____291) his door. R_____292) in the driver's seat, he then r_____293) back into his car to grab something else. Todd realized what he was doing and considered w_____294) he should try to help him. After a moment, he d_____295) to approach Greg. By this time, Greg had already pulled one thin wheel out of his car and attached it to the frame. He was now pulling a second wheel out when he looked up and saw Todd s_____296) near him. Todd said, "Hi there! Have a great weekend!" Greg seemed a bit surprised, but replied by w_____297) him a great weekend too. Then Greg added, "Thanks for letting me have my i_____298) ." "Of course," Todd said. After Todd and Ava c_____299) into their truck, Ava became curious. So she asked why he didn't offer to help the man with his wheelchair. Todd said, "Why do you i_____300) on brushing your teeth without my help?" She answered, "Because I know how to!" He said, "And the man knows how to put together his wheelchair." Ava understood that sometimes the best way to help someone is to not help at all.

토요일 아침에, Todd와 그의 다섯 살짜리 딸 Ava는 그들이 방금 구입한 식료품을 가지고 가게에서 걸어 나왔다. 그들이 주차장에서 식료품 카트를 밀면서 갈 때, 그들은 빨간 차 한 대가 그들의 픽업 트럭 옆 공간으로 들어오는 것을 보았다. Greg라는 이름의 한 젊은 남자가 운전을 하고 있었다. "저것은 멋진 차네요."라고 Ava가 그녀의 아빠에게 말했다. 그는 동의했고 Greg를 보았는데, 그는 주차를 마치고 그의 문을 열었다. Todd가 그의 식료품을 싣는 것을 끝냈을 때, Greg의 문은 열린 채로 있었다. Todd는 Greg가 그의 차에서 내리지 않은 것을 알아차렸다. 그러나 그는 그의 차에서 무엇인가를 꺼내고 있었다. 그는 그의 문 옆 바닥에 금속 프레임을 두었다. 운전석에 머무른 채, 그는 무엇인가 다른 것을 잡기 위해 그의 차 안 뒤쪽으로 손을 뻗었다. Todd는 그가 무엇을 하고 있는지를 깨닫고 그가 그를 도와야 할지를 생각했다. 잠시 후, 그는 Greg에게 다가가기로 결심했다. 그때 쯤, Greg는 이미 그의 차에서 얇은 바퀴 하나를 꺼내었고 그것을 프레임에 끼웠다. 그가 고개를 들어 그의 근처에 서 있는 Todd를 보았을 때 그는 이제 두 번째 바퀴를 꺼내는 중이었다. Todd는 "안녕하세요! 주말 잘 보내세요!"라고 말했다. Greg는 약간 놀란 것처럼 보였지만, 그에게도 좋은 주말을 보내라고 답했다. 그러자 Greg는 "내가 독립성을 가질 수 있게 해주셔서 고맙습니다."라고 덧붙였다. "물론이죠."라고 Todd가 말했다. Todd와 Ava가 그들의 트럭에 올라탄 후에, Ava는 호기심이 생겼다. 그래서 그녀는 왜 그가 그 남자에게 휠체어에 대해 도움을 제공하지 않았는지를 물었다. Todd는 "왜 너는 내 도움 없이 너의 이를 닦으려고 고집하니?"라고 말했다. 그녀는 "왜냐하면 제가 어떻게 하는지를 알기 때문이죠!"라고 답했다. 그는 "그리고 그 남자는 그의 휠체어를 어떻게 조립하는지 알고 있어."라고 말했다. Ava는 때때로 누군가를 돕는 가장 좋은 방법은 전혀 도와주지 않는 것임을 이해했다.

2024 고2 6월 모의고사 ❷ 회차 : 점 / 300점

❶ voca   ❷ text   ❸ [/]   ❹   ❺ quiz 1   ❻ quiz 2   ❼ quiz 3   ❽ quiz 4   ❾ quiz 5

18.

Dear Residents,

My name is Kari Patterson, and I'm the manager of the River View Apartments. It's time to take **a**_____ _**1)** of the sunny weather to make our community more beautiful. On Saturday, July 13 at 9 a.m., **r**_____ _**2)** will meet in the north parking lot. We will divide into teams to plant flowers and small trees, pull weeds, and put colorful decorations on the lawn. Please join us for this year's Gardening Day, and remember no special skills or tools are **r**_____ **3)** . Last year, we had a great time working together, so come out and make this year's event even better! / Warm regards, / Kari Patterson

19.

It was the championship race. Emma was the final runner on her relay team. She **a**_____ **4)** waited in her spot for her teammate to pass her the **b**_____ **5)** . Emma wasn't sure she could **p**_____ **6)** her role without making a mistake. Her hands shook as she thought, "What if I drop the baton?" She felt her heart rate increasing as her teammate **a**_____ **7)** . But as she started running, she received the baton smoothly. In the final 10 meters, she passed two other runners and crossed the finish line in first place! She raised her hands in the air, and a huge smile came across her face. As her teammates hugged her, she shouted, "We did it!" All of her hard training had been **w**_____ **8)** it.

20.

Most people resist the idea of a true **s**_____ **9)** , probably because they fear it might mean **d**_____**10)** some of their **b**_____**11)** about who they are and what they're capable of. As Goethe's maxim goes, it is a great failing "to see yourself as more than you are." How could you really be considered **s**_____**12)** if you refuse to consider your **w**_____ **13)** ? Don't fear **s**_____ **14)** because you're worried you might have to admit some things about yourself. The second half of Goethe's **m**_____**15)** is important too. He states that it is equally **d**_____ **16)** to "value yourself at **l**_____ **17)** than your true worth." We **u**_____**18)** our capabilities just as much and just as dangerously as we **o**_____ **19)** other abilities. **C**_____ **20)** the ability to **j**_____ **21)** yourself accurately and honestly. Look inward to **d**_____ **22)** what you're capable of and what it will take to unlock that **p**_____ **23)** .

21.

Take a look at some of the **m**_____ **24)** powerful, rich, and famous people in the world. Ignore the **t**_____ **25)** of their success and what they're able to buy. Look instead at what they're **f**_____ **26)** to trade in return — look at what success has **c**_____ **27)** them. **M**_____ **28)** Freedom. Their work **d**_____ **29)** they wear a suit. Their success depends on **a**_____ **30)** certain parties, kissing up to people they don't like. It will require — **i**_____ **31)** — realizing they are unable to say what they actually think. **W**__ **32)** it demands that they become a different type of person or do bad things. Sure, it might **p**_____ **33)** well — but they haven't truly **e**_____ **34)** the transaction. As Seneca put it, "Slavery **r**_____ **35)** under marble and gold." Too many successful people are prisoners in jails of their own making. Is that what you want? Is that what you're working hard toward? Let's hope not.

22.

If a firm is going to be **s**_____ 36) by the government, it might be **e**_____ 37) to concentrate on lobbying the government for more money rather than taking the harder decision of **r**_____ 38) the company to be able to be **p**_____ 39) and **v**_____ 40) in the long term. This is an example of something known as moral hazard — when government support **a**_____ 41) the decisions firms **t**_____ 42) . For example, if governments rescue banks who get into difficulty, as they did during the credit crisis of 2007-08, this could encourage banks to take greater risks in the future because they know there is a **p**_____ 43) that governments will **i**_____ 44) if they lose money. Although the government rescue may be well **i**_____ 45) it can negatively affect the behavior of banks, encouraging **r**_____ _46) and poor decision making.

23.

If there is little or no **d**_____ 47) of views, and all scientists see, think, and question the world in a similar way, then they will not, as a community, be as **o**_____ 48) as they maintain they are, or at l_____ _49) aspire to be. The solution is that there should be far greater **d**_____ 50) in the practice of science: in gender, **e**_____ 51) and social and cultural backgrounds. Science works because it is **c**_____ 52) out by people who pursue their curiosity about the natural world and test their and each other's ideas from as many **v**_____ 53) perspectives and **a**_____ 54) as possible. When science is **d**_____ 55) by a diverse group of people, and if **c**_____ 56) builds up about a particular area of scientific knowledge, then we can have more confidence in its **o**_____ 57) and truth.

24.

We tend to break up time into units, such as weeks, months, and seasons; in a series of studies **a**_____ _58) farmers in India and students in North America, **p**_____ 59) found that if a **d**_____ 60) is on the other side of a "break" — such as in the New Year — we're more **l**_____ 61) to see it as remote, and, as a result, be **l**_____ 62) ready to jump into action. What you need to do in that situation is find another way to think about the **t**_____ 63) . For example, if it's November and the deadline is in January, it's better to tell yourself you have to get it **d**_____ 64) "this winter" rather than "next year." The best **a**_____ 65) is to **v**_____ 66) deadlines as a challenge that you have to meet within a **p**_____ _67) that's **i**_____ 68) . That way the stress is more **m**_____ 69) and you have a better chance of starting — and therefore finishing — in good time.

25.

The graph **a**_____ 70) shows the amount of CO_2 **e**_____ 71) per person **a**_____ 72) selected Asian countries in 2010 and 2020. All the countries except Uzbekistan had a **g**_____ 73) amount of CO_2 emissions per person in 2020 than that in 2010. In 2010, the amount of CO_2 emissions per person of China was the **l**_____ 74) among the five countries, followed by that of Mongolia. However, in 2020, Mongolia **s**_____ 75) China in terms of the amount of CO_2 emissions per person. In 2010, Uzbekistan produced a **l**_____ 76) amount of CO_2 emissions per person than Vietnam, while the **o**_____ 77) was true in 2020. Among the five countries, India was the only one where the amount of CO_2 emissions per person was **l**_____ 78) than 2 tons in 2020.

26.

Henry David Thoreau was born in Concord, Massachusetts in 1817. When he was 16, he entered Harvard College. After **g**_____ **79)** Thoreau **w**_____ **80)** as a schoolteacher but he **q**_____ **81)** after two weeks. In June of 1838 he set up a school with his brother John. However, he had hopes of becoming a nature **p**_____ **82)** . In 1845, he **m**_____ **83)** into a small self-built house near Walden Pond. At Walden, Thoreau did an incredible amount of **r**_____ **84)** . The journal he **w**_____ **85)** there became the source of his most famous book, Walden. In his **l**_____ **86)** life, Thoreau **t**_____ **87)** to the Maine woods, to Cape Cod, and to Canada. At the age of 43, he **e**_____ **88)** his travels and **r**_____ **89)** to Concord. Although his works were not **w**_____ **90)** read during his lifetime, he never **s**_____ **91)** writing, and his works **f**_____ **92)** 20 volumes.

29.

The built-in **c**_____ **93)** for smiling is **p**_____ **94)** by the **r**_____ **95)** observation that babies who are **c**_____ **96)** both deaf and blind, who have never seen a human face, also start to smile at **a**_____ **97)** 2 months. However, **s**_____ **98)** in blind babies eventually disappears if **n**_____ **99)** is done to reinforce it. Without the right feedback, smiling dies out. But here's a **f**_____ **100)** fact: blind babies will continue to smile if they are cuddled, bounced, nudged, and tickled by an adult — anything to **l**_____ **101)** them know that they are not alone and that someone cares about them. This social feedback encourages the baby to continue **s**_____ **102)** In this way, early experience **o**_____ **103)** with our **b**_____ **104)** to establish social behaviors. In fact, you don't need the cases of blind babies to make the point. Babies with sight smile more at you when you look at them or, **b**_____ **105)** still, smile back at them.

30.

Because people tend to **a**_____ **106)** , interrupting positive things with negative ones can actually increase enjoyment. Take **c**_____ **107)** . Most people hate them, so **r**_____ **108)** them should make shows or other entertainment more enjoyable. But the **o**_____ **109)** is true. Shows are actually more enjoyable when they're **b**_____ **110)** up by **a**_____ **111)** commercials. Because these **l**_____ _**112)** enjoyable moments break up adaptation to the positive experience of the show. Think about eating chocolate chips. The first chip is delicious: sweet, melt-in-your-mouth goodness. The second chip is also pretty good. But by the fourth, fifth, or tenth chip in a row, the goodness is no **l**_____ **113)** as **p**_____ **114)** . We adapt. **I**_____ **115)** positive experiences with **l**_____ **116)** positive ones, however, can slow down adaptation. Eating a Brussels sprout between chocolate chips or viewing commercials between parts of TV shows **d**_____ **117)** the process. The less positive moment makes the **f**_____ **118)** positive one new again and **t**_____ **119)** more enjoyable.

31.

We collect stamps, coins, vintage cars e_____120) when they s_____121) no practical purpose. The post office doesn't a_____122) the old stamps, the banks don't take old coins, and the vintage cars are no longer a_____123) on the road. These are all s_____124) issues; the attraction is that they are in short s_____125) In one study, students were asked to a_____126) ten posters in order of a_____127) — with the agreement that afterward they could keep one poster as a reward for their participation. Five minutes later, they were told that the poster with the third h_____128) rating was no longer available. Then they were asked to judge all ten from s_____129) . The poster that was no longer available was suddenly c_____130) as the most beautiful. In p_____131) , this p_____132) is called reactance: when we are d_____133) of an option, we suddenly d_____134) it more attractive.

32.

If we've i_____135) in something that hasn't repaid us — be it money in a f_____136) venture, or time in an unhappy relationship — we find it very difficult to walk away. This is the s_____137) cost fallacy. Our instinct is to continue i_____138) money or time as we hope that our investment will p_____139) to be w_____140) in the end. G_____141) up would mean a_____142) that we've wasted something we can't get back, and that thought is so painful that we p_____143) to avoid it if we can. The problem, of course, is that if something really is a bad b_____144) then staying with it simply increases the amount we lose. Rather than walk away from a bad five-year relationship, for example, we turn it into a bad 10-year relationship; rather than accept that we've l_____145) a thousand dollars, we l_____146) down another thousand and lose that too. In the end, by d_____147) the pain of a_____148) our problem, we only add to it. Sometimes we just have to cut our losses.

33.

On our little world, light t_____149) , for all practical purposes, i_____150) . If a light-bulb is glowing, then of course it's physically where we see it, shining away. We r_____151) out our hand and touch it: It's there all right, and u_____152) hot. If the f_____153) fails, then the light goes out. We don't see it in the same place, glowing, illuminating the room years after the bulb b_____154) and it's r_____155) from its socket. The very notion seems n_____156) . But if we're far enough away, an entire sun can go out and we'll continue to see it shining brightly; we w_____157) learn of its death, it may be, for ages to come — in fact, for how long it takes light, which travels fast but not i_____158) fast, to cross the i_____159) v_____160) The i_____161) distances to the stars and the galaxies mean that we see everything in space in the past.

34.

Financial markets do more than take capital from the rich and l_____ 162) it to everyone else. They enable each of us to s_____ 163) consumption o_____ 164) our lifetimes, which is a fancy way of saying that we don't have to spend income at the same time we e_____ 165) it. Shakespeare may have a_____ 166) us to be n_____ 167) borrowers nor lenders; the fact is that most of us will be both at some point. If we lived in an a_____ 168) society, we would have to eat our crops r_____ 169) soon after the harvest or find some way to s_____ 170) them. Financial markets are a more s_____ 171) way of managing the harvest. We can spend income now that we have not yet earned — as by borrowing for college or a home — or we can earn income now and spend it later, as by saving for r_____ 172) . The important point is that earning income has been d_____ 173) from spending it, allowing us much more f_____ 174) in life.

35.

As the old joke goes: "Software, free. User manual, $10,000." But it's no joke. A c_____ 175) of high-p_____ 176) companies make their living selling instruction and p_____ 177) support for free software. The copy of code, being m_____ 178) bits, is free. The lines of free code become v_____ 179) to you only through support and guidance. A lot of medical and g_____ 180) information will go this route in the c_____ 181) decades. Right now getting a full copy of all your DNA is very expensive ($10,000), but soon it won't be. The price is d_____ 182) so fast, it will be $100 soon, and then the next year i_____ 183) companies will offer to s_____ 184) you for free. When a copy of your sequence costs nothing, the i_____ 185) of what it means, what you can do about it, and how to use it — the manual for your genes — will be expensive.

36.

Brains are expensive in t_____ 186) of energy. Twenty percent of the calories we c_____ 187) are used to power the brain. So brains try to o_____ 188) in the most energy-e_____ 189) way possible, and that means p_____ 190) only the m_____ 191) amount of information from our senses that we need to n_____ 192) the world. Neuroscientists weren't the first to discover that fixing your g_____ 193) on something is no guarantee of seeing it. Magicians f_____ 194) this out long ago. By directing your attention, they perform tricks with their hands in full view. Their actions should give away the game, but they can rest a_____ 195) that your brain processes only small bits of the v_____ 196) scene. This all helps to explain the p_____ 197) of traffic accidents in which drivers hit p_____ 198) in plain view, or collide with cars directly in front of them. In many of these cases, the eyes are p_____ 199) in the right direction, but the brain isn't s_____ 200) what's really out there.

37.

Buying a television is current consumption. It makes us happy today but does nothing to make us r_____201) tomorrow. Yes, money spent on a television k_____202) workers e_____203) at the television factory. But if the same money were i_____204), it would create jobs somewhere else, say for scientists in a l_____205) or workers on a c_____206) site, while also m_____207) us r_____208) in the long run. Think about college as an example. S_____209) students to college creates jobs for professors. Using the same money to buy fancy sports cars for high school graduates would c_____210) jobs for auto workers. The c_____211) difference between these s_____212) is that a college education m_____213) a young person more p_____214) for the rest of his or her life; a sports car does not. Thus, college tuition is an i_____215) ; buying a sports car is c_____216).

38.

The Net d_____217) from most of the mass media it r_____218) in an obvious and very important way: it's b_____219) . We can send messages through the network as well as receive them, which has made the system all the m_____220) useful. The ability to exchange information online, to upload as w_____221) as download, has t_____222) the Net into a t_____223) for business and c_____224) . With a few clicks, people can s_____225) virtual catalogues, place orders, track shipments, and update information in c_____226) databases. But the Net doesn't just c_____227) us with businesses; it c_____228) us with one another. It's a personal b_____229) medium as well as a c_____230) one. Millions of people use it to d_____231) their own digital creations, in the form of blogs, videos, photos, songs, and podcasts, as well as to critique, edit, or otherwise m_____232) the creations of others.

39.

Imagine that seven out of ten working Americans got f_____233) tomorrow. What would they all do? It's hard to believe you'd have an e_____234) at all if you gave pink slips to more than half the l_____235) force. But that is what the industrial r_____236) did to the w_____237) of the early 19th century. Two hundred years ago, 70 percent of American workers lived on the farm. Today a_____238) has e_____239) all but 1 percent of their jobs, r_____240) them with machines. But the d_____241) workers did not sit idle. Instead, a_____242) created hundreds of millions of jobs in e_____243) new fields. Those who once farmed were now m_____244) the factories that manufactured farm equipment, cars, and other industrial products. Since then, wave upon wave of new occupations have a_____245) a_____246) repair person, food chemist, photographer, web designer — each b_____247) on previous automation. Today, the v_____248) majority of us are doing jobs that no farmer from the 1800s could have imagined.

40.

Many things spark envy : ownership, status, health, youth, talent, popularity, beauty. It is often **c**_____ _**249)** with jealousy because the physical reactions are **i**_____ **250)** . The **d**_____ **251)** : the subject of envy is a thing (status, money, health etc.). The subject of jealousy is the behaviour of a third person. Envy needs two people. Jealousy, on the other hand, **r**_____ **252)** three: Peter is jealous of Sam because the beautiful girl next door rings him **i**_____ **253)** . **P**_____ **254)** , with envy we direct **r**_____ **255)** toward those who are **m**_____ **256)** similar to us in age, career and **r**_____ **257)** . We don't envy businesspeople from the **c**_____ **258)** before **l**_____ **259)** . We don't envy millionaires on the other **s**_____ **260)** of the globe. As a writer, I don't envy musicians, managers or dentists, but other writers. As a CEO you envy other, bigger CEOs. As a supermodel you envy more **s**_____ **261)** supermodels. Aristotle knew this: 'Potters envy potters.'

41~42.

We have **b**_____ **262)** that support our **b**_____ **263)** ! If we're **p**_____ **264)** to one option — perhaps because it's more **m**_____ **265)** , or framed to **m**_____ **266)** loss, or seemingly **c**_____ **267)** with a promising pattern — we tend to search for information that will justify **c**_____ _**268)** that option. On the one hand, it's **s**_____ **269)** to make choices that we can defend with data and a list of reasons. On the other hand, if we're not careful, we're likely to conduct an **i**_____ **270)** analysis, falling prey to a cluster of errors collectively known as "confirmation biases."

For example, nearly all companies include classic "tell me about yourself" job interviews as part of the **h**_____ **271)** process, and many **r**_____ **272)** on these interviews alone to evaluate **a**_____ **273)** . But it turns out that traditional interviews are actually one of the least useful tools for predicting an employee's future success. This is because interviewers often **s**_____ **274)** make up their minds about interviewees based on their first few moments of **i**_____ **275)** and spend the **r**_____ **276)** of the interview cherry-picking evidence and **p**_____ **277)** their questions to confirm that **i**_____ **278)** impression: "I see here you left a good position at your previous job. You must be pretty ambitious, right?" versus "You must not have been very committed, huh?" This means that interviewers can be **p**_____ **279)** to overlooking **s**_____ **280)** information that would clearly **i**_____ **281)** whether this candidate was actually the best person to hire. More structured approaches, like **o**_____ **282)** samples of a candidate's work or asking how he would respond to difficult **h**_____ **283)** situations, are dramatically better at **a**_____ **284)** future success, with a nearly **t**_____ **285)** advantage over traditional interviews.

43~45.

On Saturday morning, Todd and his 5-year-old daughter Ava **w**_____ ⁸⁶⁾ out of the store with the groceries they had just purchased. As they pushed their grocery cart through the parking lot, they saw a red car **p**_____ ²⁸⁷⁾ into the space next to their pick-up truck. A young man named Greg was driving. "That's a cool car," Ava said to her dad. He **a**_____ ²⁸⁸⁾ and looked at Greg, who finished parking and opened his door. As Todd finished **l**_____ ²⁸⁹⁾ his groceries, Greg's door **r**_____ _²⁹⁰⁾ open. Todd noticed Greg didn't get out of his car. But he was pulling something from his car. He put a metal frame on the ground **b**_____ ²⁹¹⁾ his door. **R**_____ ²⁹²⁾ in the driver's seat, he then **r**_____ ²⁹³⁾ back into his car to grab something else. Todd realized what he was doing and considered **w**_____ ²⁹⁴⁾ he should try to help him. After a moment, he **d**_____ ²⁹⁵⁾ to approach Greg. By this time, Greg had already pulled one thin wheel out of his car and attached it to the frame. He was now pulling a second wheel out when he looked up and saw Todd **s**_____ ²⁹⁶⁾ near him. Todd said, "Hi there! Have a great weekend!" Greg seemed a bit surprised, but replied by **w**_____ ²⁹⁷⁾ him a great weekend too. Then Greg added, "Thanks for letting me have my **i**_____ ²⁹⁸⁾ ." "Of course," Todd said. After Todd and Ava **c**_____ ²⁹⁹⁾ into their truck, Ava became curious. So she asked why he didn't offer to help the man with his wheelchair. Todd said, "Why do you **i**_____ ³⁰⁰⁾ on brushing your teeth without my help?" She answered, "Because I know how to!" He said, "And the man knows how to put together his wheelchair." Ava understood that sometimes the best way to help someone is to not help at all.

2024 고2 6월 모의고사

❶ voca ❷ text ❸ [/] ❹ ____ ❺ quiz 1 ❻ quiz 2 ❼ quiz 3 ❽ quiz 4 ❾ quiz 5

1. 1) 18.

Dear Residents, My name is Kari Patterson, and I'm the manager of the River View Apartments.

(A) It's time to take advantage of the sunny weather to make our community more beautiful. On Saturday, July 13 at 9 a.m., residents will meet in the north parking lot.

(B) Warm regards, Kari Patterson

(C) We will divide into teams to plant flowers and small trees, pull weeds, and put colorful decorations on the lawn.

(D) Last year, we had a great time working together, so come out and make this year's event even better!

(E) Please join us for this year's Gardening Day, and remember no special skills or tools are required.

2. 2) 19.

It was the championship race.

(A) Emma was the final runner on her relay team. She anxiously waited in her spot for her teammate to pass her the baton. Emma wasn't sure she could perform her role without making a mistake.

(B) As her teammates hugged her, she shouted, "We did it!" All of her hard training had been worth it.

(C) In the final 10 meters, she passed two other runners and crossed the finish line in first place! She raised her hands in the air, and a huge smile came across her face.

(D) Her hands shook as she thought, "What if I drop the baton?" She felt her heart rate increasing as her teammate approached. But as she started running, she received the baton smoothly.

3. 3) 20.

Most people resist the idea of a true self-estimate, probably because they fear it might mean downgrading some of their beliefs about who they are and what they're capable of.

(A) Don't fear self-assessment because you're worried you might have to admit some things about yourself. The second half of Goethe's maxim is important too.

(B) Look inward to discern what you're capable of and what it will take to unlock that potential.

(C) As Goethe's maxim goes, it is a great failing "to see yourself as more than you are." How could you really be considered self-aware if you refuse to consider your weaknesses?

(D) Cultivate the ability to judge yourself accurately and honestly.

(E) He states that it is equally damaging to "value yourself at less than your true worth." We underestimate our capabilities just as much and just as dangerously as we overestimate other abilities.

4. 4) 21.

Take a look at some of the most powerful, rich, and famous people in the world.

(A) Ignore the trappings of their success and what they're able to buy. Look instead at what they're forced to trade in return — look at what success has cost them. Mostly? Freedom. Their work demands they wear a suit.

(B) Too many successful people are prisoners in jails of their own making. Is that what you want? Is that what you're working hard toward? Let's hope not.

(C) Their success depends on attending certain parties, kissing up to people they don't like. It will require — inevitably — realizing they are unable to say what they actually think. Worse, it demands that they become a different type of person or do bad things. Sure, it might pay well — but they haven't truly examined the transaction. As Seneca put it, "Slavery resides under marble and gold."

5. 5) 22.

If a firm is going to be saved by the government, it might be easier to concentrate on lobbying the government for more money rather than taking the harder decision of restructuring the company to be able to be profitable and viable in the long term.

(A) For example, if governments rescue banks who get into difficulty, as they did during the credit crisis of 2007-08, this could encourage banks to take greater risks in the future because they know there is a possibility that governments will intervene if they lose money.

(B) Although the government rescue may be well intended, it can negatively affect the behavior of banks, encouraging risky and poor decision making.

(C) This is an example of something known as moral hazard — when government support alters the decisions firms take.

6. 6) 23.

If there is little or no diversity of views, and all scientists see, think, and question the world in a similar way, then they will not, as a community, be as objective as they maintain they are, or at least aspire to be.

(A) Science works because it is carried out by people who pursue their curiosity about the natural world and test their and each other's ideas from as many varied perspectives and angles as possible.

(B) The solution is that there should be far greater diversity in the practice of science: in gender, ethnicity, and social and cultural backgrounds.

(C) When science is done by a diverse group of people, and if consensus builds up about a particular area of scientific knowledge, then we can have more confidence in its objectivity and truth.

7. 7) 24.

We tend to break up time into units, such as weeks, months, and seasons; in a series of studies among farmers in India and students in North America, psychologists found that if a deadline is on the other side of a "break" — such as in the New Year — we're more likely to see it as remote, and, as a result, be less ready to jump into action.

(A) The best approach is to view deadlines as a challenge that you have to meet within a period that's imminent.

(B) What you need to do in that situation is find another way to think about the timeframe.

(C) For example, if it's November and the deadline is in January, it's better to tell yourself you have to get it done "this winter" rather than "next year."

(D) That way the stress is more manageable, and you have a better chance of starting — and therefore finishing — in good time.

8. 8) ^{25.}

The graph above shows the amount of CO₂ emissions per person across selected Asian countries in 2010 and 2020.

(A) All the countries except Uzbekistan had a greater amount of CO₂ emissions per person in 2020 than that in 2010. In 2010, the amount of CO₂ emissions per person of China was the largest among the five countries, followed by that of Mongolia.

(B) However, in 2020, Mongolia surpassed China in terms of the amount of CO₂ emissions per person. In 2010, Uzbekistan produced a larger amount of CO₂ emissions per person than Vietnam, while the opposite was true in 2020.

(C) Among the five countries, India was the only one where the amount of CO₂ emissions per person was less than 2 tons in 2020.

9. 9) ^{26.}

Henry David Thoreau was born in Concord, Massachusetts in 1817.

(A) In 1845, he moved into a small self-built house near Walden Pond. At Walden, Thoreau did an incredible amount of reading. The journal he wrote there became the source of his most famous book, Walden.

(B) When he was 16, he entered Harvard College. After graduating, Thoreau worked as a schoolteacher but he quit after two weeks. In June of 1838 he set up a school with his brother John. However, he had hopes of becoming a nature poet.

(C) In his later life, Thoreau traveled to the Maine woods, to Cape Cod, and to Canada. At the age of 43, he ended his travels and returned to Concord. Although his works were not widely read during his lifetime, he never stopped writing, and his works fill 20 volumes.

10. 10) ^{29.}

The built-in capacity for smiling is proven by the remarkable observation that babies who are congenitally both deaf and blind, who have never seen a human face, also start to smile at around 2 months.

(A) In fact, you don't need the cases of blind babies to make the point.

(B) But here's a fascinating fact: blind babies will continue to smile if they are cuddled, bounced, nudged, and tickled by an adult — anything to let them know that they are not alone and that someone cares about them. This social feedback encourages the baby to continue smiling.

(C) Babies with sight smile more at you when you look at them or, better still, smile back at them.

(D) However, smiling in blind babies eventually disappears if nothing is done to reinforce it. Without the right feedback, smiling dies out.

(E) In this way, early experience operates with our biology to establish social behaviors.

11. 11) 30.

Because people tend to adapt, interrupting positive things with negative ones can actually increase enjoyment.

(A) Interspersing positive experiences with less positive ones, however, can slow down adaptation. Eating a Brussels sprout between chocolate chips or viewing commercials between parts of TV shows disrupts the process. The less positive moment makes the following positive one new again and thus more enjoyable.

(B) The second chip is also pretty good. But by the fourth, fifth, or tenth chip in a row, the goodness is no longer as pleasurable. We adapt.

(C) Take commercials. Most people hate them, so removing them should make shows or other entertainment more enjoyable. But the opposite is true. Shows are actually more enjoyable when they're broken up by annoying commercials.

(D) Because these less enjoyable moments break up adaptation to the positive experience of the show. Think about eating chocolate chips. The first chip is delicious: sweet, melt-in-your-mouth goodness.

12. 12) 31.

We collect stamps, coins, vintage cars even when they serve no practical purpose.

(A) The post office doesn't accept the old stamps, the banks don't take old coins, and the vintage cars are no longer allowed on the road. These are all side issues; the attraction is that they are in short supply.

(B) In one study, students were asked to arrange ten posters in order of attractiveness — with the agreement that afterward they could keep one poster as a reward for their participation. Five minutes later, they were told that the poster with the third highest rating was no longer available.

(C) Then they were asked to judge all ten from scratch. The poster that was no longer available was suddenly classified as the most beautiful.

(D) In psychology, this phenomenon is called reactance: when we are deprived of an option, we suddenly deem it more attractive.

13. 13) 32.

If we've invested in something that hasn't repaid us — be it money in a failing venture, or time in an unhappy relationship — we find it very difficult to walk away.

(A) This is the sunk cost fallacy. Our instinct is to continue investing money or time as we hope that our investment will prove to be worthwhile in the end.

(B) Rather than walk away from a bad five-year relationship, for example, we turn it into a bad 10-year relationship; rather than accept that we've lost a thousand dollars, we lay down another thousand and lose that too.

(C) Giving up would mean acknowledging that we've wasted something we can't get back, and that thought is so painful that we prefer to avoid it if we can. The problem, of course, is that if something really is a bad bet, then staying with it simply increases the amount we lose.

(D) In the end, by delaying the pain of admitting our problem, we only add to it.

(E) Sometimes we just have to cut our losses.

14. 14) 33.

On our little world, light travels, for all practical purposes, instantaneously.

(A) The immense distances to the stars and the galaxies mean that we see everything in space in the past.

(B) If the filament fails, then the light goes out. We don't see it in the same place, glowing, illuminating the room years after the bulb breaks and it's removed from its socket.

(C) The very notion seems nonsensical. But if we're far enough away, an entire sun can go out and we'll continue to see it shining brightly; we won't learn of its death, it may be, for ages to come — in fact, for how long it takes light, which travels fast but not infinitely fast, to cross the intervening vastness.

(D) If a light-bulb is glowing, then of course it's physically where we see it, shining away. We reach out our hand and touch it: It's there all right, and unpleasantly hot.

15. 15) 34.

Financial markets do more than take capital from the rich and lend it to everyone else.

(A) We can spend income now that we have not yet earned — as by borrowing for college or a home — or we can earn income now and spend it later, as by saving for retirement. The important point is that earning income has been divorced from spending it, allowing us much more flexibility in life.

(B) If we lived in an agrarian society, we would have to eat our crops reasonably soon after the harvest or find some way to store them. Financial markets are a more sophisticated way of managing the harvest.

(C) They enable each of us to smooth consumption over our lifetimes, which is a fancy way of saying that we don't have to spend income at the same time we earn it Shakespeare may have admonished us to be neither borrowers nor lenders; the fact is that most of us will be both at some point.

16. 16) 35.

As the old joke goes: "Software, free.

(A) User manual, $10,000." But it's no joke. A couple of high-profile companies make their living selling instruction and paid support for free software.

(B) The price is dropping so fast, it will be $100 soon, and then the next year insurance companies will offer to sequence you for free. When a copy of your sequence costs nothing, the interpretation of what it means, what you can do about it, and how to use it — the manual for your genes — will be expensive.

(C) The copy of code, being mere bits, is free. The lines of free code become valuable to you only through support and guidance.

(D) A lot of medical and genetic information will go this route in the coming decades. Right now getting a full copy of all your DNA is very expensive ($10,000), but soon it won't be.

17. 17) 36.

Brains are expensive in terms of energy.

(A) This all helps to explain the prevalence of traffic accidents in which drivers hit pedestrians in plain view, or collide with cars directly in front of them. In many of these cases, the eyes are pointed in the right direction, but the brain isn't seeing what's really out there.

(B) Twenty percent of the calories we consume are used to power the brain. So brains try to operate in the most energy-efficient way possible, and that means processing only the minimum amount of information from our senses that we need to navigate the world. Neuroscientists weren't the first to discover that fixing your gaze on something is no guarantee of seeing it.

(C) Magicians figured this out long ago. By directing your attention, they perform tricks with their hands in full view. Their actions should give away the game, but they can rest assured that your brain processes only small bits of the visual scene.

18. 18) 37.

Buying a television is current consumption.

(A) The crucial difference between these scenarios is that a college education makes a young person more productive for the rest of his or her life; a sports car does not. Thus, college tuition is an investment; buying a sports car is consumption.

(B) It makes us happy today but does nothing to make us richer tomorrow. Yes, money spent on a television keeps workers employed at the television factory. But if the same money were invested, it would create jobs somewhere else, say for scientists in a laboratory or workers on a construction site, while also making us richer in the long run.

(C) Think about college as an example. Sending students to college creates jobs for professors. Using the same money to buy fancy sports cars for high school graduates would create jobs for auto workers.

19. 19) 38.

The Net differs from most of the mass media it replaces in an obvious and very important way: it's bidirectional.

(A) Millions of people use it to distribute their own digital creations, in the form of blogs, videos, photos, songs, and podcasts, as well as to critique, edit, or otherwise modify the creations of others.

(B) It's a personal broadcasting medium as well as a commercial one.

(C) But the Net doesn't just connect us with businesses; it connects us with one another.

(D) With a few clicks, people can search virtual catalogues, place orders, track shipments, and update information in corporate databases.

(E) We can send messages through the network as well as receive them, which has made the system all the more useful. The ability to exchange information online, to upload as well as download, has turned the Net into a thoroughfare for business and commerce.

20. 20) 39.

Imagine that seven out of ten working Americans got fired tomorrow.

(A) What would they all do? It's hard to believe you'd have an economy at all if you gave pink slips to more than half the labor force. But that is what the industrial revolution did to the workforce of the early 19th century. Two hundred years ago, 70 percent of American workers lived on the farm.

(B) Today automation has eliminated all but 1 percent of their jobs, replacing them with machines. But the displaced workers did not sit idle. Instead, automation created hundreds of millions of jobs in entirely new fields.

(C) Those who once farmed were now manning the factories that manufactured farm equipment, cars, and other industrial products. Since then, wave upon wave of new occupations have arrived — appliance repair person, food chemist, photographer, web designer — each building on previous automation. Today, the vast majority of us are doing jobs that no farmer from the 1800s could have imagined.

21. 21) 40.

Many things spark envy : ownership, status, health, youth, talent, popularity, beauty.

(A) As a writer, I don't envy musicians, managers or dentists, but other writers. As a CEO you envy other, bigger CEOs. As a supermodel you envy more successful supermodels. Aristotle knew this: 'Potters envy potters'.

(B) It is often confused with jealousy because the physical reactions are identical. The difference: the subject of envy is a thing (status, money, health etc.). The subject of jealousy is the behaviour of a third person. Envy needs two people.

(C) Jealousy, on the other hand, requires three: Peter is jealous of Sam because the beautiful girl next door rings him instead. Paradoxically, with envy we direct resentments toward those who are most similar to us in age, career and residence. We don't envy businesspeople from the century before last. We don't envy millionaires on the other side of the globe.

22. 22) 41~42.

We have biases that support our biases!

(A) You must be pretty ambitious, right?" versus "You must not have been very committed, huh?" This means that interviewers can be prone to overlooking significant information that would clearly indicate whether this candidate was actually the best person to hire.

(B) But it turns out that traditional interviews are actually one of the least useful tools for predicting an employee's future success. This is because interviewers often subconsciously make up their minds about interviewees based on their first few moments of interaction and spend the rest of the interview cherry-picking evidence and phrasing their questions to confirm that initial impression: "I see here you left a good position at your previous job.

(C) More structured approaches, like obtaining samples of a candidate's work or asking how he would respond to difficult hypothetical situations, are dramatically better at assessing future success, with a nearly threefold advantage over traditional interviews.

(D) On the other hand, if we're not careful, we're likely to conduct an imbalanced analysis, falling prey to a cluster of errors collectively known as "confirmation biases." For example, nearly all companies include classic "tell me about yourself" job interviews as part of the hiring process, and many rely on these interviews alone to evaluate applicants.

(E) If we're partial to one option — perhaps because it's more memorable, or framed to minimize loss, or seemingly consistent with a promising pattern — we tend to search for information that will justify choosing that option. On the one hand, it's sensible to make choices that we can defend with data and a list of reasons.

23. 23) 43~45.

On Saturday morning, Todd and his 5-year-old daughter Ava walked out of the store with the groceries they had just purchased.

(A) After a moment, he decided to approach Greg. By this time, Greg had already pulled one thin wheel out of his car and attached it to the frame. He was now pulling a second wheel out when he looked up and saw Todd standing near him. Todd said, "Hi there! Have a great weekend!"

(B) Greg seemed a bit surprised, but replied by wishing him a great weekend too. Then Greg added, "Thanks for letting me have my independence." "Of course," Todd said. After Todd and Ava climbed into their truck, Ava became curious. So she asked why he didn't offer to help the man with his wheelchair.

(C) Todd noticed Greg didn't get out of his car. But he was pulling something from his car. He put a metal frame on the ground beside his door. Remaining in the driver's seat, he then reached back into his car to grab something else. Todd realized what he was doing and considered whether he should try to help him.

(D) As they pushed their grocery cart through the parking lot, they saw a red car pulling into the space next to their pick-up truck. A young man named Greg was driving. "That's a cool car," Ava said to her dad. He agreed and looked at Greg, who finished parking and opened his door. As Todd finished loading his groceries, Greg's door remained open.

(E) Todd said, "Why do you insist on brushing your teeth without my help?" She answered, "Because I know how to!" He said, "And the man knows how to put together his wheelchair." Ava understood that sometimes the best way to help someone is to not help at all.

2024 고2 6월 모의고사

❶ voca ❷ text ❸ [/] ❹ _____ ❺ quiz 1 ❻ quiz 2 ❼ quiz 3 ❽ quiz 4 ❾ quiz 5

---

1. 1)밑줄 친 ⓐ~ⓓ 중 어법, 혹은 문맥상 어휘의 사용이 어색한 것끼리 짝지어진 것을 고르시오. 18.

Dear Residents, / My name is Kari Patterson, and I'm the manager of the River View Apartments. It's time to take advantage ⓐ **of** the sunny weather to make our community more ⓑ **beautifully**. On Saturday, July 13 at 9 a.m., residents will meet in the north parking lot. We will divide into teams to plant flowers and small trees, pull weeds, and put colorful decorations on the lawn. Please ⓒ **join in** us for this year's Gardening Day, and remember no special skills or tools ⓓ **are required**. Last year, we had a great time working together, so come out and make this year's event even better!
Warm regards, / Kari Patterson

① ⓐ, ⓒ 　② ⓐ, ⓓ 　③ ⓑ, ⓒ
④ ⓒ, ⓓ 　⑤ ⓐ, ⓒ, ⓓ

2. 2)밑줄 친 ⓐ~ⓖ 중 어법, 혹은 문맥상 어휘의 사용이 어색한 것끼리 짝지어진 것을 고르시오. 19.

It was the championship race. Emma was the final runner ⓐ **with** her relay team. She anxiously ⓑ **waited** in her spot ⓒ **of** her teammate to pass her the baton. Emma wasn't sure she could perform her role without making a mistake. Her hands shook as she thought, "What if I drop the baton"? She felt her heart rate ⓓ **to increase** as her teammate ⓔ **approached**. But as she started running, she received the baton smoothly. In the final 10 meters, she passed two other runners and crossed the finish line in first place! She ⓕ **raised** her hands in the air, and a huge smile came across her face. As her teammates hugged her, she shouted, "We did it"! All of her hard training ⓖ **have** been worth it.

① ⓕ, ⓖ 　② ⓐ, ⓑ, ⓒ 　③ ⓑ, ⓕ, ⓖ
④ ⓒ, ⓔ, ⓖ 　⑤ ⓐ, ⓒ, ⓓ, ⓖ

3. 3)밑줄 친 ⓐ~ⓗ 중 어법, 혹은 문맥상 어휘의 사용이 어색한 것끼리 짝지어진 것을 고르시오. 20.

Most people resist the idea of a true self-estimate, probably because they fear ⓐ **them** might mean ⓑ **downgrading** some of their beliefs about who they are and what they're capable of. As Goethe's maxim goes, it is a great failing "to see yourself as more than you ⓒ **do**". How could you really ⓓ **consider** self-aware if you refuse to consider your weaknesses? Don't fear self-assessment because you're worried you might have to admit some things about yourself. The second half of Goethe's maxim is important too. He states that it is equally ⓔ **damaging** to "value yourself at ⓕ **less** than your true worth". We underestimate our capabilities just as much and just as ⓖ **dangerously** as we overestimate other abilities. Cultivate the ability to judge yourself accurately and honestly. Look ⓗ **inward** to discern what you're capable of and what it will take to unlock that potential.

① ⓓ, ⓗ 　② ⓔ, ⓖ 　③ ⓐ, ⓒ, ⓓ
④ ⓐ, ⓒ, ⓕ 　⑤ ⓒ, ⓓ, ⓗ

4. ⁴⁾**밑줄 친 ⓐ~ⓕ 중 어법, 혹은 문맥상 어휘의 사용이 어색한 것끼리 짝지어진 것을 고르시오.** ^{21.}

Take a look at some of the most powerful, rich, and famous people in the world. ⓐ **To ignore** the trappings of their success and ⓑ **what** they're able to buy. Look instead at what they're forced to trade in return — look at what success has cost them. Mostly? Freedom. Their work demands they wear a suit. Their success depends on ⓒ **attending** certain parties, kissing up to people they don't like. It will require — inevitably — ⓓ **realizing** they are unable to say what they actually think. Worse, it demands that they become a different type of person or do bad things. Sure, it might pay well — but they haven't truly ⓔ **examined** the transaction. As Seneca put it, "Slavery resides under marble and gold". Too many successful people are prisoners in jails of their own making. Is that what you want? Is that what you're working ⓕ **hardly** toward? Let's hope not.

① ⓐ, ⓓ　　　　② ⓐ, ⓕ　　　　③ ⓑ, ⓓ
④ ⓒ, ⓔ, ⓕ　　⑤ ⓓ, ⓔ, ⓕ

5. ⁵⁾**밑줄 친 ⓐ~ⓕ 중 어법, 혹은 문맥상 어휘의 사용이 어색한 것끼리 짝지어진 것을 고르시오.** ^{22.}

If a firm is going to ⓐ **be saved** by the government, it might be easier to concentrate on lobbying the government for more money rather than ⓑ **taking** the harder decision of ⓒ **reconciling** the company to be able to be ⓓ **profitable** and ⓔ **variable** in the long term. This is an example of something known ⓕ **as** moral hazard — when government support alters the decisions firms take. For example, if governments rescue banks who get into difficulty, as they ⓖ **did** during the credit crisis of 2007-08, this could encourage banks to take greater risks in the future because they know there is a possibility that governments will ⓗ **intervene** if they lose money. Although the government rescue may be well intended, it can negatively affect the behavior of banks, ⓘ **to encourage** risky and poor decision making.

① ⓐ, ⓘ　　　　② ⓓ, ⓔ　　　　③ ⓐ, ⓓ, ⓗ
④ ⓑ, ⓔ, ⓗ　　⑤ ⓒ, ⓔ, ⓘ

6. ⁶⁾**밑줄 친 ⓐ~ⓖ 중 어법, 혹은 문맥상 어휘의 사용이 어색한 것끼리 짝지어진 것을 고르시오.** ^{23.}

If there is ⓐ **little** or no diversity of views, and all scientists see, think, and question the world in a ⓑ **similar** way, then they will not, as a community, be as ⓒ **objectively** as they maintain they are, or at least ⓓ **respire** to be. The solution is that there should be far greater diversity in the practice of science: in gender, ethnicity, and social and cultural backgrounds. Science works because it is carried out by people who pursue their curiosity about the natural world and test their and each other's ideas from as many ⓔ **varied** perspectives and angles as possible. When science is done by a diverse group of people, and if consensus builds up about a particular area of scientific knowledge, then we can have more confidence in ⓕ **our** ⓖ **objection** and truth.

① ⓐ, ⓖ　　　　② ⓑ, ⓓ　　　　③ ⓐ, ⓓ, ⓔ
④ ⓐ, ⓑ, ⓕ, ⓖ　⑤ ⓒ, ⓓ, ⓕ, ⓖ

7. ⁷⁾**밑줄 친 ⓐ~ⓕ 중 어법, 혹은 문맥상 어휘의 사용이 어색한 것끼리 짝지어진 것을 고르시오.** 24.

We tend to break up time into units, such as weeks, months, and seasons; in a series of studies among farmers in India and students in North America, psychologists ⓐ **founded** that if a deadline is on the other side of a "break" — such as in the New Year — we're ⓑ **less** likely to see it as remote, and, as a result, be less ready to jump into action. What you need to do in that situation is find another way to think about the timeframe. For example, if it's November and the deadline is in January, it's better to tell ⓒ **yourself** you have to get it ⓓ **done** "this winter" rather than "next year". The best approach is to view deadlines as a challenge that you have to ⓔ **meet** within a period that's imminent. That way the stress is more manageable, and you have a better chance of starting — and therefore ⓕ **finishing** — in good time.

① ⓐ, ⓑ   ② ⓐ, ⓓ   ③ ⓐ, ⓕ
④ ⓑ, ⓓ   ⑤ ⓓ, ⓔ, ⓕ

8. ⁸⁾**밑줄 친 ⓐ~ⓕ 중 어법, 혹은 문맥상 어휘의 사용이 어색한 것끼리 짝지어진 것을 고르시오.** 25.

The graph above shows the amount of CO_2 ⓐ **emissions** per person across selected Asian countries in 2010 and 2020. All the countries ⓑ **expect** Uzbekistan had a greater amount of CO_2 emissions per person in 2020 than ⓒ **those** in 2010. In 2010, the amount of CO_2 emissions per person of China was the largest among the five countries, ⓓ **followed** by that of Mongolia. However, in 2020, Mongolia ⓔ **surpassed** China in terms of the amount of CO_2 emissions per person. In 2010, Uzbekistan produced a larger amount of CO_2 emissions per person than Vietnam, while the opposite was true in 2020. Among the five countries, India was the only one ⓕ **where** the amount of CO_2 emissions per person was less than 2 tons in 2020.

① ⓑ, ⓒ   ② ⓑ, ⓓ   ③ ⓒ, ⓔ
④ ⓐ, ⓑ, ⓓ, ⓕ   ⑤ ⓐ, ⓒ, ⓓ, ⓔ

9. ⁹⁾**밑줄 친 ⓐ~ⓕ 중 어법, 혹은 문맥상 어휘의 사용이 어색한 것끼리 짝지어진 것을 고르시오.** 26.

Henry David Thoreau was born in Concord, Massachusetts in 1817. When he was 16, he ⓐ **entered into** Harvard College. After ⓑ **graduated**, Thoreau worked as a schoolteacher but he quit after two weeks. In June of 1838 he set up a school with his brother John. However, he had hopes of becoming a nature poet. In 1845, he moved into a small self-ⓒ **building** house near Walden Pond. At Walden, Thoreau did an incredible amount of reading. The journal he wrote there became the source of his most famous book, Walden. In his later life, Thoreau traveled to the Maine woods, to Cape Cod, and to Canada. At the age of 43, he ended his travels and ⓓ **was returned** to Concord. ⓔ **Although** his works were not widely read during his lifetime, he never stopped ⓕ **writing** , and his works fill 20 volumes.

① ⓐ, ⓒ, ⓔ   ② ⓐ, ⓔ, ⓕ   ③ ⓒ, ⓔ, ⓕ
④ ⓐ, ⓑ, ⓒ, ⓓ   ⑤ ⓐ, ⓑ, ⓓ, ⓔ

10. 10)밑줄 친 ⓐ~ⓖ 중 어법, 혹은 문맥상 어휘의 사용이 어색한 것끼리 짝지어진 것을 고르시오.
29.

The built-in capacity for smiling is ⓐ **proven** by the remarkable observation that babies who are ⓑ **cognitively** both deaf and blind, who have never seen a human face, also start to smile at around 2 months. However, smiling in blind babies eventually ⓒ **is disappeared** if nothing ⓓ **done** to reinforce it. Without the right feedback, smiling dies out. But here's a fascinating fact: blind babies will continue to smile if they are cuddled, bounced, nudged, and tickled by an adult — anything to let ⓔ **them** know that they are not alone and that someone cares about them. This social feedback ⓕ **discourages** the baby to continue smiling. In this way, early experience operates with our biology to establish social behaviors. In fact, you don't need the cases of blind babies to make the point. Babies with sight smile more at you when you look at them or, better still, smile back at ⓖ **them**.

① ⓐ, ⓑ   ② ⓒ, ⓕ, ⓖ   ③ ⓐ, ⓑ, ⓓ, ⓔ
④ ⓐ, ⓒ, ⓓ, ⓕ   ⑤ ⓑ, ⓒ, ⓓ, ⓕ

11. 11)밑줄 친 ⓐ~ⓘ 중 어법, 혹은 문맥상 어휘의 사용이 어색한 것끼리 짝지어진 것을 고르시오.
30.

Because people tend to ⓐ **adopt**, interrupting positive things with negative ⓑ **ones** can actually ⓒ **decrease** enjoyment. Take commercials. Most people hate them, so removing them should make shows or other entertainment more enjoyable. But the ⓓ **opposite** is true. Shows are actually more enjoyable when they're broken up by annoying commercials. Because these ⓔ **more** enjoyable moments break up ⓕ **adaptation** to the positive experience of the show. Think about eating chocolate chips. The first chip is delicious: sweet, melt-in-your-mouth goodness. The second chip is also pretty good. But by the fourth, fifth, or tenth chip in a row, the goodness is no longer as pleasurable. We ⓖ **adopt**. ⓗ **Interspersing** positive experiences with less positive ones, however, can slow down adaptation. Eating a Brussels sprout between chocolate chips or viewing commercials between parts of TV shows ⓘ **disrupts** the process. The less positive moment makes the following positive one new again and thus more enjoyable.

① ⓐ, ⓑ, ⓖ   ② ⓐ, ⓖ, ⓗ   ③ ⓓ, ⓖ, ⓘ
④ ⓐ, ⓑ, ⓓ, ⓘ   ⑤ ⓐ, ⓒ, ⓔ, ⓖ

12. 12)밑줄 친 ⓐ~ⓖ 중 어법, 혹은 문맥상 어휘의 사용이 어색한 것끼리 짝지어진 것을 고르시오.
31.

We collect stamps, coins, vintage cars even when they serve no practical purpose. The post office doesn't accept the old stamps, the banks don't take old coins, and the vintage cars are no longer ⓐ **allowed** on the road. These are all side issues; the attraction is that they are in ⓑ **full** supply. In one study, students ⓒ **were asked** to arrange ten posters in order of attractiveness — with the agreement that afterward they could keep one poster as a reward for ⓓ **its** participation. Five minutes later, they ⓔ **were told** that the poster with the third highest rating was no longer available. Then they were asked to judge all ten from scratch. The poster that was no longer available was suddenly classified as the most beautiful. In psychology, this phenomenon is called reactance: when we are ⓕ **full** of an option, we suddenly deem it more ⓖ **attractive**.

① ⓐ, ⓓ   ② ⓐ, ⓑ, ⓔ   ③ ⓐ, ⓒ, ⓓ
④ ⓑ, ⓓ, ⓕ   ⑤ ⓒ, ⓔ, ⓖ

13. 13)밑줄 친 ⓐ~ⓘ 중 어법, 혹은 문맥상 어휘의 사용이 어색한 것끼리 짝지어진 것을 고르시오.
32.

If we've ⓐ **invested** in something that hasn't repaid us — be it money in a failing venture, or time in an ⓑ **unhappy** relationship — we find ⓒ **them** very difficult to walk away. This is the sunk cost fallacy. Our instinct is to continue investing money or time as we hope that our investment will ⓓ **prove** to be worthwhile in the end. Giving up would mean ⓔ **acknowledging** that we've wasted something we can't get back, and ⓕ **which** thought is so painful that we prefer to avoid ⓖ **them** if we can. The problem, of course, is that if something really is a bad bet, then staying with it simply increases the amount we lose. Rather than walk away from a bad five-year relationship, for example, we turn it into a bad 10-year relationship; rather than accept that we've lost a thousand dollars, we ⓗ **lie** down another thousand and lose that too. In the end, by ⓘ **delaying** the pain of admitting our problem, we only add to it. Sometimes we just have to cut our losses.

① ⓓ, ⓖ   ② ⓐ, ⓓ, ⓘ   ③ ⓔ, ⓖ, ⓗ
④ ⓕ, ⓖ, ⓘ   ⑤ ⓒ, ⓕ, ⓖ, ⓗ

14. 14)밑줄 친 ⓐ~ⓗ 중 어법, 혹은 문맥상 어휘의 사용이 어색한 것끼리 짝지어진 것을 고르시오.
33.

On our little world, light travels, for all practical purposes, ⓐ **simultaneously**. If a light-bulb is glowing, then of course it's ⓑ **psychologically** where we see it, shining away. We reach out our hand and touch it: It's there all right, and unpleasantly hot. If the filament fails, then the light goes out. We don't see ⓒ **them** in the same place, glowing, illuminating the room years after the bulb breaks and it's removed from its socket.

The very notion seems ⓓ **nonsensical**. But if we're far enough away, an entire sun can go out and we'll continue to see it ⓔ **shining** brightly; we won't learn of its death, it may be, for ages to come — in fact, for how long it takes light, which travels fast but not infinitely fast, to cross the ⓕ **intervened** vastness. The ⓖ **immense** distances to the stars and the galaxies mean ⓗ **that** we see everything in space in the past.

① ⓔ, ⓕ, ⓖ   ② ⓐ, ⓑ, ⓒ, ⓕ   ③ ⓐ, ⓑ, ⓒ, ⓗ
④ ⓐ, ⓔ, ⓖ, ⓗ   ⑤ ⓒ, ⓔ, ⓖ, ⓗ

15. 15)밑줄 친 ⓐ~ⓕ 중 어법, 혹은 문맥상 어휘의 사용이 어색한 것끼리 짝지어진 것을 고르시오.
34.

Financial markets do more than take capital from the rich and lend ⓐ **it** to everyone else. They enable each of us to smooth consumption over our lifetimes, ⓑ **which** is a fancy way of saying that we don't have to spend income at the same time we earn it. Shakespeare may have ⓒ **abnomalised** us to be neither borrowers nor lenders; the fact is that most of us will be both at some point. If we lived in an agrarian society, we would have to eat our crops reasonably soon after the harvest or find some way to store ⓓ **them**. Financial markets are a more sophisticated way of managing the harvest. We can spend income now that we have not yet earned — as by borrowing for college or a home — or we can earn income now and spend it later, as by saving for retirement. The important point is that earning income has ⓔ **divorced** from spending it, allowing us much more ⓕ **flexibility** in life.

① ⓑ, ⓒ   ② ⓒ, ⓓ   ③ ⓒ, ⓔ
④ ⓒ, ⓕ   ⑤ ⓐ, ⓔ, ⓕ

16. ¹⁶⁾**밑줄 친 ⓐ~ⓕ 중 어법, 혹은 문맥상 어휘의 사용이 어색한 것끼리 짝지어진 것을 고르시오.**
35.

As the old joke goes: "Software, free. User manual, $10,000". But it's no joke. A couple of high-profile companies ⓐ **make** their living selling instruction and ⓑ **pahing** support for free software. The copy of code, being mere bits, ⓒ **is** free. The lines of free code become valuable to you only through support and guidance. A lot of medical and genetic information will go this route in the coming decades. Right now getting a full copy of all your DNA is very expensive ($10,000), but soon it won't be. The price is ⓓ **dropping** so fast, it will be $100 soon, and then the next year insurance companies will offer ⓔ **sequecing** you for free. When a copy of your sequence costs nothing, the interpretation of ⓕ **what** it means, what you can do about it, and how to use it — the manual for your genes — will be expensive.

① ⓐ, ⓓ   ② ⓐ, ⓔ   ③ ⓑ, ⓔ
④ ⓒ, ⓔ   ⑤ ⓒ, ⓕ

17. ¹⁷⁾**밑줄 친 ⓐ~ⓖ 중 어법, 혹은 문맥상 어휘의 사용이 어색한 것끼리 짝지어진 것을 고르시오.**
36.

Brains are expensive in terms of energy. Twenty percent of the calories we consume ⓐ **used** to power the brain. So brains try to operate in the most energy-efficient way possible, and ⓑ **which** means processing only the ⓒ **maximum** amount of information from our senses that we need to navigate the world. Neuroscientists weren't the first to discover that fixing your gaze on something is ⓓ **no** guarantee of seeing it. Magicians figured this out long ago. By directing your attention, they perform tricks with their hands in full view. Their actions should give away the game, but they can rest ⓔ **assured** that your brain processes only small bits of the visual scene. This all helps to ⓕ **explain** the prevalence of traffic accidents in ⓖ **what** drivers hit pedestrians in plain view, or collide with cars directly in front of them. In many of these cases, the eyes are pointed in the right direction, but the brain isn't seeing what's really out there.

① ⓐ, ⓓ   ② ⓐ, ⓑ, ⓒ, ⓖ   ③ ⓐ, ⓑ, ⓕ, ⓖ
④ ⓑ, ⓒ, ⓓ, ⓕ   ⑤ ⓒ, ⓔ, ⓕ, ⓖ

18. ¹⁸⁾**밑줄 친 ⓐ~ⓔ 중 어법, 혹은 문맥상 어휘의 사용이 어색한 것끼리 짝지어진 것을 고르시오.**
37.

Buying a television is current consumption. It makes us ⓐ **happy** today but does nothing to make us richer tomorrow. Yes, money ⓑ **spent** on a television keeps workers employed at the television factory. But if the same money ⓒ **is** invested, it would create jobs somewhere else, say for scientists in a laboratory or workers on a construction site, while also making us richer in the long run. Think about college as an example. Sending students to college ⓓ **create** jobs for professors. Using the same money to buy fancy sports cars for high school graduates would create jobs for auto workers. The crucial difference between these scenarios ⓔ **are** that a college education makes a young person more productive for the rest of his or her life; a sports car does not. Thus, college tuition is an investment; buying a sports car is consumption.

① ⓐ, ⓑ, ⓔ   ② ⓐ, ⓒ, ⓓ   ③ ⓑ, ⓒ, ⓓ
④ ⓑ, ⓓ, ⓔ   ⑤ ⓒ, ⓓ, ⓔ

19. 19)밑줄 친 ⓐ~ⓕ 중 어법, 혹은 문맥상 어휘의 사용이 어색한 것끼리 짝지어진 것을 고르시오.
38.

The Net differs from most of the mass media it replaces in an obvious and very important way: it's bidirectional. We can send messages through the network as well as receive them, ⓐ **which** has made the system all the more ⓑ **useful**. The ability to exchange information online, to upload as well as download, ⓒ **has** turned the Net into a thoroughfare for business and commerce. With a few clicks, people can search virtual catalogues, place orders, track shipments, and update information in ⓓ **cooperate** databases. But the Net doesn't just connect us with businesses; it connects us with one another. It's a personal broadcasting ⓔ **medium** as well as a commercial one. Millions of people use ⓕ **them** to distribute their own digital creations, in the form of blogs, videos, photos, songs, and podcasts, as well as to critique, edit, or otherwise modify the creations of others.

① ⓐ, ⓓ   ② ⓑ, ⓒ   ③ ⓑ, ⓓ
④ ⓓ, ⓔ   ⑤ ⓓ, ⓕ

20. 20)밑줄 친 ⓐ~ⓖ 중 어법, 혹은 문맥상 어휘의 사용이 어색한 것끼리 짝지어진 것을 고르시오.
39.

Imagine that seven out of ten working Americans got fired tomorrow. What would they all do? It's hard to believe you'd have an economy at all if you gave pink slips to more than half the labor force. But that is what the industrial ⓐ **revolution** did to the workforce of the early 19th century. Two hundred years ago, 70 percent of American workers lived on the farm. Today ⓑ **anatomy** has ⓒ **eliminated** all but 1 percent of their jobs, replacing ⓓ **them** with machines. But the displaced workers did not sit ⓔ **idle**. Instead, automation created hundreds of millions of jobs in entirely new fields. Those who once farmed were now manning the factories that manufactured farm equipment, cars, and other industrial products. Since then, wave upon wave of new occupations have ⓕ **been arrived** — ⓖ **applicants** repair person, food chemist, photographer, web designer — each building on previous automation. Today, the vast majority of us are doing jobs that no farmer from the 1800s could have imagined.

① ⓒ, ⓓ   ② ⓒ, ⓖ   ③ ⓑ, ⓒ, ⓕ
④ ⓑ, ⓒ, ⓖ   ⑤ ⓑ, ⓕ, ⓖ

21. 21)밑줄 친 ⓐ~ⓕ 중 어법, 혹은 문맥상 어휘의 사용이 어색한 것끼리 짝지어진 것을 고르시오.
40.

Many things spark envy : ownership, status, health, youth, talent, popularity, beauty. It is often ⓐ **confused** with jealousy because the ⓑ **psychological** reactions are ⓒ **identical**. The difference: the subject of envy is a thing (status, money, health etc.). The subject of jealousy is the behaviour of a third person. Envy needs two people. Jealousy, on the other hand, requires three: Peter is jealous of Sam because the beautiful girl next door rings him instead. Paradoxically, with envy we ⓓ **indirect** resentments toward those who are most ⓔ **similar** to us in age, career and residence. We don't envy businesspeople from the century before last. We don't envy millionaires on the other side of the globe. As a writer, I don't envy musicians, managers or dentists, but other writers. As a CEO you envy other, bigger CEOs. As a supermodel you envy more ⓕ **successful** supermodels. Aristotle knew this. 'Potters envy potters'.

① ⓐ, ⓓ   ② ⓑ, ⓒ   ③ ⓑ, ⓓ
④ ⓓ, ⓔ   ⑤ ⓐ, ⓒ, ⓔ, ⓕ

22. ²²⁾**밑줄 친 ⓐ~ⓜ 중 어법, 혹은 문맥상 어휘의 사용이 어색한 것끼리 짝지어진 것을 고르시오.**
41~42.

We have biases that support our biases! If we're ⓐ **partial** to one option — perhaps because it's more memorable, or ⓑ **framed** to minimize loss, or seemingly consistent with a ⓒ **promising** pattern — we tend to search for information that will justify choosing that option. On the one hand, it's ⓓ **sensible** to make choices that we can defend with data and a list of reasons. On the other hand, if we're not careful, we're likely to conduct an ⓔ **balanced** analysis, falling prey to a cluster of errors collectively known ⓕ **as** "confirmation biases".

For example, nearly all companies include classic "tell me about yourself" job interviews as part of the hiring process, and many rely on these interviews ⓖ **alone** to evaluate ⓗ **appliances**. But it turns out that traditional interviews are actually one of the least useful tools for predicting an employee's future success. This is ⓘ **because** interviewers often subconsciously make up their minds about interviewees based on their first few moments of interaction and spend the rest of the interview cherry-picking evidence and phrasing their questions to ⓙ **confirm** that initial impression: "I see here you left a good position at your previous job. You must be pretty ambitious, right"? versus "You must not have been very committed, huh"? This means that interviewers can be prone to ⓚ **overlooking** significant information that would clearly indicate whether this candidate was actually the best person to hire. More structured approaches, like obtaining samples of a candidate's work or asking how he would respond to difficult hypothetical situations, ⓛ **are** dramatically better at ⓜ **assessment** future success, with a nearly threefold advantage over traditional interviews.

① ⓛ, ⓜ ② ⓑ, ⓔ, ⓚ ③ ⓔ, ⓕ, ⓚ
④ ⓔ, ⓖ, ⓗ ⑤ ⓔ, ⓗ, ⓜ

23. ²³⁾**밑줄 친 ⓐ~ⓙ 중 어법, 혹은 문맥상 어휘의 사용이 어색한 것끼리 짝지어진 것을 고르시오.**
43~45.

On Saturday morning, Todd and his 5-year-old daughter Ava walked out of the store with the groceries they ⓐ **had** just purchased. As they pushed their grocery cart through the parking lot, they saw a red car ⓑ **to pull** into the space next to their pick-up truck. A young man named Greg was driving. "That's a cool car", Ava said to her dad. He agreed and looked at Greg, who finished ⓒ **parking** and opened his door. As Todd finished loading his groceries, Greg's door ⓓ **was remained** open. Todd noticed Greg didn't get out of his car. But he was pulling something from his car. He put a metal frame on the ground beside his door. ⓔ **Remaining** in the driver's seat, he then reached back into his car to grab something else. Todd realized ⓕ **what** he was doing and considered whether he should try to help him. After a moment, he decided to ⓖ **approach to** Greg. By this time, Greg had already pulled one thin wheel out of his car and attached ⓗ **them** to the frame. He was now pulling a second wheel out when he looked up and saw Todd standing near him. Todd said, "Hi there! Have a great weekend"! Greg seemed a bit surprised, but replied by wishing him a great weekend too. Then Greg added, "Thanks for letting me ⓘ **have** my independence". "Of course", Todd said. After Todd and Ava climbed into their truck, Ava became curious. So she asked ⓙ **why** he didn't offer to help the man with his wheelchair. Todd said, "Why do you insist on brushing your teeth without my help"? She answered, "Because I know how to"! He said, "And the man knows how to put together his wheelchair". Ava understood that sometimes the best way to help someone is to not help at all.

① ⓒ, ⓕ ② ⓒ, ⓖ ③ ⓐ, ⓑ, ⓒ, ⓘ
④ ⓐ, ⓑ, ⓕ, ⓙ ⑤ ⓑ, ⓓ, ⓖ, ⓗ

2024 고2 6월 모의고사

❶ voca ❷ text ❸ [/] ❹ ____ ❺ quiz 1 ❻ quiz 2 ❼ quiz 3 ❽ quiz 4 ❾ quiz 5

☑ 밑줄 친 부분 중 어법, 혹은 문맥상 어휘의 사용
이 어색한 것은 모두 몇 개인가?

24. 1) 18.

Dear Residents,

My name is Kari Patterson, and I'm the manager of the River View Apartments. It's time to take advantage ① **to** the sunny weather to make our community more ② **beautiful**. On Saturday, July 13 at 9 a.m., residents will meet in the north parking lot. We will divide into teams to plant flowers and small trees, pull weeds, and put colorful decorations on the lawn. Please ③ **join in** us for this year's Gardening Day, and remember no special skills or tools ④ **are required**. Last year, we had a great time working together, so come out and make this year's event even better!

Warm regards, / Kari Patterson

① 없음 ② 1개 ③ 2개 ④ 3개 ⑤ 4개

25. 2) 19.

It was the championship race. Emma was the final runner ① **with** her relay team. She anxiously ② **awaited** in her spot ③ **for** her teammate to pass her the baton. Emma wasn't sure she could perform her role without making a mistake. Her hands shook as she thought, "What if I drop the baton"? She felt her heart rate ④ **increasing** as her teammate ⑤ **was approched**. But as she started running, she received the baton smoothly. In the final 10 meters, she passed two other runners and crossed the finish line in first place! She ⑥ **raised** her hands in the air, and a huge smile came across her face. As her teammates hugged her, she shouted, "We did it"! All of her hard training ⑦ **have** been worth it.

① 1개 ② 4개 ③ 5개 ④ 6개 ⑤ 7개

26. 3) 20.

Most people resist the idea of a true self-estimate, probably because they fear ① **it** might mean ② **to downgrade** some of their beliefs about who they are and what they're capable of. As Goethe's maxim goes, it is a great failing "to see yourself as more than you ③ **do**". How could you really ④ **be considered** self-aware if you refuse to consider your weaknesses? Don't fear self-assessment because you're worried you might have to admit some things about yourself. The second half of Goethe's maxim is important too. He states that it is equally ⑤ **damaged** to "value yourself at ⑥ **more** than your true worth". We underestimate our capabilities just as much and just as ⑦ **dangerously** as we overestimate other abilities. Cultivate the ability to judge yourself accurately and honestly. Look ⑧ **forward** to discern what you're capable of and what it will take to unlock that potential.

① 1개 ② 5개 ③ 6개 ④ 7개 ⑤ 8개

27. 4) 21.

Take a look at some of the most powerful, rich, and famous people in the world. ① **To ignore** the trappings of their success and ② **that** they're able to buy. Look instead at what they're forced to trade in return — look at what success has cost them. Mostly? Freedom. Their work demands they wear a suit. Their success depends on ③ **attending** certain parties, kissing up to people they don't like. It will require — inevitably — ④ **realizing** they are unable to say what they actually think. Worse, it demands that they become a different type of person or do bad things. Sure, it might pay well — but they haven't truly ⑤ **examined** the transaction. As Seneca put it, "Slavery resides under marble and gold". Too many successful people are prisoners in jails of their own making. Is that what you want? Is that what you're working ⑥ **hardly** toward? Let's hope not.

① 없음   ② 1개   ③ 3개   ④ 4개   ⑤ 5개

28. 5) 22.

If a firm is going to ① **be saved** by the government, it might be easier to concentrate on lobbying the government for more money rather than ② **taking** the harder decision of ③ **reconciling** the company to be able to be ④ **proficient** and ⑤ **variable** in the long term. This is an example of something known ⑥ **as** moral hazard — when government support alters the decisions firms take. For example, if governments rescue banks who get into difficulty, as they ⑦ **did** during the credit crisis of 2007-08, this could encourage banks to take greater risks in the future because they know there is a possibility that governments will ⑧ **interlcok** if they lose money. Although the government rescue may be well intended, it can negatively affect the behavior of banks, ⑨ **encouraging** risky and poor decision making.

① 없음   ② 2개   ③ 3개   ④ 4개   ⑤ 8개

29. 6) 23.

If there is ① **little** or no diversity of views, and all scientists see, think, and question the world in a ② **different** way, then they will not, as a community, be as ③ **objectively** as they maintain they are, or at least ④ **respire** to be. The solution is that there should be far greater diversity in the practice of science: in gender, ethnicity, and social and cultural backgrounds. Science works because it is carried out by people who pursue their curiosity about the natural world and test their and each other's ideas from as many ⑤ **varied** perspectives and angles as possible. When science is done by a diverse group of people, and if consensus builds up about a particular area of scientific knowledge, then we can have more confidence in ⑥ **our** ⑦ **objection** and truth.

① 없음   ② 1개   ③ 3개   ④ 5개   ⑤ 7개

30. 7) 24.

We tend to break up time into units, such as weeks, months, and seasons; in a series of studies among farmers in India and students in North America, psychologists ① **founded** that if a deadline is on the other side of a "break" — such as in the New Year — we're ② **more** likely to see it as remote, and, as a result, be less ready to jump into action. What you need to do in that situation is find another way to think about the timeframe. For example, if it's November and the deadline is in January, it's better to tell ③ **yourself** you have to get it ④ **to do** "this winter" rather than "next year". The best approach is to view deadlines as a challenge that you have to ⑤ **meet** within a period that's imminent. That way the stress is more manageable, and you have a better chance of starting — and therefore ⑥ **finishing** — in good time.

① 없음   ② 1개   ③ 2개   ④ 3개   ⑤ 6개

31. 8) 25.

The graph above shows the amount of CO₂ ① **omissions** per person across selected Asian countries in 2010 and 2020. All the countries ② **except** Uzbekistan had a greater amount of CO₂ emissions per person in 2020 than ③ **those** in 2010. In 2010, the amount of CO₂ emissions per person of China was the largest among the five countries, ④ **following** by that of Mongolia. However, in 2020, Mongolia ⑤ **was surpassed** China in terms of the amount of CO₂ emissions per person. In 2010, Uzbekistan produced a larger amount of CO₂ emissions per person than Vietnam, while the opposite was true in 2020. Among the five countries, India was the only one ⑥ **which** the amount of CO₂ emissions per person was less than 2 tons in 2020.

① 없음   ② 2개   ③ 3개   ④ 4개   ⑤ 5개

32. 9) 26.

Henry David Thoreau was born in Concord, Massachusetts in 1817. When he was 16, he ① **entered into** Harvard College. After ② **graduating**, Thoreau worked as a schoolteacher but he quit after two weeks. In June of 1838 he set up a school with his brother John. However, he had hopes of becoming a nature poet. In 1845, he moved into a small self-③ **building** house near Walden Pond. At Walden, Thoreau did an incredible amount of reading. The journal he wrote there became the source of his most famous book, Walden. In his later life, Thoreau traveled to the Maine woods, to Cape Cod, and to Canada. At the age of 43, he ended his travels and ④ **returned** to Concord. ⑤ **Despite** his works were not widely read during his lifetime, he never stopped ⑥ **to write** , and his works fill 20 volumes.

① 1개   ② 2개   ③ 4개   ④ 5개   ⑤ 6개

33. 10) 29.

The built-in capacity for smiling is ① **proved** by the remarkable observation that babies who are ② **congenitally** both deaf and blind, who have never seen a human face, also start to smile at around 2 months. However, smiling in blind babies eventually ③ **disappears** if nothing ④ **done** to reinforce it. Without the right feedback, smiling dies out. But here's a fascinating fact: blind babies will continue to smile if they are cuddled, bounced, nudged, and tickled by an adult — anything to let ⑤ **them** know that they are not alone and that someone cares about them. This social feedback ⑥ **encourages** the baby to continue smiling. In this way, early experience operates with our biology to establish social behaviors. In fact, you don't need the cases of blind babies to make the point. Babies with sight smile more at you when you look at them or, better still, smile back at ⑦ **themselves**.

① 없음   ② 3개   ③ 5개   ④ 6개   ⑤ 7개

34. 11) 30.

Because people tend to ① **adapt**, interrupting positive things with negative ② **ones** can actually ③ **decrease** enjoyment. Take commercials. Most people hate them, so removing them should make shows or other entertainment more enjoyable. But the ④ **same** is true. Shows are actually more enjoyable when they're broken up by annoying commercials. Because these ⑤ **more** enjoyable moments break up ⑥ **aoption** to the positive experience of the show. Think about eating chocolate chips. The first chip is delicious: sweet, melt-in-your-mouth goodness. The second chip is also pretty good. But by the fourth, fifth, or tenth chip in a row, the goodness is no longer as pleasurable. We ⑦ **adapt**. ⑧ **Interfering** positive experiences with less positive ones, however, can slow down adaptation. Eating a Brussels sprout between chocolate chips or viewing commercials between parts of TV shows ⑨ **disrupts** the process. The less positive moment makes the following positive one new again and thus more enjoyable.

① 1개   ② 2개   ③ 3개   ④ 4개   ⑤ 5개

35. 12) 31.

We collect stamps, coins, vintage cars even when they serve no practical purpose. The post office doesn't accept the old stamps, the banks don't take old coins, and the vintage cars are no longer ① **allowed** on the road. These are all side issues; the attraction is that they are in ② **short** supply. In one study, students ③ **asked** to arrange ten posters in order of attractiveness — with the agreement that afterward they could keep one poster as a reward for ④ **its** participation. Five minutes later, they ⑤ **told** that the poster with the third highest rating was no longer available. Then they were asked to judge all ten from scratch. The poster that was no longer available was suddenly classified as the most beautiful. In psychology, this phenomenon is called reactance: when we are ⑥ **deprived** of an option, we suddenly deem it more ⑦ **attractively**.

① 없음　　② 2개　　③ 3개　　④ 4개　　⑤ 6개

36. 13) 32.

If we've ① **invested** in something that hasn't repaid us — be it money in a failing venture, or time in an ② **unhappy** relationship — we find ③ **them** very difficult to walk away. This is the sunk cost fallacy. Our instinct is to continue investing money or time as we hope that our investment will ④ **disprove** to be worthwhile in the end. Giving up would mean ⑤ **acknowledging** that we've wasted something we can't get back, and ⑥ **which** thought is so painful that we prefer to avoid ⑦ **them** if we can. The problem, of course, is that if something really is a bad bet, then staying with it simply increases the amount we lose. Rather than walk away from a bad five-year relationship, for example, we turn it into a bad 10-year relationship; rather than accept that we've lost a thousand dollars, we ⑧ **lay** down another thousand and lose that too. In the end, by ⑨ **accepting** the pain of admitting our problem, we only add to it. Sometimes we just have to cut our losses.

① 3개　　② 5개　　③ 6개　　④ 8개　　⑤ 9개

37. 14) 33.

On our little world, light travels, for all practical purposes, ① **instantaneously**. If a light-bulb is glowing, then of course it's ② **psychologically** where we see it, shining away. We reach out our hand and touch it: It's there all right, and unpleasantly hot. If the filament fails, then the light goes out. We don't see ③ **it** in the same place, glowing, illuminating the room years after the bulb breaks and it's removed from its socket. The very notion seems ④ **nonsensical**. But if we're far enough away, an entire sun can go out and we'll continue to see it ⑤ **to shine** brightly; we won't learn of its death, it may be, for ages to come — in fact, for how long it takes light, which travels fast but not infinitely fast, to cross the ⑥ **intervened** vastness. The ⑦ **immense** distances to the stars and the galaxies mean ⑧ **that** we see everything in space in the past.

① 2개　　② 3개　　③ 4개　　④ 5개　　⑤ 7개

38. 15) 34.

Financial markets do more than take capital from the rich and lend ① **them** to everyone else. They enable each of us to smooth consumption over our lifetimes, ② **which** is a fancy way of saying that we don't have to spend income at the same time we earn it. Shakespeare may have ③ **admonished** us to be neither borrowers nor lenders; the fact is that most of us will be both at some point. If we lived in an agrarian society, we would have to eat our crops reasonably soon after the harvest or find some way to store ④ **them**. Financial markets are a more sophisticated way of managing the harvest. We can spend income now that we have not yet earned — as by borrowing for college or a home — or we can earn income now and spend it later, as by saving for retirement. The important point is that earning income has ⑤ **divorced** from spending it, allowing us much more ⑥ **flexibility** in life.

① 없음　　② 1개　　③ 2개　　④ 3개　　⑤ 5개

39. 16) 35.

As the old joke goes: "Software, free. User manual, $10,000". But it's no joke. A couple of high-profile companies ① **makes** their living selling instruction and ② **paid** support for free software. The copy of code, being mere bits, ③ **are** free. The lines of free code become valuable to you only through support and guidance. A lot of medical and genetic information will go this route in the coming decades. Right now getting a full copy of all your DNA is very expensive ($10,000), but soon it won't be. The price is ④ **dropped** so fast, it will be $100 soon, and then the next year insurance companies will offer ⑤ **to sequence** you for free. When a copy of your sequence costs nothing, the interpretation of ⑥ **what** it means, what you can do about it, and how to use it — the manual for your genes — will be expensive.

① 없음　　② 1개　　③ 2개　　④ 3개　　⑤ 4개

40. 17) 36.

Brains are expensive in terms of energy. Twenty percent of the calories we consume ① **are used** to power the brain. So brains try to operate in the most energy-efficient way possible, and ② **that** means processing only the ③ **maximum** amount of information from our senses that we need to navigate the world. Neuroscientists weren't the first to discover that fixing your gaze on something is ④ **x** guarantee of seeing it. Magicians figured this out long ago. By directing your attention, they perform tricks with their hands in full view. Their actions should give away the game, but they can rest ⑤ **assuring** that your brain processes only small bits of the visual scene. This all helps to ⑥ **explain** the prevalence of traffic accidents in ⑦ **what** drivers hit pedestrians in plain view, or collide with cars directly in front of them. In many of these cases, the eyes are pointed in the right direction, but the brain isn't seeing what's really out there.

① 2개　　② 3개　　③ 4개　　④ 5개　　⑤ 7개

41. 18) 37.

Buying a television is current consumption. It makes us ① **happy** today but does nothing to make us richer tomorrow. Yes, money ② **is spent** on a television keeps workers employed at the television factory. But if the same money ③ **is** invested, it would create jobs somewhere else, say for scientists in a laboratory or workers on a construction site, while also making us richer in the long run. Think about college as an example. Sending students to college ④ **creates** jobs for professors. Using the same money to buy fancy sports cars for high school graduates would create jobs for auto workers. The crucial difference between these scenarios ⑤ **is** that a college education makes a young person more productive for the rest of his or her life; a sports car does not. Thus, college tuition is an investment; buying a sports car is consumption.

① 없음　　② 2개　　③ 3개　　④ 4개　　⑤ 5개

42. 19) 38.

The Net differs from most of the mass media it replaces in an obvious and very important way: it's bidirectional. We can send messages through the network as well as receive them, ① **which** has made the system all the more ② **useful**. The ability to exchange information online, to upload as well as download, ③ **having** turned the Net into a thoroughfare for business and commerce. With a few clicks, people can search virtual catalogues, place orders, track shipments, and update information in ④ **corporate** databases. But the Net doesn't just connect us with businesses; it connects us with one another. It's a personal broadcasting ⑤ **medium** as well as a commercial one. Millions of people use ⑥ **them** to distribute their own digital creations, in the form of blogs, videos, photos, songs, and podcasts, as well as to critique, edit, or otherwise modify the creations of others.

① 1개　　② 2개　　③ 4개　　④ 5개　　⑤ 6개

43. 20) 39.

Imagine that seven out of ten working Americans got fired tomorrow. What would they all do? It's hard to believe you'd have an economy at all if you gave pink slips to more than half the labor force. But that is what the industrial ① **evolution** did to the workforce of the early 19th century. Two hundred years ago, 70 percent of American workers lived on the farm. Today ② **anatomy** has ③ **been eliminated** all but 1 percent of their jobs, replacing ④ **them** with machines. But the displaced workers did not sit ⑤ **idle**. Instead, automation created hundreds of millions of jobs in entirely new fields. Those who once farmed were now manning the factories that manufactured farm equipment, cars, and other industrial products. Since then, wave upon wave of new occupations have ⑥ **been arrived** — ⑦ **appliance** repair person, food chemist, photographer, web designer — each building on previous automation. Today, the vast majority of us are doing jobs that no farmer from the 1800s could have imagined.

① 없음　　② 2개　　③ 3개　　④ 4개　　⑤ 7개

44. 21) 40.

Many things spark envy : ownership, status, health, youth, talent, popularity, beauty. It is often ① **confused** with jealousy because the ② **physical** reactions are ③ **identical**. The difference: the subject of envy is a thing (status, money, health etc.). The subject of jealousy is the behaviour of a third person. Envy needs two people. Jealousy, on the other hand, requires three: Peter is jealous of Sam because the beautiful girl next door rings him instead. Paradoxically, with envy we ④ **indirect** resentments toward those who are most ⑤ **similar** to us in age, career and residence. We don't envy businesspeople from the century before last. We don't envy millionaires on the other side of the globe. As a writer, I don't envy musicians, managers or dentists, but other writers. As a CEO you envy other, bigger CEOs. As a supermodel you envy more ⑥ **successful** supermodels. Aristotle knew this: 'Potters envy potters'.

① 1개　　② 2개　　③ 3개　　④ 4개　　⑤ 5개

45. 22) ^{41~42.}

We have biases that support our biases! If we're ① **partial** to one option — perhaps because it's more memorable, or ② **framed** to minimize loss, or seemingly consistent with a ③ **promising** pattern — we tend to search for information that will justify choosing that option. On the one hand, it's ④ **sensible** to make choices that we can defend with data and a list of reasons. On the other hand, if we're not careful, we're likely to conduct an ⑤ **balanced** analysis, falling prey to a cluster of errors collectively known ⑥ **to** "confirmation biases".

For example, nearly all companies include classic "tell me about yourself" job interviews as part of the hiring process, and many rely on these interviews ⑦ **lonely** to evaluate ⑧ **appliances**. But it turns out that traditional interviews are actually one of the least useful tools for predicting an employee's future success. This is ⑨ **because** interviewers often subconsciously make up their minds about interviewees based on their first few moments of interaction and spend the rest of the interview cherry-picking evidence and phrasing their questions to ⑩ **confirm** that initial impression: "I see here you left a good position at your previous job. You must be pretty ambitious, right"? versus "You must not have been very committed, huh"? This means that interviewers can be prone to ⑪ **overlook** significant information that would clearly indicate whether this candidate was actually the best person to hire. More structured approaches, like obtaining samples of a candidate's work or asking how he would respond to difficult hypothetical situations, ⑫ **being** dramatically better at ⑬ **assessment** future success, with a nearly threefold advantage over traditional interviews.

① 3개   ② 7개   ③ 9개   ④ 10개   ⑤ 12개

46. 23) ^{43~45.}

On Saturday morning, Todd and his 5-year-old daughter Ava walked out of the store with the groceries they ① **had** just purchased. As they pushed their grocery cart through the parking lot, they saw a red car ② **to pull** into the space next to their pick-up truck. A young man named Greg was driving. "That's a cool car", Ava said to her dad. He agreed and looked at Greg, who finished ③ **to park** and opened his door. As Todd finished loading his groceries, Greg's door ④ **remained** open. Todd noticed Greg didn't get out of his car. But he was pulling something from his car. He put a metal frame on the ground beside his door. ⑤ **Remained** in the driver's seat, he then reached back into his car to grab something else. Todd realized ⑥ **that** he was doing and considered whether he should try to help him. After a moment, he decided to ⑦ **approach** Greg. By this time, Greg had already pulled one thin wheel out of his car and attached ⑧ **them** to the frame. He was now pulling a second wheel out when he looked up and saw Todd standing near him. Todd said, "Hi there! Have a great weekend"! Greg seemed a bit surprised, but replied by wishing him a great weekend too. Then Greg added, "Thanks for letting me ⑨ **have** my independence". "Of course", Todd said. After Todd and Ava climbed into their truck, Ava became curious. So she asked ⑩ **why** he didn't offer to help the man with his wheelchair. Todd said, "Why do you insist on brushing your teeth without my help"? She answered, "Because I know how to"! He said, "And the man knows how to put together his wheelchair". Ava understood that sometimes the best way to help someone is to not help at all.

① 없음   ② 1개   ③ 2개   ④ 5개   ⑤ 9개

2024 고2 6월 모의고사

❶ voca ❷ text ❸ [/] ❹ ____ ❺ quiz 1 ❻ quiz 2 ❼ quiz 3 ❽ quiz 4 ❾ quiz 5

47. 1)**밑줄 부분 중 어법, 혹은 문맥상 어휘의 쓰임이 어색한 것을 올바르게 고쳐 쓰시오. (3개)** 18.

Dear Residents,

My name is Kari Patterson, and I'm the manager of the River View Apartments. It's time to take advantage ① **to** the sunny weather to make our community more ② **beautifully**. On Saturday, July 13 at 9 a.m., residents will meet in the north parking lot. We will divide into teams to plant flowers and small trees, pull weeds, and put colorful decorations on the lawn. Please ③ **join** us for this year's Gardening Day, and remember no special skills or tools ④ **require**. Last year, we had a great time working together, so come out and make this year's event even better!

Warm regards, / Kari Patterson

기호	어색한 표현		올바른 표현
( )	_____	⇨	_____
( )	_____	⇨	_____
( )	_____	⇨	_____

48. 2)**밑줄 부분 중 어법, 혹은 문맥상 어휘의 쓰임이 어색한 것을 올바르게 고쳐 쓰시오. (6개)** 19.

It was the championship race. Emma was the final runner ① **on** her relay team. She anxiously ② **awaited** in her spot ③ **of** her teammate to pass her the baton. Emma wasn't sure she could perform her role without making a mistake. Her hands shook as she thought, "What if I drop the baton"? She felt her heart rate ④ **to increase** as her teammate ⑤ **was approched**. But as she started running, she received the baton smoothly. In the final 10 meters, she passed two other runners and crossed the finish line in first place! She ⑥ **roused** her hands in the air, and a huge smile came across her face. As her teammates hugged her, she shouted, "We did it"! All of her hard training ⑦ **have** been worth it.

기호	어색한 표현		올바른 표현
( )	_____	⇨	_____
( )	_____	⇨	_____
( )	_____	⇨	_____
( )	_____	⇨	_____
( )	_____	⇨	_____
( )	_____	⇨	_____

49. 3)밑줄 부분 중 어법, 혹은 문맥상 어휘의 쓰임이 어색한 것을 올바르게 고쳐 쓰시오. (2개) 20.

Most people resist the idea of a true self-estimate, probably because they fear ① **them** might mean ② **downgrading** some of their beliefs about who they are and what they're capable of. As Goethe's maxim goes, it is a great failing "to see yourself as more than you ③ **are**". How could you really ④ **be considered** self-aware if you refuse to consider your weaknesses? Don't fear self-assessment because you're worried you might have to admit some things about yourself. The second half of Goethe's maxim is important too. He states that it is equally ⑤ **damaging** to "value yourself at ⑥ **more** than your true worth". We underestimate our capabilities just as much and just as ⑦ **dangerously** as we overestimate other abilities. Cultivate the ability to judge yourself accurately and honestly. Look ⑧ **inward** to discern what you're capable of and what it will take to unlock that potential.

기호	어색한 표현		올바른 표현
( )	_____	⇨	_____
( )	_____	⇨	_____

50. 4)밑줄 부분 중 어법, 혹은 문맥상 어휘의 쓰임이 어색한 것을 올바르게 고쳐 쓰시오. (1개) 21.

Take a look at some of the most powerful, rich, and famous people in the world. ① **Ignore** the trappings of their success and ② **what** they're able to buy. Look instead at what they're forced to trade in return — look at what success has cost them. Mostly? Freedom. Their work demands they wear a suit. Their success depends on ③ **attending** certain parties, kissing up to people they don't like. It will require — inevitably — ④ **realizing** they are unable to say what they actually think. Worse, it demands that they become a different type of person or do bad things. Sure, it might pay well — but they haven't truly ⑤ **examined** the

transaction. As Seneca put it, "Slavery resides under marble and gold". Too many successful people are prisoners in jails of their own making. Is that what you want? Is that what you're working ⑥ **hardly** toward? Let's hope not.

기호	어색한 표현		올바른 표현
( )	_____	⇨	_____

51. 5)밑줄 부분 중 어법, 혹은 문맥상 어휘의 쓰임이 어색한 것을 올바르게 고쳐 쓰시오. (9개) 22.

If a firm is going to ① **save** by the government, it might be easier to concentrate on lobbying the government for more money rather than ② **to take** the harder decision of ③ **reconciling** the company to be able to be ④ **proficient** and ⑤ **variable** in the long term. This is an example of something known ⑥ **to** moral hazard — when government support alters the decisions firms take. For example, if governments rescue banks who get into difficulty, as they ⑦ **were** during the credit crisis of 2007-08, this could encourage banks to take greater risks in the future because they know there is a possibility that governments will ⑧ **interlcok** if they lose money. Although the government rescue may be well intended, it can negatively affect the behavior of banks, ⑨ **to encourage** risky and poor decision making.

기호	어색한 표현		올바른 표현
( )	_____	⇨	_____
( )	_____	⇨	_____
( )	_____	⇨	_____
( )	_____	⇨	_____
( )	_____	⇨	_____
( )	_____	⇨	_____
( )	_____	⇨	_____
( )	_____	⇨	_____
( )	_____	⇨	_____

52. 6)밑줄 부분 중 어법, 혹은 문맥상 어휘의 쓰임이 어색한 것을 올바르게 고쳐 쓰시오. (2개) 23.

If there is ① **little** or no diversity of views, and all scientists see, think, and question the world in a ② **similar** way, then they will not, as a community, be as ③ **objectively** as they maintain they are, or at least ④ **aspire** to be. The solution is that there should be far greater diversity in the practice of science: in gender, ethnicity, and social and cultural backgrounds. Science works because it is carried out by people who pursue their curiosity about the natural world and test their and each other's ideas from as many ⑤ **varying** perspectives and angles as possible. When science is done by a diverse group of people, and if consensus builds up about a particular area of scientific knowledge, then we can have more confidence in ⑥ **its** ⑦ **objectivity** and truth.

기호	어색한 표현		올바른 표현
( )	_____	⇨	_____
( )	_____	⇨	_____

53. 7)밑줄 부분 중 어법, 혹은 문맥상 어휘의 쓰임이 어색한 것을 올바르게 고쳐 쓰시오. (2개) 24.

We tend to break up time into units, such as weeks, months, and seasons; in a series of studies among farmers in India and students in North America, psychologists ① **found** that if a deadline is on the other side of a "break" — such as in the New Year — we're ② **more** likely to see it as remote, and, as a result, be less ready to jump into action. What you need to do in that situation is find another way to think about the timeframe. For example, if it's November and the deadline is in January, it's better to tell ③ **yourself** you have to get it ④ **to do** "this winter" rather than "next year". The best approach is to view deadlines as a challenge that you have to ⑤ **be met** within a period that's imminent. That way the stress is

more manageable, and you have a better chance of starting — and therefore ⑥ **finishing** — in good time.

기호	어색한 표현		올바른 표현
( )	_____	⇨	_____
( )	_____	⇨	_____

54. 8)밑줄 부분 중 어법, 혹은 문맥상 어휘의 쓰임이 어색한 것을 올바르게 고쳐 쓰시오. (4개) 25.

The graph above shows the amount of CO_2 ① **emissions** per person across selected Asian countries in 2010 and 2020. All the countries ② **expect** Uzbekistan had a greater amount of CO_2 emissions per person in 2020 than ③ **those** in 2010. In 2010, the amount of CO_2 emissions per person of China was the largest among the five countries, ④ **following** by that of Mongolia. However, in 2020, Mongolia ⑤ **was surpassed** China in terms of the amount of CO_2 emissions per person. In 2010, Uzbekistan produced a larger amount of CO_2 emissions per person than Vietnam, while the opposite was true in 2020. Among the five countries, India was the only one ⑥ **where** the amount of CO_2 emissions per person was less than 2 tons in 2020.

기호	어색한 표현		올바른 표현
( )	_____	⇨	_____
( )	_____	⇨	_____
( )	_____	⇨	_____
( )	_____	⇨	_____

55. ⁹⁾**밑줄 부분 중 어법, 혹은 문맥상 어휘의 쓰임이 어색한 것을 올바르게 고쳐 쓰시오. (2개)** ^{26.}

Henry David Thoreau was born in Concord, Massachusetts in 1817. When he was 16, he ① **entered** Harvard College. After ② **graduated**, Thoreau worked as a schoolteacher but he quit after two weeks. In June of 1838 he set up a school with his brother John. However, he had hopes of becoming a nature poet. In 1845, he moved into a small self-③ **built** house near Walden Pond. At Walden, Thoreau did an incredible amount of reading. The journal he wrote there became the source of his most famous book, Walden. In his later life, Thoreau traveled to the Maine woods, to Cape Cod, and to Canada. At the age of 43, he ended his travels and ④ **was returned** to Concord. ⑤ **Although** his works were not widely read during his lifetime, he never stopped ⑥ **writing** , and his works fill 20 volumes.

기호	어색한 표현		올바른 표현
( )	_____	⇨	_____
( )	_____	⇨	_____

56. ¹⁰⁾**밑줄 부분 중 어법, 혹은 문맥상 어휘의 쓰임이 어색한 것을 올바르게 고쳐 쓰시오. (2개)** ^{29.}

The built-in capacity for smiling is ① **proved** by the remarkable observation that babies who are ② **congenitally** both deaf and blind, who have never seen a human face, also start to smile at around 2 months. However, smiling in blind babies eventually ③ **disappears** if nothing ④ **done** to reinforce it. Without the right feedback, smiling dies out. But here's a fascinating fact: blind babies will continue to smile if they are cuddled, bounced, nudged, and tickled by an adult — anything to let ⑤ **them** know that they are not alone and that someone cares about them. This social feedback ⑥ **encourages** the baby to continue smiling. In this way, early experience operates with our biology to establish social behaviors. In fact, you don't need the cases of blind babies to make the point. Babies with sight smile more at you when you look at them or, better still, smile back at ⑦ **them**.

기호	어색한 표현		올바른 표현
( )	_____	⇨	_____
( )	_____	⇨	_____

57. ¹¹⁾**밑줄 부분 중 어법, 혹은 문맥상 어휘의 쓰임이 어색한 것을 올바르게 고쳐 쓰시오. (1개)** ^{30.}

Because people tend to ① **adapt**, interrupting positive things with negative ② **ones** can actually ③ **decrease** enjoyment. Take commercials. Most people hate them, so removing them should make shows or other entertainment more enjoyable. But the ④ **opposite** is true. Shows are actually more enjoyable when they're broken up by annoying commercials. Because these ⑤ **less** enjoyable moments break up ⑥ **adaptation** to the positive experience of the show. Think about eating chocolate chips. The first chip is delicious: sweet, melt-in-your-mouth goodness. The second chip is also pretty good. But by the fourth, fifth, or tenth chip in a row, the goodness is no longer as pleasurable. We ⑦ **adapt**. ⑧ **Interspersing** positive experiences with less positive ones, however, can slow down adaptation. Eating a Brussels sprout between chocolate chips or viewing commercials between parts of TV shows ⑨ **disrupts** the process. The less positive moment makes the following positive one new again and thus more enjoyable.

기호	어색한 표현		올바른 표현
( )	_____	⇨	_____

58. 12)밑줄 부분 중 어법, 혹은 문맥상 어휘의 쓰임이 어색한 것을 올바르게 고쳐 쓰시오. (5개) 31.

We collect stamps, coins, vintage cars even when they serve no practical purpose. The post office doesn't accept the old stamps, the banks don't take old coins, and the vintage cars are no longer ① **to allow** on the road. These are all side issues; the attraction is that they are in ② **short** supply. In one study, students ③ **asked** to arrange ten posters in order of attractiveness — with the agreement that afterward they could keep one poster as a reward for ④ **its** participation. Five minutes later, they ⑤ **were told** that the poster with the third highest rating was no longer available. Then they were asked to judge all ten from scratch. The poster that was no longer available was suddenly classified as the most beautiful. In psychology, this phenomenon is called reactance: when we are ⑥ **full** of an option, we suddenly deem it more ⑦ **attractively**.

기호	어색한 표현		올바른 표현
( )	_____	⇨	_____
( )	_____	⇨	_____
( )	_____	⇨	_____
( )	_____	⇨	_____
( )	_____	⇨	_____

59. 13)밑줄 부분 중 어법, 혹은 문맥상 어휘의 쓰임이 어색한 것을 올바르게 고쳐 쓰시오. (3개) 32.

If we've ① **invested** in something that hasn't repaid us — be it money in a failing venture, or time in an ② **unhappy** relationship — we find ③ **them** very difficult to walk away. This is the sunk cost fallacy. Our instinct is to continue investing money or time as we hope that our investment will ④ **prove** to be worthwhile in the end. Giving up would mean ⑤ **acknowledging** that we've wasted something we can't get back, and ⑥ **which** thought is so painful that we prefer to avoid ⑦ **them** if we can. The problem, of course, is that if something really is a bad bet, then staying with it simply increases the amount we lose. Rather than walk away from a bad five-year relationship, for

example, we turn it into a bad 10-year relationship; rather than accept that we've lost a thousand dollars, we ⑧ **lay** down another thousand and lose that too. In the end, by ⑨ **delaying** the pain of admitting our problem, we only add to it. Sometimes we just have to cut our losses.

기호	어색한 표현		올바른 표현
( )	_____	⇨	_____
( )	_____	⇨	_____
( )	_____	⇨	_____

60. 14)밑줄 부분 중 어법, 혹은 문맥상 어휘의 쓰임이 어색한 것을 올바르게 고쳐 쓰시오. (8개) 33.

On our little world, light travels, for all practical purposes, ① **simultaneously**. If a light-bulb is glowing, then of course it's ② **psychologically** where we see it, shining away. We reach out our hand and touch it: It's there all right, and unpleasantly hot. If the filament fails, then the light goes out. We don't see ③ **them** in the same place, glowing, illuminating the room years after the bulb breaks and it's removed from its socket. The very notion seems ④ **nonsesically**. But if we're far enough away, an entire sun can go out and we'll continue to see it ⑤ **to shine** brightly; we won't learn of its death, it may be, for ages to come — in fact, for how long it takes light, which travels fast but not infinitely fast, to cross the ⑥ **intervened** vastness. The ⑦ **immediate** distances to the stars and the galaxies mean ⑧ **what** we see everything in space in the past.

기호	어색한 표현		올바른 표현
( )	_____	⇨	_____
( )	_____	⇨	_____
( )	_____	⇨	_____
( )	_____	⇨	_____
( )	_____	⇨	_____
( )	_____	⇨	_____
( )	_____	⇨	_____
( )	_____	⇨	_____

61. 15)**밑줄 부분 중 어법, 혹은 문맥상 어휘의 쓰임이 어색한 것을 올바르게 고쳐 쓰시오. (5개)** 34.

Financial markets do more than take capital from the rich and lend ① **it** to everyone else. They enable each of us to smooth consumption over our lifetimes, ② **that** is a fancy way of saying that we don't have to spend income at the same time we earn it. Shakespeare may have ③ **abnomalised** us to be neither borrowers nor lenders; the fact is that most of us will be both at some point. If we lived in an agrarian society, we would have to eat our crops reasonably soon after the harvest or find some way to store ④ **it**. Financial markets are a more sophisticated way of managing the harvest. We can spend income now that we have not yet earned — as by borrowing for college or a home — or we can earn income now and spend it later, as by saving for retirement. The important point is that earning income has ⑤ **divorced** from spending it, allowing us much more ⑥ **fixedness** in life.

기호	어색한 표현		올바른 표현
( )	_____	⇒	_____
( )	_____	⇒	_____
( )	_____	⇒	_____
( )	_____	⇒	_____
( )	_____	⇒	_____

62. 16)**밑줄 부분 중 어법, 혹은 문맥상 어휘의 쓰임이 어색한 것을 올바르게 고쳐 쓰시오. (3개)** 35.

As the old joke goes: "Software, free. User manual, $10,000". But it's no joke. A couple of high-profile companies ① **make** their living selling instruction and ② **pahing** support for free software. The copy of code, being mere bits, ③ **is** free. The lines of free code become valuable to you only through support and guidance. A lot of medical and genetic information will go this route in the coming decades. Right now getting a full copy of all your DNA is very expensive ($10,000), but soon it won't be. The price is ④ **dropped** so fast, it will be $100 soon, and then the next year insurance companies will offer ⑤ **to sequence** you for free. When a copy of your sequence costs nothing, the interpretation of ⑥ **which** it means, what you can do about it, and how to use it — the manual for your genes — will be expensive.

기호	어색한 표현		올바른 표현
( )	_____	⇒	_____
( )	_____	⇒	_____
( )	_____	⇒	_____

63. 17)**밑줄 부분 중 어법, 혹은 문맥상 어휘의 쓰임이 어색한 것을 올바르게 고쳐 쓰시오. (3개)** 36.

Brains are expensive in terms of energy. Twenty percent of the calories we consume ① **are used** to power the brain. So brains try to operate in the most energy-efficient way possible, and ② **that** means processing only the ③ **minimum** amount of information from our senses that we need to navigate the world. Neuroscientists weren't the first to discover that fixing your gaze on something is ④ **x** guarantee of seeing it. Magicians figured this out long ago. By directing your attention, they perform tricks with their hands in full view. Their actions should give away the game, but they can rest ⑤ **assuring** that your brain processes only small bits of the visual scene. This all helps to ⑥ **explain about** the prevalence of traffic accidents in ⑦ **which** drivers hit pedestrians in plain view, or collide with cars directly in front of them. In many of these cases, the eyes are pointed in the right direction, but the brain isn't seeing what's really out there.

기호	어색한 표현		올바른 표현
( )	_____	⇒	_____
( )	_____	⇒	_____
( )	_____	⇒	_____

64. [18]**밑줄 부분 중 어법, 혹은 문맥상 어휘의 쓰임이 어색한 것을 올바르게 고쳐 쓰시오. (4개)** [37.]

Buying a television is current consumption. It makes us ① **happily** today but does nothing to make us richer tomorrow. Yes, money ② **is spent** on a television keeps workers employed at the television factory. But if the same money ③ **is** invested, it would create jobs somewhere else, say for scientists in a laboratory or workers on a construction site, while also making us richer in the long run. Think about college as an example. Sending students to college ④ **create** jobs for professors. Using the same money to buy fancy sports cars for high school graduates would create jobs for auto workers. The crucial difference between these scenarios ⑤ **is** that a college education makes a young person more productive for the rest of his or her life; a sports car does not. Thus, college tuition is an investment; buying a sports car is consumption.

기호	어색한 표현		올바른 표현
( )	_____	⇨	_____
( )	_____	⇨	_____
( )	_____	⇨	_____
( )	_____	⇨	_____

65. [19]**밑줄 부분 중 어법, 혹은 문맥상 어휘의 쓰임이 어색한 것을 올바르게 고쳐 쓰시오. (1개)** [38.]

The Net differs from most of the mass media it replaces in an obvious and very important way: it's bidirectional. We can send messages through the network as well as receive them, ① **that** has made the system all the more ② **useful**. The ability to exchange information online, to upload as well as download, ③ **has** turned the Net into a thoroughfare for business and commerce. With a few clicks, people can search virtual catalogues, place orders, track shipments, and update information in ④ **corporate** databases. But the Net doesn't just connect us with businesses; it connects us with one another. It's a personal

broadcasting ⑤ **medium** as well as a commercial one. Millions of people use ⑥ **it** to distribute their own digital creations, in the form of blogs, videos, photos, songs, and podcasts, as well as to critique, edit, or otherwise modify the creations of others.

기호	어색한 표현		올바른 표현
( )	_____	⇨	_____

66. [20]**밑줄 부분 중 어법, 혹은 문맥상 어휘의 쓰임이 어색한 것을 올바르게 고쳐 쓰시오. (7개)** [39.]

Imagine that seven out of ten working Americans got fired tomorrow. What would they all do? It's hard to believe you'd have an economy at all if you gave pink slips to more than half the labor force. But that is what the industrial ① **evolution** did to the workforce of the early 19th century. Two hundred years ago, 70 percent of American workers lived on the farm. Today ② **anatomy** has ③ **been eliminated** all but 1 percent of their jobs, replacing ④ **themselves** with machines. But the displaced workers did not sit ⑤ **ideal**. Instead, automation created hundreds of millions of jobs in entirely new fields. Those who once farmed were now manning the factories that manufactured farm equipment, cars, and other industrial products. Since then, wave upon wave of new occupations have ⑥ **been arrived** — ⑦ **applicants** repair person, food chemist, photographer, web designer — each building on previous automation. Today, the vast majority of us are doing jobs that no farmer from the 1800s could have imagined.

기호	어색한 표현		올바른 표현
( )	_____	⇨	_____
( )	_____	⇨	_____
( )	_____	⇨	_____
( )	_____	⇨	_____
( )	_____	⇨	_____
( )	_____	⇨	_____
( )	_____	⇨	_____

67. 21)밑줄 부분 중 어법, 혹은 문맥상 어휘의 쓰임이 어색한 것을 올바르게 고쳐 쓰시오. (3개) 40.

Many things spark envy : ownership, status, health, youth, talent, popularity, beauty. It is often ① **confused** with jealousy because the ② **psychological** reactions are ③ **identical**. The difference: the subject of envy is a thing (status, money, health etc.). The subject of jealousy is the behaviour of a third person. Envy needs two people. Jealousy, on the other hand, requires three: Peter is jealous of Sam because the beautiful girl next door rings him instead. Paradoxically, with envy we ④ **indirect** resentments toward those who are most ⑤ **similar** to us in age, career and residence. We don't envy businesspeople from the century before last. We don't envy millionaires on the other side of the globe. As a writer, I don't envy musicians, managers or dentists, but other writers. As a CEO you envy other, bigger CEOs. As a supermodel you envy more ⑥ **successibe** supermodels. Aristotle knew this: 'Potters envy potters'.

기호	어색한 표현		올바른 표현
( )	＿＿＿＿＿＿	⇨	＿＿＿＿＿＿
( )	＿＿＿＿＿＿	⇨	＿＿＿＿＿＿
( )	＿＿＿＿＿＿	⇨	＿＿＿＿＿＿

68. 22)밑줄 부분 중 어법, 혹은 문맥상 어휘의 쓰임이 어색한 것을 올바르게 고쳐 쓰시오. (10개)
41~42.

We have biases that support our biases! If we're ① **impartial** to one option — perhaps because it's more memorable, or ② **framing** to minimize loss, or seemingly consistent with a ③ **promising** pattern — we tend to search for information that will justify choosing that option. On the one hand, it's ④ **sensitive** to make choices that we can defend with data and a list of reasons. On the

other hand, if we're not careful, we're likely to conduct an ⑤ **balanced** analysis, falling prey to a cluster of errors collectively known ⑥ **to** "confirmation biases".

For example, nearly all companies include classic "tell me about yourself" job interviews as part of the hiring process, and many rely on these interviews ⑦ **lonely** to evaluate ⑧ **appliances**. But it turns out that traditional interviews are actually one of the least useful tools for predicting an employee's future success. This is ⑨ **why** interviewers often subconsciously make up their minds about interviewees based on their first few moments of interaction and spend the rest of the interview cherry-picking evidence and phrasing their questions to ⑩ **confirm** that initial impression: "I see here you left a good position at your previous job. You must be pretty ambitious, right"? versus "You must not have been very committed, huh"? This means that interviewers can be prone to ⑪ **overlooking** significant information that would clearly indicate whether this candidate was actually the best person to hire. More structured approaches, like obtaining samples of a candidate's work or asking how he would respond to difficult hypothetical situations, ⑫ **being** dramatically better at ⑬ **assessment** future success, with a nearly threefold advantage over traditional interviews.

기호	어색한 표현		올바른 표현
( )	＿＿＿＿＿＿	⇨	＿＿＿＿＿＿
( )	＿＿＿＿＿＿	⇨	＿＿＿＿＿＿
( )	＿＿＿＿＿＿	⇨	＿＿＿＿＿＿
( )	＿＿＿＿＿＿	⇨	＿＿＿＿＿＿
( )	＿＿＿＿＿＿	⇨	＿＿＿＿＿＿
( )	＿＿＿＿＿＿	⇨	＿＿＿＿＿＿
( )	＿＿＿＿＿＿	⇨	＿＿＿＿＿＿
( )	＿＿＿＿＿＿	⇨	＿＿＿＿＿＿
( )	＿＿＿＿＿＿	⇨	＿＿＿＿＿＿
( )	＿＿＿＿＿＿	⇨	＿＿＿＿＿＿

69. ²³⁾**밑줄 부분 중 어법, 혹은 문맥상 어휘의 쓰임이 어색한 것을 올바르게 고쳐 쓰시오. (4개)**

43~45.

On Saturday morning, Todd and his 5-year-old daughter Ava walked out of the store with the groceries they ① **had** just purchased. As they pushed their grocery cart through the parking lot, they saw a red car ② **to pull** into the space next to their pick-up truck. A young man named Greg was driving. "That's a cool car", Ava said to her dad. He agreed and looked at Greg, who finished ③ **to park** and opened his door. As Todd finished loading his groceries, Greg's door ④ **remained** open. Todd noticed Greg didn't get out of his car. But he was pulling something from his car. He put a metal frame on the ground beside his door. ⑤ **Remaining** in the driver's seat, he then reached back into his car to grab something else. Todd realized ⑥ **that** he was doing and considered whether he should try to help him. After a moment, he decided to ⑦ **approach** Greg. By this time, Greg had already pulled one thin wheel out of his car and attached ⑧ **them** to the frame. He was now pulling a second wheel out when he looked up and saw Todd standing near him. Todd said, "Hi there! Have a great weekend"! Greg seemed a bit surprised, but replied by wishing him a great weekend too. Then Greg added, "Thanks for letting me ⑨ **have** my independence". "Of course", Todd said. After Todd and Ava climbed into their truck, Ava became curious. So she asked ⑩ **why** he didn't offer to help the man with his wheelchair. Todd said, "Why do you insist on brushing your teeth without my help"? She answered, "Because I know how to"! He said, "And the man knows how to put together his wheelchair". Ava understood that sometimes the best way to help someone is to not help at all.

기호	어색한 표현		올바른 표현
( )	_____	⇨	_____
( )	_____	⇨	_____
( )	_____	⇨	_____
( )	_____	⇨	_____

2024 고2 6월 모의고사

❶ voca   ❷ text   ❸ [/]   ❹ _____   ❺ quiz 1   ❻ quiz 2   ❼ quiz 3   ❽ quiz 4   ❾ quiz 5

☑ 다음 글을 읽고 물음에 답하시오. (18)

Dear Residents, My name is Kari Patterson, and I'm the manager of the River View Apartments. It's time to ^{~을 이용하다, 3단어} _____ the sunny weather to make our community more beautiful. On Saturday, July 13 at 9 a.m., residents will meet in the north parking lot. We will divide into teams to plant flowers and small trees, pull weeds, and put colorful ^{장식} _____ on the ^{잔디밭} _____. ⓐ Please join us for this year's Gardening Day, and remember no special skills or tools required. Last year, we had a great time working together, so coming out and make this year's event even better! Warm regards, Kari Patterson

1. 1)힌트를 참고하여 각 빈칸에 알맞은 단어를 쓰시오.

2. 2)밑줄 친 ⓐ에서, 어법 혹은 문맥상 어색한 부분을 찾아 올바르게 고쳐 쓰시오.

   ⓐ   잘못된 표현   바른 표현

   (   ) ⇨ (   )

   (   ) ⇨ (   )

☑ 다음 글을 읽고 물음에 답하시오. (19.)

It was the championship race. Emma was the final runner on her relay team. She ^{초조하게} _____ waited in her spot for her teammate to pass her the baton. Emma wasn't sure she could perform her role without making a mistake. Her hands shook as she thought, "What if I drop the baton"? She felt her heart rate increasing as her teammate approached. ⓐ But as she started running, she received the baton smooth. In the final 10 meters, she passed two other runners and crossed the finish line in first place! She rose her hands in the air, and a huge smile came across her face. As her teammates hugged her, she shouted, "We did it"! All of her hard training had been worthy it.

3. 3)힌트를 참고하여 각 빈칸에 알맞은 단어를 쓰시오.

4. 4)밑줄 친 ⓐ에서, 어법 혹은 문맥상 어색한 부분을 찾아 올바르게 고쳐 쓰시오.

   ⓐ   잘못된 표현   바른 표현

   (   ) ⇨ (   )

   (   ) ⇨ (   )

   (   ) ⇨ (   )

☑ **다음 글을 읽고 물음에 답하시오.** (20.)

Most people resist the idea of a true self-estimate, probably because they fear it might mean ᴺᴬᴷᶜʰᵘᵈᵃ낮추다 _____ some of their beliefs about who they are and what they're capable of. As Goethe's maxim goes, it is a great failing "to see yourself as more than you are". How could you really ᶜᵒⁿˢⁱᵈᵉʳ의 바른 형태 _____ self-aware if you refuse to consider your weaknesses? Don't fear self-assessment because you're worried you might have to admit some things about yourself. The second half of Goethe's maxim is important too. ⓐ <u>He states that it is equally damaging to "value you at more than your true worth". We overestimate our capabilities just as much and just as dangerously as we underestimate other abilities. Cultivating the ability to judge yourself accurately and honestly.</u> (가) 네가 할 수 있는 것과 너의 잠재력을 열기 위해 필요한 것을 파악하기 위해 내면을 들여다 봐라.

5. ⁵⁾힌트를 참고하여 각 <u>빈칸에 알맞은</u> 단어를 쓰시오.

6. ⁶⁾밑줄 친 ⓐ에서, 어법 혹은 문맥상 어색한 부분을 찾아 올바르게 고쳐 쓰시오.

ⓐ	잘못된 표현		바른 표현
(	)	⇨ (	)
(	)	⇨ (	)
(	)	⇨ (	)
(	)	⇨ (	)
(	)	⇨ (	)

7. ⁷⁾위 글에 주어진 (가)의 한글과 같은 의미를 가지도록, 각각의 주어진 단어들을 알맞게 배열하시오.

(가) to / capable / unlock / you're / take / it / what / discern / that / will / and / to / of / inward / potential. / Look / what

☑ **다음 글을 읽고 물음에 답하시오.** (21.)

Take a look at some of the most powerful, rich, and famous people in the world. (가) 그들의 성공의 장식과 그들이 살 수 있는 것을 무시해라. ⓐ <u>Look instead at that they're forced to trade in return — look at that success has cost it. Mostly? Freedom. Their work demands they wear a suit. Their success depends on attending certain parties, kissing up to people they don't like. It will require — evitably — realizing they are unable to say they they actually think.</u> Worse, it demands that they become a different type of person or do bad things. Sure, it might pay well — but they haven't truly examined the ᵍᵉⁿᵃ거래 _____. As Seneca put it, "Slavery resides under marble and gold". Too many successful people are prisoners in jails of their own making. Is that what you want? Is that what you're working hard toward? Let's hope not.

8. ⁸⁾힌트를 참고하여 각 빈칸에 알맞은 단어를 쓰시오.

9. ⁹⁾밑줄 친 ⓐ에서, 어법 혹은 문맥상 어색한 부분을 찾아 올바르게 고쳐 쓰시오.

ⓐ	잘못된 표현	바른 표현
(	) ⇨ (	)
(	) ⇨ (	)
(	) ⇨ (	)
(	) ⇨ (	)
(	) ⇨ (	)

10. ¹⁰⁾위 글에 주어진 (가)의 한글과 같은 의미를 가지도록, 각각의 주어진 단어들을 알맞게 배열하시오.

(가) Ignore / the trappings / to buy. / and what / success / able / their / of / they're

☑ 다음 글을 읽고 물음에 답하시오. ⁽²²·⁾

ⓐ If a firm is going to save the government, it might be easier to concentrate on lobbying the government for more money rather than take the harder decision of restructuring the company to be able to be profitable and viable in the long term. This is an example of something known as moral hazard — when government support alters the decisions firms taking. For example, if governments rescue banks who get into difficulty, as they did during the credit crisis of 2007-08, this could encourage banks to take greater risks in the future because they know there is a possibility that governments will ᵏ끼어들다 _____ if they lose money. (가) 정부의 구제는 좋은 의도일지라도, 그것은 은행의 행동에 부정적으로 영향을 미쳐, 위험하고 형편없는 의사 결정을 조장할 수 있다.

11. ¹¹⁾힌트를 참고하여 각 빈칸에 알맞은 단어를 쓰시오.

12. ¹²⁾밑줄 친 ⓐ에서, 어법 혹은 문맥상 어색한 부분을 찾아 올바르게 고쳐 쓰시오.

ⓐ	잘못된 표현	바른 표현
(	) ⇨ (	)
(	) ⇨ (	)
(	) ⇨ (	)

13. ¹³⁾위 글에 주어진 (가)의 한글과 같은 의미를 가지도록, 각각의 주어진 단어들을 알맞게 배열하시오.

(가) be / Although / can negatively / the government / and poor / well intended, / affect / of banks, / may / risky / rescue / encouraging / the behavior / decision making. / it

☑ **다음 글을 읽고 물음에 답하시오.** (23)

If there is little or no ^{다양성} _____ of views, and all scientists see, think, and question the world in a similar way, then (가) <u>그러면 그들은, 하나의 공동체로서, 자신들이 주장하는 것만큼, 혹은 적어도 그렇게 되기를 열망하는 것만큼, 객관적이지 않을 것이다</u> The solution is that there should be far greater diversity in the practice of science: in gender, ethnicity, and social and cultural backgrounds. Science works because it is carried out by people who pursue their ^{호기심} _____ about the natural world and test their and each other's ideas from as many varied ^{관점} _____ and angles as possible. When science is done by a diverse group of people, and if ^{의견 일치} _____ builds up about a particular area of scientific knowledge, then we can have more ^{자신감} _____ in its ^{객관성} _____ and truth.

14. 14)힌트를 참고하여 각 <u>빈칸에</u> 알맞은 단어를 쓰시오.

15. 15)위 글에 주어진 (가)의 한글과 같은 의미를 가지도록, 각각의 주어진 단어들을 알맞게 배열하시오.

(가) as / as they / they are, / be / will not, / aspire to / objective / they / as a community, / maintain / or at least / be.

☑ **다음 글을 읽고 물음에 답하시오.** (24.)

ⓐ <u>We tend to break up time into units, such as weeks, months, and seasons; in a series of studies among farmers in India and students in North America, psychologists found that if a deadline is on the other side of a "break" — such as in the New Year — we're less likely to see it as remote, and, as a result, be more ready to jump into action. That you need to do in that situation is find the same way to think about the timeframe.</u> For example, if it's November and the deadline is in January, it's better to tell yourself you have to get it done "this winter" rather than "next year". The best approach is to view deadlines as a ^{도전} _____ that you have to meet within a period that's imminent. (가) <u>그런 식으로 스트레스는 더 잘 관리될 수 있고, 적시에 작업을 시작 — 따라서 마무리 — 할 수 있는 가능성이 높아진다.</u>

16. 16)힌트를 참고하여 각 <u>빈칸에</u> 알맞은 단어를 쓰시오.

17. 17)밑줄 친 ⓐ에서, 어법 혹은 문맥상 어색한 부분을 찾아 올바르게 고쳐 쓰시오.

ⓐ	잘못된 표현		바른 표현
	(	) ⇨ (	)
	(	) ⇨ (	)
	(	) ⇨ (	)
	(	) ⇨ (	)

18. 18)위 글에 주어진 (가)의 한글과 같은 의미를 가지도록, 각각의 주어진 단어들을 알맞게 배열하시오.

(가) in good time. / That / and therefore / more / finishing / chance of / have / manageable, / starting / a better / / way / and you / is / the stress

☑ **다음 글을 읽고 물음에 답하시오.** (25.)

The graph above shows the amount of CO_2 ^{뜻: emissions} ___ per person across selected Asian countries in 2010 and 2020. All the countries except Uzbekistan had a greater amount of CO_2 emissions per person in 2020 than ^{의미하는바: that} _____ in 2010. In 2010, the amount of CO_2 emissions per person of China was the largest among the five countries, followed by that of Mongolia. However, in 2020, Mongolia ^{능가한} _____ China ^{~에 있어서} _____ the amount of CO_2 emissions per person. In 2010, Uzbekistan produced a larger amount of CO_2 emissions per person than Vietnam, while the opposite was true in 2020. Among the five countries, India was the only one where the amount of CO_2 emissions per person was less than 2 tons in 2020..

19. 19)힌트를 참고하여 각 빈칸에 알맞은 단어를 쓰시오.

☑ **다음 글을 읽고 물음에 답하시오.** (26.)

Henry David Thoreau was born in Concord, Massachusetts in 1817. When he was 16, he entered Harvard College. After graduating, Thoreau worked as a schoolteacher but he ^{그만두다} ____ after two weeks. In June of 1838 he set up a school with his brother John. However, he had hopes of becoming a nature poet. In 1845, he moved into a small self-built house near Walden Pond. At Walden, Thoreau did an incredible amount of reading. The journal he wrote there became the source of his most famous book, Walden. ⓐ <u>In his later life, Thoreau traveled the Maine woods, to Cape Cod, and to Canada. At the age of 43, he ended his travels and returned to Concord. Despite his works were not widely read during his lifetime, he never stopped to write, and his works fill 20 volumes.</u>

20. 20)힌트를 참고하여 각 빈칸에 알맞은 단어를 쓰시오.

21. 21)밑줄 친 ⓐ에서, 어법 혹은 문맥상 어색한 부분을 찾아 올바르게 고쳐 쓰시오.

ⓐ	잘못된 표현		바른 표현	
	(	) ⇨ (		)
	(	) ⇨ (		)
	(	) ⇨ (		)

☑ **다음 글을 읽고 물음에 답하시오.** (29)

The ᵍ선천적인 _____ ᵍ능력 _____ for smiling is proven by the remarkable observation that babies who are ᵍ선천적으로 _____ both ᵍ청각장애 _____ and blind, who have never seen a human face, also start to smile at around 2 months. (가) 그러나, 시각장애를 가진 아기의 미소 짓기는 그것을 강화하기 위해 아무것도 행해지지 않으면 결국 사라진다. Without the right feedback, smiling dies out. But here's a fascinating fact: blind babies will continue to smile if they are cuddled, bounced, nudged, and tickled by an adult — (나) 그들이 혼자가 아니며 누군가 그들에게 관심을 갖고 있다는 것을 알게 하는 것 This social feedback ᵍ격려하다 _____ the baby to continue smiling. In this way, early experience operates with our biology to establish social behaviors. In fact, you don't need the cases of blind babies to make the point. Babies with sight smile more at you when you look at them or, better still, smile back at them.

22. ²²⁾힌트를 참고하여 각 <u>빈칸</u>에 알맞은 단어를 쓰시오.

23. ²³⁾위 글에 주어진 (가) ~ (나)의 한글과 같은 의미를 가지도록, 각각의 주어진 단어들을 알맞게 배열하시오.

(가) in blind / if nothing / babies / eventually disappears / to / reinforce it. / smiling / However, / is done

(나) them. / anything / they / that someone / cares about / and / them / know that / are / to let / not alone

☑ **다음 글을 읽고 물음에 답하시오.** (30)

Because people tend to adapt, interrupting positive things with negative ones can actually increase enjoyment. Take ᵍ광고 _____. Most people hate them, so removing them should make shows or other entertainment more enjoyable. But the opposite is true. (가) 쇼는 그것들이 성가신 광고들에 의해 중단될 때 실제로 더 즐거워진다. Because these less enjoyable moments break up adaptation to the positive experience of the show. Think about eating chocolate chips. The first chip is delicious: sweet, melt-in-your-mouth goodness. The second chip is also pretty good. But by the fourth, fifth, or tenth chip in a row, the goodness is no longer as ᵍ즐거운 _____. We adapt. Interspersing positive experiences with less positive ones, however, can slow down ᵍ적응 _____. Eating a Brussels sprout between chocolate chips or viewing commercials between parts of TV shows ᵍ방해하다 _____ the process. (나) 덜 긍정적인 순간은 뒤에 오는 긍정적인 순간을 다시 새롭게 만들어서 더 즐겁게 만든다.

24. ²⁴⁾힌트를 참고하여 각 <u>빈칸</u>에 알맞은 단어를 쓰시오.

25. 25)위 글에 주어진 (가) ~ (나)의 한글과 같은 의미를 가지도록, 각각의 주어진 단어들을 알맞게 배열하시오.

(가) actually / are / enjoyable when / broken up / more / commercials. / they're / by annoying / Shows

(나) moment / new / makes / more / enjoyable. / again / and thus / positive / the following / positive one / The less

☑ **다음 글을 읽고 물음에 답하시오.** (31)

We collect stamps, coins, vintage cars even when they serve no ^{실용적인} _____ purpose. The post office doesn't accept the old stamps, the banks don't take old coins, and the vintage cars are no longer allowed on the road. These are all side issues; the attraction is that they are in short supply. In one study, students were asked to arrange ten posters in order of attractiveness — with the agreement that afterward they could keep one poster as a reward for their participation. Five minutes later, they were told that the poster with the third highest rating was no longer available. Then they were asked to judge all ten from scratch. ⓐ <u>The poster that was no longer available was suddenly classifying as the most beautiful. In psychology, this phenomenon is called reactance: when we deprived of an option, we suddenly deem it less attractive.</u>

26. 26)힌트를 참고하여 각 빈칸에 알맞은 단어를 쓰시오.

27. 27)밑줄 친 ⓐ에서, 어법 혹은 문맥상 어색한 부분을 찾아 올바르게 고쳐 쓰시오.

ⓐ 잘못된 표현		바른 표현
( )	⇨	( )
( )	⇨	( )
( )	⇨	( )

☑ **다음 글을 읽고 물음에 답하시오.** (32)

If we've invested in something that hasn't ^{보답하다} _____ us — be it money in a failing venture, or time in an unhappy relationship — we find it very difficult to walk away. This is the sunk cost ^{오류} _____. (가) 우리의 본능은 결국에는 우리의 투자가 가치 있는 것으로 입증될 것이라고 희망하면서 돈이나 시간에 투자를 계속 하는 것이다. Giving up would mean ^{인정하다} _____ that we've wasted something we can't get back, and that thought is so painful that we prefer to avoid it if we can. ⓐ The problem, of course, is that if something really is a bad bet, then stay with it simply increases the amount we lose. Rather than waking away from a bad five-year relationship, for example, we turn it into a bad 10-year relationship; rather than accepting that we've lost a thousand dollars, we lay down another thousand and lose that too. In the end, by ^{늦추기} _____ the pain of ^{인정하기} _____ our problem, we only add to it. Sometimes we just have to cut our losses.

28. ²⁸⁾힌트를 참고하여 각 빈칸에 알맞은 단어를 쓰시오.

29. ²⁹⁾밑줄 친 ⓐ에서, 어법 혹은 문맥상 어색한 부분을 찾아 올바르게 고쳐 쓰시오.

   ⓐ   잘못된 표현   바른 표현

   (   ) ⇨ (   )

   (   ) ⇨ (   )

   (   ) ⇨ (   )

30. ³⁰⁾위 글에 주어진 (가)의 한글과 같은 의미를 가지도록, 각각의 주어진 단어들을 알맞게 배열하시오.

(가) to / continue investing / hope that / or time / will / in the end. / money / Our instinct is / worthwhile / be / as we / our investment / prove to

☑ **다음 글을 읽고 물음에 답하시오.** (33.)

On our little world, light travels, for all practical purposes, ^{순간적으로} _____. If a light-bulb is glowing, then of course it's physically where we see it, shining away. We reach out our hand and touch it: It's there all right, and ^{불쾌하게} _____ hot. If the filament fails, then the light goes out. We don't see it in the same place, glowing, illuminating the room years after the bulb breaks and it's removed from its socket. ^{바로 그} _____ notion seems ^{말도 안 되는} _____. But if we're far enough away, an entire sun can go out and we'll continue to see it shining brightly; we won't learn of its death, it may be, for ages to come — in fact, for how long it takes light, which travels fast but not infinitely fast, to cross the intervening ^{광대함} _____. (가) 별과 은하까지의 엄청난 거리는 우리가 우주 공간의 모든 것을 과거의 모습으로 보고 있다는 것을 의미한다.

31. 31)힌트를 참고하여 각 빈칸에 알맞은 단어를 쓰시오.

32. 32)위 글에 주어진 (가)의 한글과 같은 의미를 가지도록, 각각의 주어진 단어들을 알맞게 배열하시오.

(가) we / stars / that / and the galaxies / to / in the past. / in / everything / space / The immense distances / the / see / mean

☑ **다음 글을 읽고 물음에 답하시오.** (34.)

(가) 금융 시장은 부자들로부터 자본을 받아 다른 모든 사람들에게 그것을 빌려주는 것 이상을 한다. They enable each of us to smooth consumption over our lifetimes, which is a fancy way of saying that we don't have to spend income at the same time we earn it. Shakespeare may have admonished us to be neither borrowers nor lenders; the fact is that most of us will be both at some point. If we lived in an ^{농경사회} _____, we would have to eat our crops ^{합리적으로} _____ soon after the harvest or find some way to store them. Financial markets are a more ^{정교한} _____ way of managing the harvest. We can spend income now that we have not yet earned — as by borrowing for college or a home — or we can earn income now and spend it later, as by saving for retirement. (나) 중요한 점은 소득을 버는 것이 그것을 소비하는 것과 분리되어 있다는 것이고, 이는 우리에게 삶에서 훨씬 더 많은 유연성을 허용해준다.

33. 33)힌트를 참고하여 각 빈칸에 알맞은 단어를 쓰시오.

34. 34)위 글에 주어진 (가) ~ (나)의 한글과 같은 의미를 가지도록, 각각의 주어진 단어들을 알맞게 배열하시오.

(가) and / to / else. / Financial / markets / do more / from / capital / lend it / than take / the rich / everyone

(나) has been / divorced from / earning / The important point / that / is / more / spending it, / allowing / income / us much / flexibility / in life.

☑ **다음 글을 읽고 물음에 답하시오.** (35.)

As the old joke goes: "Software, free. User manual, $10,000". But it's no joke. A couple of high-profile companies make their living selling instruction and paid support for free software. The copy of code, being mere bits, is free. The lines of free code become ^{가치있는} _____ to you only through support and ^{안내} _____. A lot of medical and ^{유전의} _____ information will go this route in the coming decades. Right now getting a full copy of all your DNA is very expensive ($10,000), but soon it won't be. The price is dropping so fast, it will be $100 soon, and then the next year ^{보험} _____ companies will offer to sequence you for free. ⓐ <u>That a copy of your sequence costs nothing, the interpretation of that it means, that you can do about it, and what to use it —the manual for your genes— will be expensive.</u>

35. 35)힌트를 참고하여 각 <u>빈칸에 알맞은</u> 단어를 쓰시오.

36. 36)밑줄 친 ⓐ에서, 어법 혹은 문맥상 어색한 부분을 찾아 올바르게 고쳐 쓰시오.

ⓐ 　　　　잘못된 표현　　　　　　　바른 표현
(　　　　　　　) ⇨ (　　　　　　　)
(　　　　　　　) ⇨ (　　　　　　　)
(　　　　　　　) ⇨ (　　　　　　　)
(　　　　　　　) ⇨ (　　　　　　　)

☑ **다음 글을 읽고 물음에 답하시오.** (36.)

Brains are expensive in terms of energy. Twenty percent of the calories we consume are used to power the brain. So brains try to ^{작동하다} _____ in the most energy-efficient way possible, and that means processing only the minimum amount of information from our senses that we need to ^{항해하다} _____ the world. Neuroscientists weren't the first to discover that fixing your ^{시선} ____ on something is no guarantee of seeing it. Magicians figured this out long ago. By directing your attention, they perform tricks with their hands in full view. Their actions should give away the game, but they can rest assured that your brain processes only small bits of the visual scene. (가) <u>이 모든 것은 운전자가 명백한 시야에 있는 보행자들을 치거나, 바로 앞에 있는 차량들과 충돌하는 교통사고의 빈번함을 설명하는 데 도움이 된다.</u> In many of these cases, the eyes are pointed in the right direction, but the brain isn't seeing what's really out there.

37. 37)힌트를 참고하여 각 <u>빈칸에 알맞은</u> 단어를 쓰시오.

38. 38)위 글에 주어진 (가)의 한글과 같은 의미를 가지도록, 각각의 주어진 단어들을 알맞게 배열하시오.

(가) in plain view, / pedestrians / directly in front / to explain / the prevalence / of / collide / This / all helps / them. / of traffic / with cars / or / which / accidents in / drivers hit

☑ **다음 글을 읽고 물음에 답하시오.** (37.)

Buying a television is current ^{소비}_____. It makes us happy today but does nothing to make us richer tomorrow. Yes, money spent on a television keeps workers employed at the television factory. But if the same money were invested, it would create jobs somewhere else, say for scientists in a laboratory or workers on a construction site, while also making us richer in the long run. Think about college as an example. ⓐ Send students to college creates jobs for professors. Use the same money to buy fancy sports cars for high school graduates would create jobs for auto workers. The crucial difference between these scenarios are that a college education makes a young person less productive for the rest of his or her life; a sports car is not. Thus, college tuition is an consumption; buying a sports car is investment.

39. 39)힌트를 참고하여 각 빈칸에 알맞은 단어를 쓰시오.

40. 40)밑줄 친 ⓐ에서, 어법 혹은 문맥상 어색한 부분을 찾아 올바르게 고쳐 쓰시오.

ⓐ	잘못된 표현		바른 표현
	( )	⇨ (	)
	( )	⇨ (	)
	( )	⇨ (	)
	( )	⇨ (	)
	( )	⇨ (	)
	( )	⇨ (	)
	( )	⇨ (	)

☑ **다음 글을 읽고 물음에 답하시오.** (38.)

The Net differs from most of the mass media it replaces in an obvious and very important way: it's ^{두 방향으로} _____. (가) <u>우리는 네트워크를 통해 메시지들을 받을 수 있을 뿐만 아니라 그것들을 보낼 수도 있는데, 이것은 그 시스템을 훨씬 더 유용하게 만들었다.</u> The ability to ^{교환하다} _____ information online, to upload as well as download, has turned the Net into a thoroughfare for business and commerce. With a few clicks, people can search ^{가상의} _____ catalogues, place orders, track shipments, and update information in corporate databases. But the Net doesn't just connect us with businesses; it connects us with one another. It's a personal broadcasting medium as well as a commercial one. Millions of people use it to ^{배포하다} _____ their own digital creations, in the form of blogs, videos, photos, songs, and podcasts, as well as to critique, edit, or ^{그렇지 않으면} _____ ^{수정하다} _____ the creations of others.

41. ⁴¹⁾힌트를 참고하여 각 <u>빈칸에 알맞은</u> 단어를 쓰시오.

42. ⁴²⁾위 글에 주어진 (가)의 한글과 같은 의미를 가지도록, 각각의 주어진 단어들을 알맞게 배열하시오.

(가) We / well as / receive / all / through the / send messages / which / the system / as / network / them, / useful. / made / has / the more / can

☑ **다음 글을 읽고 물음에 답하시오.** (39.)

Imagine that seven out of ten working Americans got fired tomorrow. What would they all do? (가) <u>노동력의 절반 이상에게 해고 통지서를 보낸다면 경제가 유지될 것이라고 믿기 어려울 것이다.</u> But that is what the industrial revolution did to the workforce of the early 19th century. Two hundred years ago, 70 percent of American workers lived on the farm. Today ^{자동화} _____ has eliminated all but 1 percent of their jobs, replacing them with machines. But the ^{대체된} _____ workers did not sit ^{놀고 있는} _____. Instead, automation created hundreds of millions of jobs in entirely new fields. Those who once farmed were now manning the factories that manufactured farm equipment, cars, and other industrial products. Since then, wave upon wave of new occupations have arrived — appliance repair person, food chemist, photographer, web designer — each building on previous automation. Today, (나) <u>우리 중 대다수는 1800년대의 농부들은 상상도 할 수 없었던 일을 하고 있다.</u>

43. ⁴³⁾힌트를 참고하여 각 <u>빈칸에 알맞은</u> 단어를 쓰시오.

44. 44)위 글에 주어진 (가) ~ (나)의 한글과 같은 의미를 가지도록, 각각의 주어진 단어들을 알맞게 배열하시오.

(가) than / you'd / pink / half the labor / have an economy / force. / believe / at all / to more / slips / if / It's / you gave / hard to

(나) no farmer / could / the vast / imagined. / majority / the 1800s / jobs / from / have / that / us / doing / of / are

☑ **다음 글을 읽고 물음에 답하시오.** (40.)

Many things spark 부러움 _____ : ownership, status, health, youth, talent, popularity, beauty. ⓐ <u>It is often confusing with jealousy because the physical reactions are different. The difference: the subject of envy is a thing (status, money, health etc.). The subject of envy is the behaviour of a third person. Jealousy needs two people.</u> Jealousy, on the other hand, requires three: Peter is jealous of Sam because the beautiful girl next door rings him instead. 역설적이게도 _____, with envy we direct 불쾌감 _____ toward those who are most similar to us in age, career and residence. We don't envy businesspeople from the century before last. We don't envy millionaires on the other side of the globe. As a writer, I don't envy musicians, managers or dentists, but other writers. As a CEO you envy other, bigger CEOs. As a supermodel you envy more successful supermodels. Aristotle knew this: 'Potters envy potters'.

45. 45)힌트를 참고하여 각 빈칸에 알맞은 단어를 쓰시오.

46. 46)밑줄 친 ⓐ에서, 어법 혹은 문맥상 어색한 부분을 찾아 올바르게 고쳐 쓰시오.

ⓐ	잘못된 표현		바른 표현
(	)	⇨ (	)
(	)	⇨ (	)
(	)	⇨ (	)
(	)	⇨ (	)

☑ **다음 글을 읽고 물음에 답하시오.** (41~42.)

We have biases that support our biases! If we're ^{편향된}_____ to one option — perhaps because it's more memorable, or framed to minimize loss, or seemingly ^{한결같은}_____ with a ^{유망한}_____ pattern — we tend to search for information that will ^{정당화하다}_____ choosing that option. On the one hand, it's sensible to make choices that we can defend with data and a list of reasons. ⓐ On the other hand, if we're not careful, we're likely to conduct an balanced analysis, falling prey to a cluster of errors collective known as "confirmation biases". For example, nearly all companies include classic "tell me about yourself" job interviews as part of the hiring process, and many rely on these interviews alone to evaluate applicants. But (가) 전통적인 면접은 실제로 직원의 미래 성공을 예측하는 데 가장 유용하지 않은 도구 중 하나라는 것으로 판명된다. This is because interviewers often ^{잠재의식적으로}_____ make up their minds about interviewees based on their first few moments of interaction and spend the rest of the interview cherry-picking evidence and phrasing their questions to confirm that ^{처음의}_____ impression: "I see here you left a good position at your previous job. You must be pretty ^{야망있는}_____, right"? versus "You must not have been very committed, huh"? This means that (나) 면접관이 이 지원자가 실제로 채용하기에 가장 좋은 사람인지 여부를 명확하게 보여줄 수 있는 중요한 정보를 간과하기 쉽다. More structured approaches, like obtaining samples of a candidate's work or asking how he would respond to difficult ^{가정적인}_____ situations, are dramatically better at assessing future success, with a nearly threefold advantage over traditional interviews.

47. ⁴⁷⁾힌트를 참고하여 각 빈칸에 알맞은 단어를 쓰시오.

48. ⁴⁸⁾밑줄 친 ⓐ에서, 어법 혹은 문맥상 어색한 부분을 찾아 올바르게 고쳐 쓰시오.

　　ⓐ　　　　잘못된 표현　　　　　　　　바른 표현

　　　(　　　　　　　　) ⇨ (　　　　　　　　)

　　　(　　　　　　　　) ⇨ (　　　　　　　　)

49. ⁴⁹⁾위 글에 주어진 (가) ~ (나)의 한글과 같은 의미를 가지도록, 각각의 주어진 단어들을 알맞게 배열하시오.

(가) an employee's / one of / it / for / that traditional / success. / future / useful / the least / are actually / predicting / tools / turns out / interviews

(나) this candidate / can be / prone to / whether / interviewers / information that / the best / was / clearly indicate / to hire. / actually / person / would / overlooking / significant

☑ 다음 글을 읽고 물음에 답하시오. ^(43~45.)

On Saturday morning, Todd and his 5-year-old daughter Ava walked out of the store with the ^{식료품} _____ they had just purchased. As they pushed their grocery cart through the parking lot, they saw a red car pulling into the space next to their pick-up truck. A young man named Greg was driving. "That's a cool car", Ava said to her dad. He agreed and looked at Greg, who finished parking and opened his door. As Todd finished loading his groceries, ⓐ <u>Greg's door remained opened. Todd noticed Greg didn't get out of his car. But he was pulling something from his car. He put a metal frame on the ground beside his door. Remained in the driver's seat, he then reached back into his car to grab something else.</u> (가)<u>Todd는 그가 무엇을 하고 있는지를 깨닫고 그가 그를 도와야 할지를 생각했다.</u> After a moment, he decided to approach Greg. By this time, Greg had already pulled one thin wheel out of his car and attached it to the frame. He was now pulling a second wheel out when he looked up and saw Todd standing near him. Todd said, "Hi there! Have a great weekend"! Greg seemed a bit surprised, but replied by wishing him a great weekend too. Then Greg added, "Thanks for letting me have my ^{독립성} _____". "Of course", Todd said. After Todd and Ava climbed into their truck, Ava became ^{궁금해하는} _____. So she asked why he didn't offer to help the man with his wheelchair. Todd said, "Why do you insist on brushing your teeth without my help"? She answered, "Because I know how to"! He said, "And the man knows how to put together his wheelchair". Ava understood that sometimes the best way to help someone is to not help at all.

50. ⁵⁰⁾힌트를 참고하여 각 빈칸에 알맞은 단어를 쓰시오.

51. ⁵¹⁾밑줄 친 ⓐ에서, 어법 혹은 문맥상 어색한 부분을 찾아 올바르게 고쳐 쓰시오.

　　ⓐ　　　잘못된 표현　　　　　　바른 표현

　　(　　　　　　　) ⇨ (　　　　　　　　　)

　　(　　　　　　　) ⇨ (　　　　　　　　　)

52. ⁵²⁾위 글에 주어진 (가)의 한글과 같은 의미를 가지도록, 각각의 주어진 단어들을 알맞게 배열하시오.

(가) him. / doing / to help / Todd / what he / whether / he should / and considered / try / was / realized

정답

WORK BOOK

2024년 고2 6월 모의고사 내신대비용 WorkBook & 변형문제

Prac 1 **Answers**

1) to make
2) meet
3) put
4) remember
5) make
6) to pass
7) making
8) smoothly
9) other
10) crossed
11) because
12) what
13) yourself
14) be considered
15) because
16) damaging
17) other
18) accurately
19) honestly
20) what
21) Take
22) what
23) what
24) to trade
25) them
26) attending
27) require
28) what
29) that
30) examined
31) resides
32) successful
33) be saved
34) lobbying
35) restructuring
36) moral
37) take
38) did
39) to take
40) intervene
41) negatively
42) encouraging
43) little
44) objective
45) aspire
46) greater
47) is carried out
48) test
49) varied
50) builds
51) objectivity
52) break
53) that
54) more
55) less
56) What
57) another
58) meet
59) imminent

60) starting
61) finishing
62) selected
63) followed
64) surpassed
65) opposite
66) where
67) was born
68) becoming
69) near
70) returned
71) during
72) writing
73) is proven
74) that
75) disappears
76) it
77) are
78) know
79) encourages
80) social
81) with
82) positive
83) negative
84) them
85) more
86) true
87) annoying
88) less
89) break
90) pleasurable
91) less
92) disrupts
93) more
94) practical
95) allowed
96) that
97) were asked
98) reward
99) were told
100) were asked
101) classified
102) is called
103) suddenly
104) more
105) that
106) to walk
107) instinct
108) prove
109) acknowledging
110) avoid
111) it
112) from
113) another
114) delaying
115) where
116) touch
117) unpleasantly
118) removed
119) nonsensical
120) far enough
121) which
122) immense

123) everything
124) it
125) to smooth
126) don't
127) neither
128) lived
129) reasonably
130) them
131) more
132) it
133) that
134) allowing
135) paid
136) mere
137) become
138) getting
139) dropping
140) nothing
141) expensive
142) are
143) to operate
144) minimum
145) navigate
146) that
147) this out
148) assured
149) in which
150) directly
151) what's
152) current
153) employed
154) were invested
155) making
156) creates
157) crucial
158) more
159) tuition
160) obvious
161) bidirectional
162) receive
163) which
164) exchange
165) a few
166) update
167) personal
168) it
169) modify
170) got fired
171) what
172) did
173) has eliminated
174) replacing
175) displaced
176) entirely
177) that
178) have
179) confused
180) needs
181) requires
182) because
183) similar
184) the other
185) other

186) successful
187) partial
188) because
189) that
190) sensible
191) imbalanced
192) nearly
193) tools
194) because
195) phrasing
196) confirm
197) overlooking
198) asking
199) are
200) had
201) opened
202) beside
203) what
204) approach
205) it
206) pulling
207) replied
208) have
209) curious
210) brushing

Prac 1 **Answers**

1) to make
2) meet
3) put
4) remember
5) make
6) to pass
7) making
8) smoothly
9) other
10) crossed
11) because
12) what
13) yourself
14) be considered
15) because
16) damaging
17) other
18) accurately
19) honestly
20) what
21) Take
22) what
23) what
24) to trade
25) them
26) attending
27) require
28) what
29) that
30) examined
31) resides
32) successful
33) be saved
34) lobbying
35) restructuring
36) moral
37) take
38) did
39) to take
40) intervene
41) negatively
42) encouraging
43) little
44) objective
45) aspire
46) greater
47) is carried out
48) test
49) varied
50) builds
51) objectivity
52) break
53) that
54) more
55) less
56) What
57) another
58) meet
59) imminent

60) starting
61) finishing
62) selected
63) followed
64) surpassed
65) opposite
66) where
67) was born
68) becoming
69) near
70) returned
71) during
72) writing
73) is proven
74) that
75) disappears
76) it
77) are
78) know
79) encourages
80) social
81) with
82) positive
83) negative
84) them
85) more
86) true
87) annoying
88) less
89) break
90) pleasurable
91) less
92) disrupts
93) more
94) practical
95) allowed
96) that
97) were asked
98) reward
99) were told
100) were asked
101) classified
102) is called
103) suddenly
104) more
105) that
106) to walk
107) instinct
108) prove
109) acknowledging
110) avoid
111) it
112) from
113) another
114) delaying
115) where
116) touch
117) unpleasantly
118) removed
119) nonsensical
120) far enough
121) which
122) immense

123) everything
124) it
125) to smooth
126) don't
127) neither
128) lived
129) reasonably
130) them
131) more
132) it
133) that
134) allowing
135) paid
136) mere
137) become
138) getting
139) dropping
140) nothing
141) expensive
142) are
143) to operate
144) minimum
145) navigate
146) that
147) this out
148) assured
149) in which
150) directly
151) what's
152) current
153) employed
154) were invested
155) making
156) creates
157) crucial
158) more
159) tuition
160) obvious
161) bidirectional
162) receive
163) which
164) exchange
165) a few
166) update
167) personal
168) it
169) modify
170) got fired
171) what
172) did
173) has eliminated
174) replacing
175) displaced
176) entirely
177) that
178) have
179) confused
180) needs
181) requires
182) because
183) similar
184) the other
185) other

186) successful
187) partial
188) because
189) that
190) sensible
191) imbalanced
192) nearly
193) tools
194) because
195) phrasing
196) confirm
197) overlooking
198) asking
199) are
200) had
201) opened
202) beside
203) what
204) approach
205) it
206) pulling
207) replied
208) have
209) curious
210) brushing

Prac 2 **Answers**

1) advantage
2) residents
3) required
4) anxiously
5) baton
6) perform
7) approached
8) worth
9) self-estimate
10) downgrading
11) beliefs
12) self-aware
13) weaknesses
14) self-assessment
15) maxim
16) damaging
17) less
18) underestimate
19) overestimate
20) Cultivate
21) judge
22) discern
23) potential
24) most
25) trappings
26) forced
27) cost
28) Mostly?
29) demands
30) attending
31) inevitably
32) Worse,
33) pay

34) examined
35) resides
36) saved
37) easier
38) restructuring
39) profitable
40) viable
41) alters
42) take.
43) possibility
44) intervene
45) intended,
46) risky
47) diversity
48) objective
49) least
50) diversity
51) ethnicity,
52) carried
53) varied
54) angles
55) done
56) consensus
57) objectivity
58) among
59) psychologists
60) deadline
61) likely
62) less
63) timeframe.
64) done
65) approach
66) view
67) period
68) imminent.
69) manageable,
70) above
71) emissions
72) across
73) greater
74) largest
75) surpassed
76) larger
77) opposite
78) less
79) graduating,
80) worked
81) quit
82) poet.
83) moved
84) reading.
85) wrote
86) later
87) traveled
88) ended
89) returned
90) widely
91) stopped
92) fill
93) capacity
94) proven
95) remarkable
96) congenitally

97) around
98) smiling
99) nothing
100) fascinating
101) let
102) smiling.
103) operates
104) biology
105) better
106) adapt
107) commercials
108) removing
109) opposite
110) broken
111) annoying
112) less
113) longer
114) pleasurable.
115) Interspersing
116) less
117) disrupts
118) following
119) thus
120) even
121) serve
122) accept
123) allowed
124) side
125) supply.
126) arrange
127) attractiveness
128) highest
129) scratch
130) classified
131) psychology
132) phenomenon
133) deprived
134) deem
135) invested
136) failing
137) sunk
138) investing
139) prove
140) worthwhile
141) Giving
142) acknowledging
143) prefer
144) bet,
145) lost
146) lay
147) delaying
148) admitting
149) travels
150) instantaneously
151) reach
152) unpleasantly
153) filament
154) breaks
155) removed
156) nonsensical
157) won't
158) infinitely
159) intervening

160) vastness.
161) immense
162) lend
163) smooth
164) over
165) earn
166) admonished
167) neither
168) agrarian
169) reasonably
170) store
171) sophisticated
172) retirement
173) divorced
174) flexibility
175) couple
176) profile
177) paid
178) mere
179) valuable
180) genetic
181) coming
182) dropping
183) insurance
184) sequence
185) interpretation
186) terms
187) consume
188) operate
189) efficient
190) processing
191) minimum
192) navigate
193) gaze
194) figured
195) assured
196) visual
197) prevalence
198) pedestrians
199) pointed
200) seeing
201) richer
202) keeps
203) employed
204) invested
205) laboratory
206) construction
207) making
208) richer
209) Sending
210) create
211) crucial
212) scenarios
213) makes
214) productive
215) investment
216) consumption
217) differs
218) replaces
219) bidirectional
220) more
221) well
222) turned

223) thoroughfare
224) commerce
225) search
226) corporate
227) connect
228) connects
229) broadcasting
230) commercial
231) distribute
232) modify
233) fired
234) economy
235) labor
236) revolution
237) workforce
238) automation
239) eliminated
240) replacing
241) displaced
242) automation
243) entirely
244) manning
245) arrived
246) appliance
247) building
248) vast
249) confused
250) identical
251) difference
252) requires
253) instead
254) Paradoxically,
255) resentments
256) most
257) residence
258) century
259) last
260) side
261) successful
262) biases
263) biases
264) partial
265) memorable
266) minimize
267) consistent
268) choosing
269) sensible
270) imbalanced
271) hiring
272) rely
273) applicants
274) subconsciously
275) interaction
276) rest
277) phrasing
278) initial
279) prone
280) significant
281) indicate
282) obtaining
283) hypothetical
284) assessing
285) threefold

286) walked
287) pulling
288) agreed
289) loading
290) remained
291) beside
292) Remaining
293) reached
294) whether
295) decided
296) standing
297) wishing
298) independence
299) climbed
300) insist

Prac 2 **Answers**

1) advantage
2) residents
3) required
4) anxiously
5) baton
6) perform
7) approached
8) worth
9) self-estimate
10) downgrading
11) beliefs
12) self-aware
13) weaknesses
14) self-assessment
15) maxim
16) damaging
17) less
18) underestimate
19) overestimate
20) Cultivate
21) judge
22) discern
23) potential
24) most
25) trappings
26) forced
27) cost
28) Mostly?
29) demands
30) attending
31) inevitably
32) Worse,
33) pay
34) examined
35) resides
36) saved
37) easier
38) restructuring
39) profitable
40) viable
41) alters
42) take.
43) possibility

44) intervene
45) intended,
46) risky
47) diversity
48) objective
49) least
50) diversity
51) ethnicity,
52) carried
53) varied
54) angles
55) done
56) consensus
57) objectivity
58) among
59) psychologists
60) deadline
61) likely
62) less
63) timeframe.
64) done
65) approach
66) view
67) period
68) imminent.
69) manageable,
70) above
71) emissions
72) across
73) greater
74) largest
75) surpassed
76) larger
77) opposite
78) less
79) graduating,
80) worked
81) quit
82) poet.
83) moved
84) reading.
85) wrote
86) later
87) traveled
88) ended
89) returned
90) widely
91) stopped
92) fill
93) capacity
94) proven
95) remarkable
96) congenitally
97) around
98) smiling
99) nothing
100) fascinating
101) let
102) smiling.
103) operates
104) biology
105) better
106) adapt

107) commercials
108) removing
109) opposite
110) broken
111) annoying
112) less
113) longer
114) pleasurable.
115) Interspersing
116) less
117) disrupts
118) following
119) thus
120) even
121) serve
122) accept
123) allowed
124) side
125) supply.
126) arrange
127) attractiveness
128) highest
129) scratch
130) classified
131) psychology
132) phenomenon
133) deprived
134) deem
135) invested
136) failing
137) sunk
138) investing
139) prove
140) worthwhile
141) Giving
142) acknowledging
143) prefer
144) bet,
145) lost
146) lay
147) delaying
148) admitting
149) travels
150) instantaneously
151) reach
152) unpleasantly
153) filament
154) breaks
155) removed
156) nonsensical
157) won't
158) infinitely
159) intervening
160) vastness.
161) immense
162) lend
163) smooth
164) over
165) earn
166) admonished
167) neither
168) agrarian
169) reasonably

170) store
171) sophisticated
172) retirement
173) divorced
174) flexibility
175) couple
176) profile
177) paid
178) mere
179) valuable
180) genetic
181) coming
182) dropping
183) insurance
184) sequence
185) interpretation
186) terms
187) consume
188) operate
189) efficient
190) processing
191) minimum
192) navigate
193) gaze
194) figured
195) assured
196) visual
197) prevalence
198) pedestrians
199) pointed
200) seeing
201) richer
202) keeps
203) employed
204) invested
205) laboratory
206) construction
207) making
208) richer
209) Sending
210) create
211) crucial
212) scenarios
213) makes
214) productive
215) investment
216) consumption
217) differs
218) replaces
219) bidirectional
220) more
221) well
222) turned
223) thoroughfare
224) commerce
225) search
226) corporate
227) connect
228) connects
229) broadcasting
230) commercial
231) distribute
232) modify

233) fired
234) economy
235) labor
236) revolution
237) workforce
238) automation
239) eliminated
240) replacing
241) displaced
242) automation
243) entirely
244) manning
245) arrived
246) appliance
247) building
248) vast
249) confused
250) identical
251) difference
252) requires
253) instead
254) Paradoxically,
255) resentments
256) most
257) residence
258) century
259) last
260) side
261) successful
262) biases
263) biases
264) partial
265) memorable
266) minimize
267) consistent
268) choosing
269) sensible
270) imbalanced
271) hiring
272) rely
273) applicants
274) subconsciously
275) interaction
276) rest
277) phrasing
278) initial
279) prone
280) significant
281) indicate
282) obtaining
283) hypothetical
284) assessing
285) threefold
286) walked
287) pulling
288) agreed
289) loading
290) remained
291) beside
292) Remaining
293) reached
294) whether
295) decided

296) standing
297) wishing
298) independence
299) climbed
300) insist

Quiz 1 Answers

1) (A)-(C)-(E)-(D)-(B)
2) (A)-(D)-(C)-(B)
3) (C)-(A)-(E)-(D)-(B)
4) (A)-(C)-(B)
5) (C)-(A)-(B)
6) (B)-(A)-(C)
7) (B)-(C)-(A)-(D)
8) (A)-(B)-(C)
9) (B)-(A)-(C)
10) (D)-(B)-(E)-(A)-(C)
11) (C)-(D)-(B)-(A)
12) (A)-(B)-(C)-(D)
13) (A)-(C)-(B)-(D)-(E)
14) (D)-(B)-(C)-(A)
15) (C)-(B)-(A)
16) (A)-(C)-(D)-(B)
17) (B)-(C)-(A)
18) (B)-(C)-(A)
19) (E)-(D)-(C)-(B)-(A)
20) (A)-(B)-(C)
21) (B)-(C)-(A)
22) (E)-(D)-(B)-(A)-(C)
23) (D)-(C)-(A)-(B)-(E)

Quiz 2 Answers

1)
[정답] ③ ⓑ, ⓒ
[해설]
ⓑ beautifully ⇨ beautiful
ⓒ join in ⇨ join

2)
[정답] ⑤ ⓐ, ⓒ, ⓓ, ⓖ
[해설]
ⓐ with ⇨ on
ⓒ of ⇨ for
ⓓ to increase ⇨ increasing
ⓖ have ⇨ had

3)
[정답] ③ ⓐ, ⓒ, ⓓ
[해설]
ⓐ them ⇨ it
ⓒ do ⇨ are
ⓓ consider ⇨ be considered

4)
[정답] ② ⓐ, ⓕ
[해설]
ⓐ To ignore ⇨ Ignore
ⓕ hardly ⇨ hard

5)
[정답] ⑤ ⓒ, ⓔ, ⓕ
[해설]
ⓒ reconciling ⇨ restructuring
ⓔ variable ⇨ viable
ⓕ to encourage ⇨ encouraging

6)

[정답] ⑤ ⓒ, ⓓ, ⓕ, ⓖ
[해설]
ⓒ objectively ⇨ objective
ⓓ respire ⇨ aspire
ⓕ our ⇨ its
ⓖ objection ⇨ objectivity

7)
[정답] ① ⓐ, ⓑ
[해설]
ⓐ founded ⇨ found
ⓑ less ⇨ more

8)
[정답] ① ⓑ, ⓒ
[해설]
ⓑ expect ⇨ except
ⓒ those ⇨ that

9)
[정답] ④ ⓐ, ⓑ, ⓒ, ⓓ
[해설]
ⓐ entered into ⇨ entered
ⓑ graduated ⇨ graduating
ⓒ building ⇨ built
ⓓ was returned ⇨ returned

10)
[정답] ⑤ ⓑ, ⓒ, ⓓ, ⓕ
[해설]
ⓑ cognitively ⇨ congenitally
ⓒ is disappeared ⇨ disappears
ⓓ done ⇨ is done
ⓕ discourages ⇨ encourages

11)
[정답] ⑤ ⓐ, ⓒ, ⓔ, ⓖ
[해설]
ⓐ adopt ⇨ adapt
ⓒ decrease ⇨ increase
ⓔ more ⇨ less
ⓖ adopt ⇨ adapt

12)
[정답] ④ ⓑ, ⓓ, ⓕ
[해설]
ⓑ full ⇨ short
ⓓ its ⇨ their
ⓕ full ⇨ deprived

13)
[정답] ⑤ ⓒ, ⓕ, ⓖ, ⓗ
[해설]
ⓒ them ⇨ it
ⓕ which ⇨ that
ⓖ them ⇨ it
ⓗ lie ⇨ lay

14)
[정답] ② ⓐ, ⓑ, ⓒ, ⓕ
[해설]
ⓐ simultaneously ⇨ instantaneously
ⓑ psychologically ⇨ physically
ⓒ them ⇨ it
ⓕ intervened ⇨ intervening

15)
[정답] ③ ⓒ, ⓔ
[해설]
ⓒ abnomalised ⇨ admonished
ⓔ divorced ⇨ been divorced

16)
[정답] ③ ⓑ, ⓔ
[해설]
ⓑ pahing ⇨ paid
ⓔ sequecing ⇨ to sequence

17)
[정답] ② ⓐ, ⓑ, ⓒ, ⓖ
[해설]
ⓐ used ⇨ are used
ⓑ which ⇨ that
ⓒ maximum ⇨ minimum
ⓖ what ⇨ which

18)
[정답] ⑤ ⓒ, ⓓ, ⓔ
[해설]
ⓒ is ⇨ were
ⓓ create ⇨ creates
ⓔ are ⇨ is

19)
[정답] ⑤ ⓓ, ⓕ
[해설]
ⓓ cooperate ⇨ corporate
ⓕ them ⇨ it

20)
[정답] ⑤ ⓑ, ⓕ, ⓖ
[해설]
ⓑ anatomy ⇨ automation
ⓕ been arrived ⇨ arrived
ⓖ applicants ⇨ appliance

21)
[정답] ③ ⓑ, ⓓ
[해설]
ⓑ psychological ⇨ physical
ⓓ indirect ⇨ direct

22)
[정답] ⑤ ⓔ, ⓗ, ⓜ
[해설]
ⓔ balanced ⇨ imbalanced
ⓗ appliances ⇨ applicants
ⓜ assessment ⇨ assessing

23)
[정답] ⑤ ⓑ, ⓓ, ⓖ, ⓗ
[해설]
ⓑ to pull ⇨ pulling
ⓓ was remained ⇨ remained
ⓖ approach to ⇨ approach
ⓗ them ⇨ it

Answer Keys

Quiz 2 Answers

1)
[정답] ③
[해설]
2개
① to ⇨ of
③ join in ⇨ join

2)
[정답] ②
[해설]
4개
① with ⇨ on
② awaited ⇨ waited
⑤ was approched ⇨ approached
⑦ have ⇨ had

3)
[정답] ②
[해설]
5개
② to downgrade ⇨ downgrading
③ do ⇨ are
⑤ damaged ⇨ damaging
⑥ more ⇨ less
⑧ forward ⇨ inward

4)
[정답] ③
[해설]
3개
① To ignore ⇨ Ignore
② that ⇨ what
⑥ hardly ⇨ hard

5)
[정답] ④
[해설]
4개
③ reconciling ⇨ restructuring
④ proficient ⇨ profitable
⑤ variable ⇨ viable
⑧ interlcok ⇨ intervene

6)
[정답] ④
[해설]
5개
② different ⇨ similar
③ objectively ⇨ objective
④ respire ⇨ aspire
⑥ our ⇨ its
⑦ objection ⇨ objectivity

7)
[정답] ③
[해설]
2개
① founded ⇨ found
④ to do ⇨ done

8)
[정답] ⑤

[해설]
5개
① omissions ⇨ emissions
③ those ⇨ that
④ following ⇨ followed
⑤ was surpassed ⇨ surpassed
⑥ which ⇨ where

9)
[정답] ③
[해설]
4개
① entered into ⇨ entered
③ building ⇨ built
⑤ Despite ⇨ Although
⑥ to write ⇨ writing

10)
[정답] ②
[해설]
3개
① proved ⇨ proven
④ done ⇨ is done
⑦ themselves ⇨ them

11)
[정답] ⑤
[해설]
5개
③ decrease ⇨ increase
④ same ⇨ opposite
⑤ more ⇨ less
⑥ aoption ⇨ adaptation
⑧ Interfering ⇨ Interspersing

12)
[정답] ④
[해설]
4개
③ asked ⇨ were asked
④ its ⇨ their
⑤ told ⇨ were told
⑦ attractively ⇨ attractive

13)
[정답] ②
[해설]
5개
③ them ⇨ it
④ disprove ⇨ prove
⑥ which ⇨ that
⑦ them ⇨ it
⑨ accepting ⇨ delaying

14)
[정답] ②
[해설]
3개
② psychologically ⇨ physically
⑤ to shine ⇨ shining
⑥ intervened ⇨ intervening

15)
[정답] ③

[해설]
2개
① them ⇨ it
⑤ divorced ⇨ been divorced

16)
[정답] ④
[해설]
3개
① makes ⇨ make
③ are ⇨ is
④ dropped ⇨ dropping

17)
[정답] ③
[해설]
4개
③ maximum ⇨ minimum
④ x ⇨ no
⑤ assuring ⇨ assured
⑦ what ⇨ which

18)
[정답] ②
[해설]
2개
② is spent ⇨ spent
③ is ⇨ were

19)
[정답] ②
[해설]
2개
③ having ⇨ has
⑥ them ⇨ it

20)
[정답] ④
[해설]
4개
① evolution ⇨ revolution
② anatomy ⇨ automation
③ been eliminated ⇨ eliminated
⑥ been arrived ⇨ arrived

21)
[정답] ①
[해설]
1개
④ indirect ⇨ direct

22)
[정답] ②
[해설]
7개
⑤ balanced ⇨ imbalanced
⑥ to ⇨ as
⑦ lonely ⇨ alone
⑧ appliances ⇨ applicants
⑪ overlook ⇨ overlooking
⑫ being ⇨ are
⑬ assessment ⇨ assessing

23)
[정답] ④

[해설]
5개
② to pull ⇨ pulling
③ to park ⇨ parking
⑤ Remained ⇨ Remaining
⑥ that ⇨ what
⑧ them ⇨ it

Quiz 3 Answers

1)
[정답]
① to ⇨ of
② beautifully ⇨ beautiful
④ require ⇨ are required

2)
[정답]
② awaited ⇨ waited
③ of ⇨ for
④ to increase ⇨ increasing
⑤ was approched ⇨ approached
⑥ roused ⇨ raised
⑦ have ⇨ had

3)
[정답]
① them ⇨ it
⑥ more ⇨ less

4)
[정답]
⑥ hardly ⇨ hard

5)
[정답]
① save ⇨ be saved
② to take ⇨ taking
③ reconciling ⇨ restructuring
④ proficient ⇨ profitable
⑤ variable ⇨ viable
⑥ to ⇨ as
⑦ were ⇨ did
⑧ interlcok ⇨ intervene
⑨ to encourage ⇨ encouraging

6)
[정답]
③ objectively ⇨ objective
⑤ varying ⇨ varied

7)
[정답]
④ to do ⇨ done
⑤ be met ⇨ meet

8)
[정답]
② expect ⇨ except
③ those ⇨ that
④ following ⇨ followed
⑤ was surpassed ⇨ surpassed

9)
[정답]
② graduated ⇨ graduating
④ was returned ⇨ returned

10)
[정답]
① proved ⇨ proven
④ done ⇨ is done

11)
[정답]
③ decrease ⇨ increase

12)
[정답]
① to allow ⇨ allowed
③ asked ⇨ were asked
④ its ⇨ their
⑥ full ⇨ deprived
⑦ attractively ⇨ attractive

13)
[정답]
③ them ⇨ it
⑥ which ⇨ that
⑦ them ⇨ it

14)
[정답]
① simultaneously ⇨ instantaneously
② psychologically ⇨ physically
③ them ⇨ it
④ nonsesically ⇨ nonsensical
⑤ to shine ⇨ shining
⑥ intervened ⇨ intervening
⑦ immediate ⇨ immense
⑧ what ⇨ that

15)
[정답]
② that ⇨ which
③ abnomalised ⇨ admonished
④ it ⇨ them
⑤ divorced ⇨ been divorced
⑥ fixedness ⇨ flexibility

16)
[정답]
② pahing ⇨ paid
④ dropped ⇨ dropping
⑥ which ⇨ what

17)
[정답]
④ x ⇨ no
⑤ assuring ⇨ assured
⑥ explain about ⇨ explain

18)
[정답]
① happily ⇨ happy
② is spent ⇨ spent
③ is ⇨ were
④ create ⇨ creates

19)
[정답]
① that ⇨ which

20)
[정답]
① evolution ⇨ revolution
② anatomy ⇨ automation
③ been eliminated ⇨ eliminated
④ themselves ⇨ them
⑤ ideal ⇨ idle
⑥ been arrived ⇨ arrived
⑦ applicants ⇨ appliance

21)
[정답]
② psychological ⇨ physical
④ indirect ⇨ direct
⑥ successibe ⇨ successful

22)
[정답]
① impartial ⇨ partial
② framing ⇨ framed
④ sensitive ⇨ sensible
⑤ balanced ⇨ imbalanced
⑥ to ⇨ as
⑦ lonely ⇨ alone
⑧ appliances ⇨ applicants
⑨ why ⇨ because
⑫ being ⇨ are
⑬ assessment ⇨ assessing

23)
[정답]
② to pull ⇨ pulling
③ to park ⇨ parking
⑥ that ⇨ what
⑧ them ⇨ it

Quiz 5 Answers

1) ~을 이용하다, 3단어 - take advantage of // 장식 - decorations
   // 잔디밭 - lawn
2)
   ⓐ
   required ⇨ are required
   coming ⇨ come
3) 초조하게 - anxiously
4)
   ⓐ
   smooth ⇨ smoothly
   rose ⇨ raised
   worthy ⇨ worth
5) 낮추다 - downgrading // consider의 바른 형태 - be considered
6)
   ⓐ
   you ⇨ yourself
   more ⇨ less
   overestimate ⇨ underestimate
   underestimate ⇨ overestimate
   Cultivating ⇨ Cultivate
7)
   (가) Look inward to discern what you're capable of and what it

will take to unlock that potential.
8) 거래 - transaction
9)

ⓐ

that ⇨ what

that ⇨ what

it ⇨ them

evitably ⇨ inevitably

they ⇨ what

10)

(가) Ignore the trappings of their success and what they're able to buy.

11) 끼어들다 - intervene
12)

ⓐ

save ⇨ be saved by

take ⇨ taking

taking ⇨ take

13)

(가) Although the government rescue may be well intended, it can negatively affect the behavior of banks, encouraging risky and poor decision making.

14) 다양성 - diversity // 호기심 - curiosity // 관점 - perspectives // 의견 일치 - consensus // 자신감 - confidence // 객관성 - objectivity

15)

(가) they will not, as a community, be as objective as they maintain they are, or at least aspire to be.

16) 도전 - challenge
17)

ⓐ

less ⇨ more

more ⇨ less

That ⇨ What

the same ⇨ another

18)

(가) That way the stress is more manageable, and you have a better chance of starting and therefore finishing in good time.

19) 뜻: emissions - 배출량 // 의미하는바: that - amount of CO_2 emissions per person // 능가한 - surpassed // ~에 있어서 - in terms of

20) 그만두다 - quit
21)

ⓐ

traveled ⇨ traveled to

Despite ⇨ Although

to write ⇨ writing

22) 선천적인 - built-in // 능력 - capacity // 선천적으로 - congenitally // 청각장애 - deaf // 격려하다 - encourages

23)

(가) However, smiling in blind babies eventually disappears if nothing is done to reinforce it.

(나) anything to let them know that they are not alone and that someone cares about them.

24) 광고 - commercials // 즐거운 - pleasurable // 적응 - adaptation // 방해하다 - disrupts

25)

(가) Shows are actually more enjoyable when they're broken up by annoying commercials.

(나) The less positive moment makes the following positive one new again and thus more enjoyable.

26) 실용적인 - practical
27)

ⓐ

classifying ⇨ classified

deprived ⇨ are deprived

less ⇨ more

28) 보답하다 - repaid // 오류 - fallacy // 인정하다 - acknowledging // 늦추기 - delaying // 인정하기 - admitting

29)

ⓐ

stay ⇨ staying

waking ⇨ walk

accepting ⇨ accept

30)

(가) Our instinct is to continue investing money or time as we hope that our investment will prove to be worthwhile in the end.

31) 순간적으로 - instantaneously // 불쾌하게 - unpleasantly // 바로 그 - The very // 말도 안 되는 - nonsensical // 광대함 - vastness

32)

(가) The immense distances to the stars and the galaxies mean that we see everything in space in the past.

33) 농경사회 - agrarian society // 합리적으로 - reasonably // 정교한 - sophisticated

34)

(가) Financial markets do more than take capital from the rich and lend it to everyone else.

(나) The important point is that earning income has been divorced from spending it, allowing us much more flexibility in life.

35) 가치있는 - valuable // 안내 - guidance // 유전의 - genetic // 보험 - insurance

36)

ⓐ

That ⇨ When

that ⇨ what

that ⇨ what

what ⇨ how

37) 작동하다 - operate // 항해하다 - navigate // 시선 - gaze
38)

(가) This all helps to explain the prevalence of traffic accidents in which drivers hit pedestrians in plain view, or collide with cars directly in front of them.

39) 소비 - consumption
40)

ⓐ

Send ⇨ Sending

Use ⇨ Using

are ⇨ is

less ⇨ more

is ⇨ does

consumption ⇨ investment

investment ⇨ consumption

41) 두 방향으로 - bidirectional // 교환하다 - exchange // 가상의 - virtual // 배포하다 - distribute // 그렇지 않으면 - otherwise // 수정하다 - modify

42)

(가) We can send messages through the network as well as receive them, which has made the system all the more useful.

43) 자동화 - automation // 대체된 - displaced // 놀고 있는 - idle
44)

(가) It's hard to believe you'd have an economy at all if you gave pink slips to more than half the labor force

(나) the vast majority of us are doing jobs that no farmer from the 1800s could have imagined.

45) 부러움 - envy // 역설적이게도 - Paradoxically // 불쾌감 - resentments

46)

ⓐ

confusing ⇨ confused

different ⇨ identical

envy ⇨ jealousy

Jealousy ⇨ Envy

47) 편향된 - partial // 한결같은 - consistent // 유망한 - promising // 정당화하다 - justify // 잠재의식적으로 - subconsciously // 처음의 - initial // 야망있는 - ambitious // 가정적인 - hypothetical

48)

49)
ⓐ
balanced ⇨ imbalanced
collective ⇨ collectively

(가) it turns out that traditional interviews are actually one of the least useful tools for predicting an employee's future success.

(나) interviewers can be prone to overlooking significant information that would clearly indicate whether this candidate was actually the best person to hire.

50) 식료품 - groceries // 독립성 - independence // 궁금해하는 - curious

51)
ⓐ
opened ⇨ open
Remained ⇨ Remaining

52) (가) Todd realized what he was doing and considered whether he should try to help him.